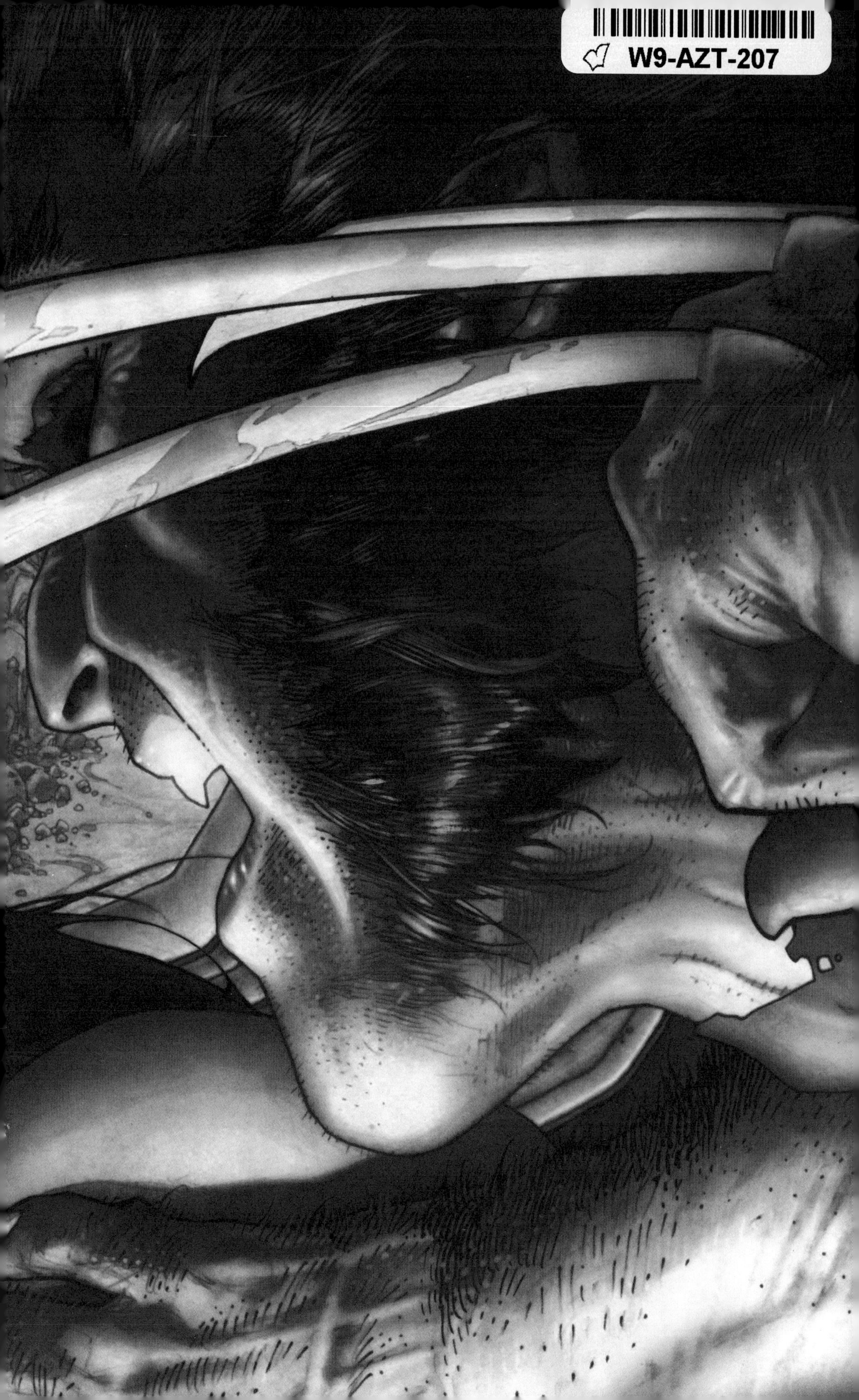

MARVEL COMICS

P R E S E N T S

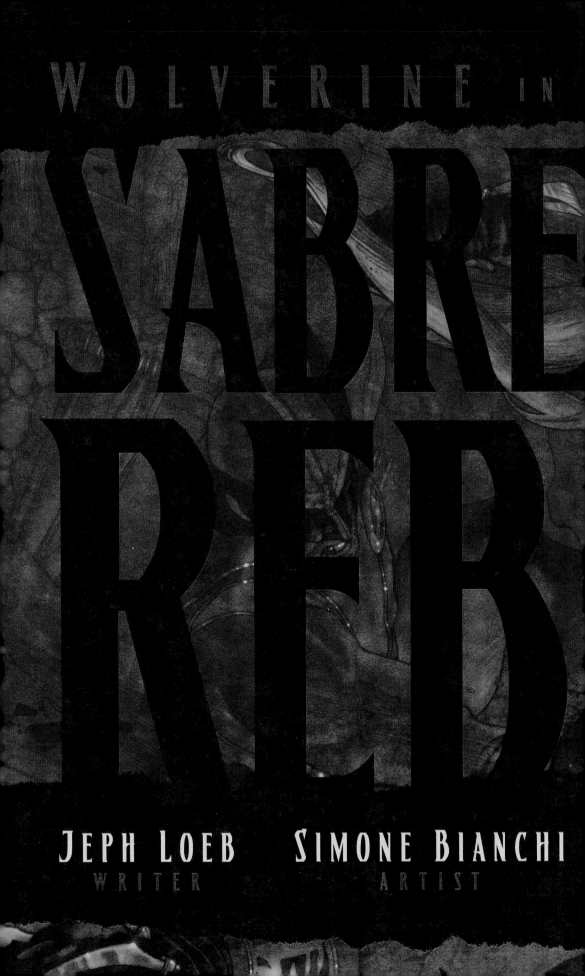

WOLVERINE IN

SABRE RED

JEPH LOEB
WRITER

SIMONE BIANCHI
ARTIST

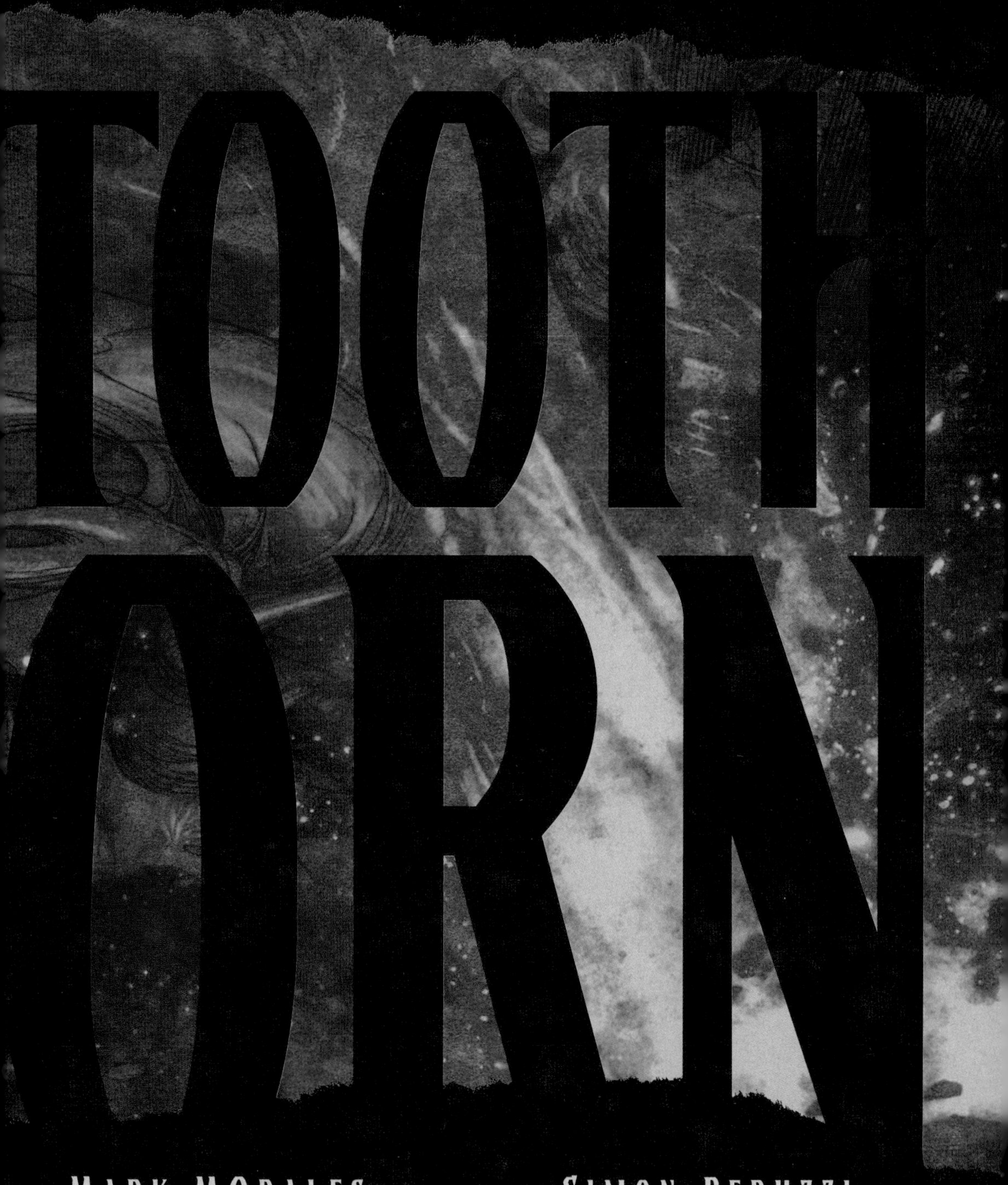

MARK MORALES
INKER - CHAPTER 2

COMICRAFT'S ALBERT DESCHESNE
LETTERING

SIMON PERUZZI WITH JASON KEITH, MORRY HOLLOWELL & GURU-EFX
COLOR ARTISTS

Jennifer M. Smith
ASSISTANT EDITOR

Jeanine Schaefer
EDITOR

Nick Lowe
SENIOR EDITOR

Jennifer Grunwald
COLLECTION EDITOR

Alex Starbuck & Nelson Ribeiro
ASSISTANT EDITORS

Mark D. Beazley
EDITOR, SPECIAL PROJECTS

Jeff Youngquist
SENIOR EDITOR, SPECIAL PROJECTS

David Gabriel
SENIOR VICE PRESIDENT OF SALES

Michael Pasciullo
SVP OF BRAND PLANNING
& COMMUNICATIONS

John Roshell of Comicraft
BOOK DESIGN

Axel Alonso
EDITOR IN CHIEF

Joe Quesada
CHIEF CREATIVE OFFICER

Dan Buckley
PUBLISHER

Alan Fine
EXECUTIVE PRODUCER

WOLVERINE: SABRETOOTH REBORN. Contains material originally published in magazine form as WOLVERINE #310-313. First printing 2013. Hardcover ISBN# 978-0-7851-6325-1. Softcover ISBN# 978-0-7851-6326-8. Published by MARVEL WORLDWIDE, INC., a subsidiary of MARVEL ENTERTAINMENT, LLC. OFFICE OF PUBLICATION: 135 West 50th Street, New York, NY 10020. Copyright © 2012 and 2013 Marvel Characters, Inc. All rights reserved. All characters featured in this issue and the distinctive names and likenesses thereof, and all related indicia are trademarks of Marvel Characters, Inc. No similarity between any of the names, characters, persons, and/or institutions in this magazine with those of any living or dead person or institution is intended, and any such similarity which may exist is purely coincidental. **Printed in the U.S.A.** ALAN FINE, EVP - Office of the President, Marvel Worldwide, Inc. and EVP & CMO Marvel Characters B.V.; DAN BUCKLEY, Publisher & President - Print, Animation & Digital Divisions; JOE QUESADA, Chief Creative Officer; TOM BREVOORT, SVP of Publishing; DAVID BOGART, SVP of Operations & Procurement, Publishing; RUWAN JAYATILLEKE, SVP & Associate Publisher, Publishing; C.B. CEBULSKI, SVP of Creator & Content Development; DAVID GABRIEL, SVP of Publishing Sales & Circulation; MICHAEL PASCIULLO, SVP of Brand Planning & Communications; JIM O'KEEFE, VP of Operations & Logistics; DAN CARR, Executive Director of Publishing Technology; SUSAN CRESPI, Editorial Operations Manager; ALEX MORALES, Publishing Operations Manager; STAN LEE, Chairman Emeritus. For information regarding advertising in Marvel Comics or on Marvel.com, please contact Niza Disla, Director of Marvel Partnerships, at ndisla@marvel.com. For Marvel subscription inquiries, please call 800-217-9158. Manufactured between 11/26/2012 and 1/7/2013 (hardcover), and 11/26/2012 and 10/28/2013 (softcover), by R.R. DONNELLEY, INC., SALEM, VA, USA.

10 9 8 7 6 5 4 3 2 1

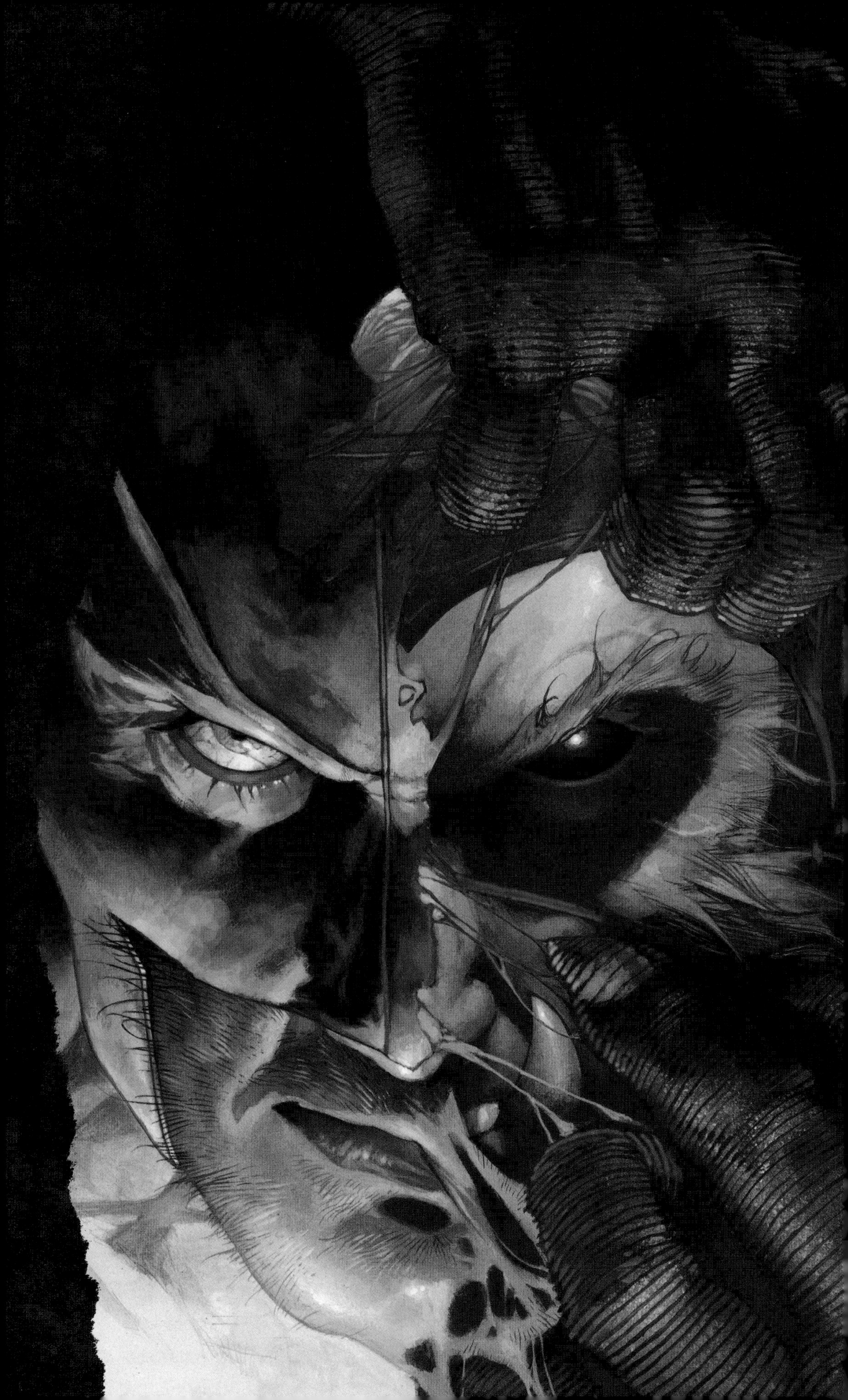

CHAPTER ONE:

OUT OF THE DARKNESS

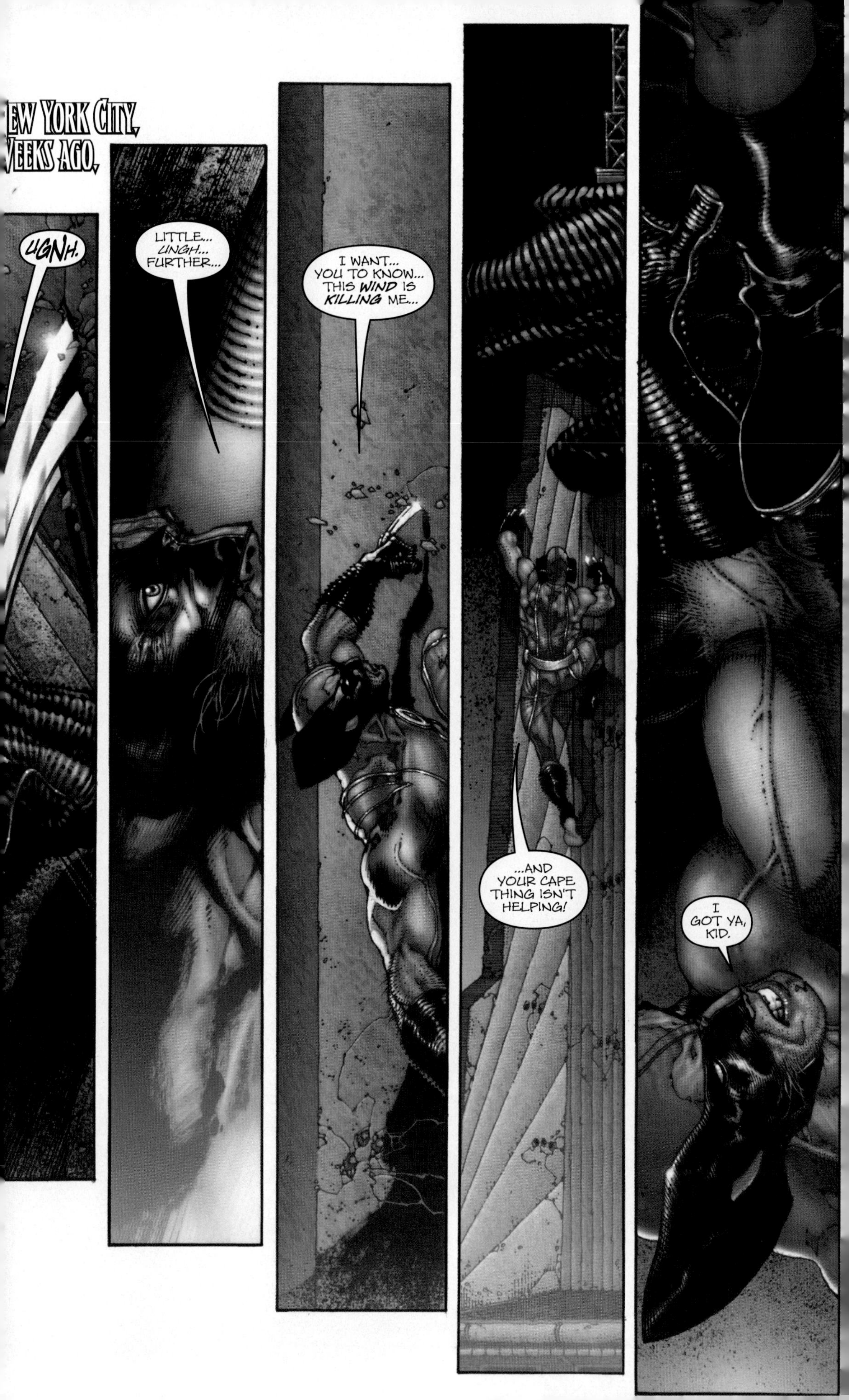
EW YORK CITY, VEEKS AGO,
UGNH.
LITTLE... UNGH... FURTHER...
I WANT... YOU TO KNOW... THIS WIND IS KILLING ME...
...AND YOUR CAPE THING ISN'T HELPING!
I GOT YA, KID.

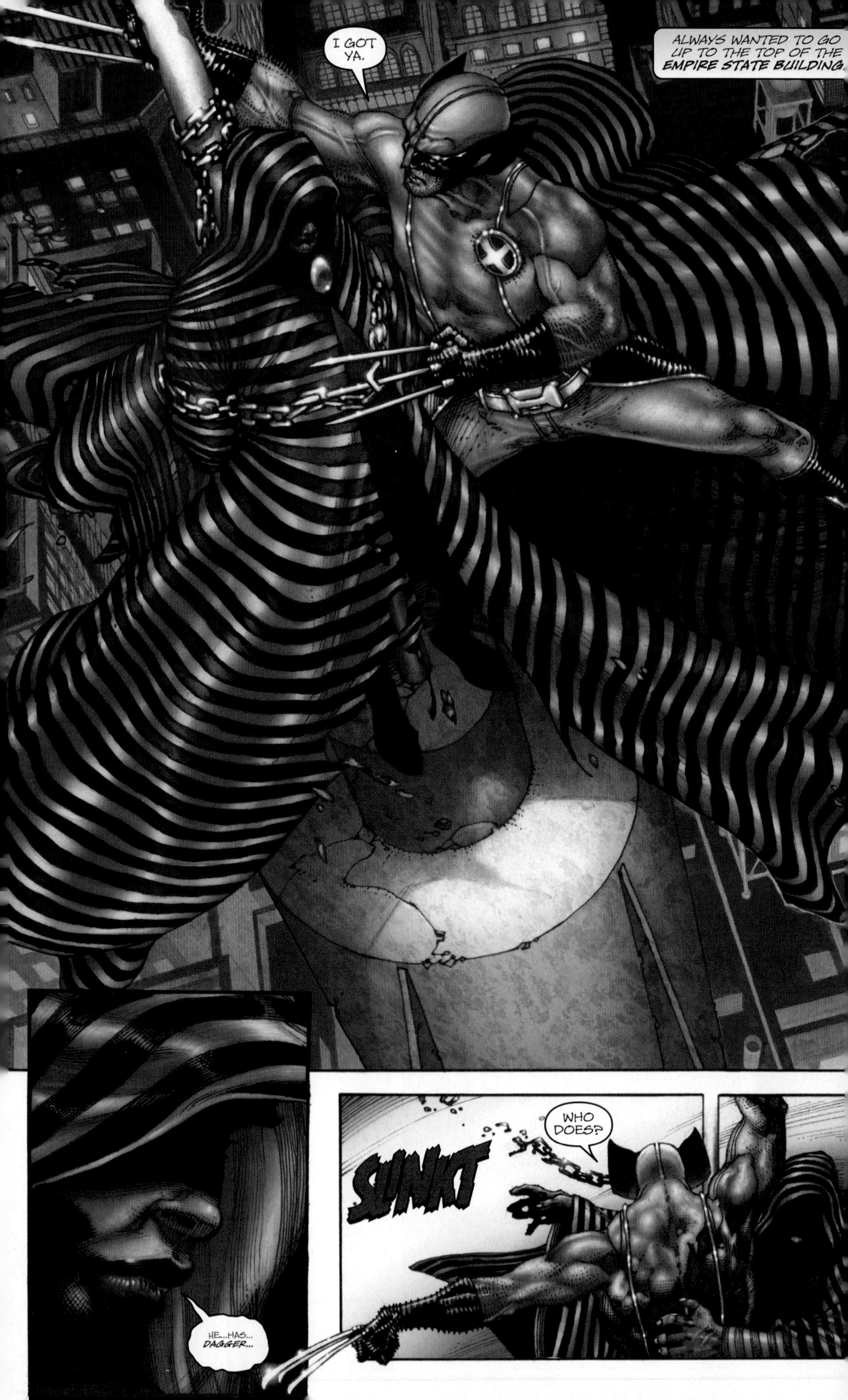
ALWAYS WANTED TO GO UP TO THE TOP OF THE EMPIRE STATE BUILDING.
I GOT YA.
HE...HAS... DAGGER...
SLNKT
WHO DOES?

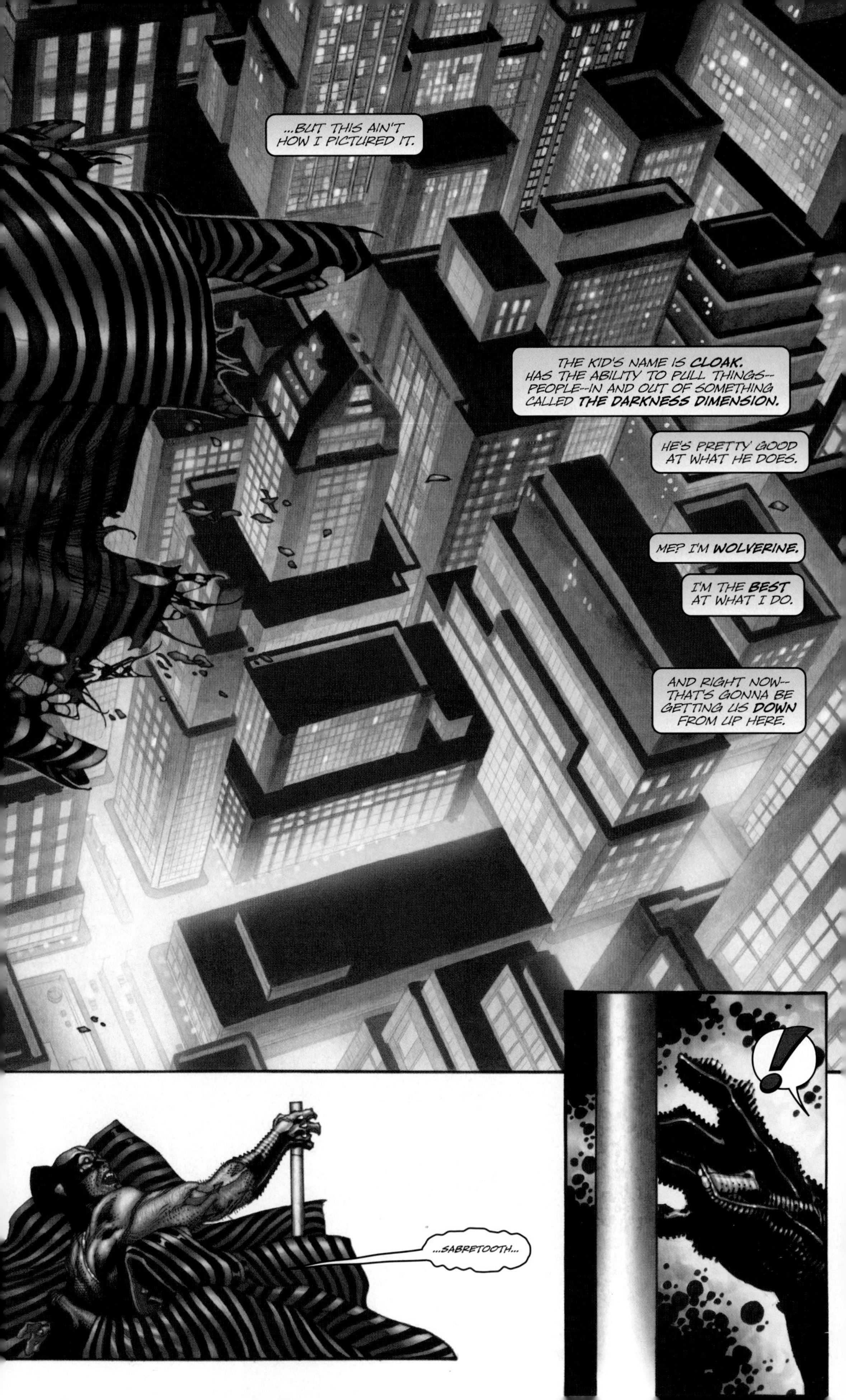
...BUT THIS AIN'T HOW I PICTURED IT.
THE KID'S NAME IS CLOAK. HAS THE ABILITY TO PULL THINGS-- PEOPLE--IN AND OUT OF SOMETHING CALLED THE DARKNESS DIMENSION.
HE'S PRETTY GOOD AT WHAT HE DOES.
ME? I'M WOLVERINE.
I'M THE BEST AT WHAT I DO.
AND RIGHT NOW-- THAT'S GONNA BE GETTING US DOWN FROM UP HERE.
...SABRETOOTH...
!

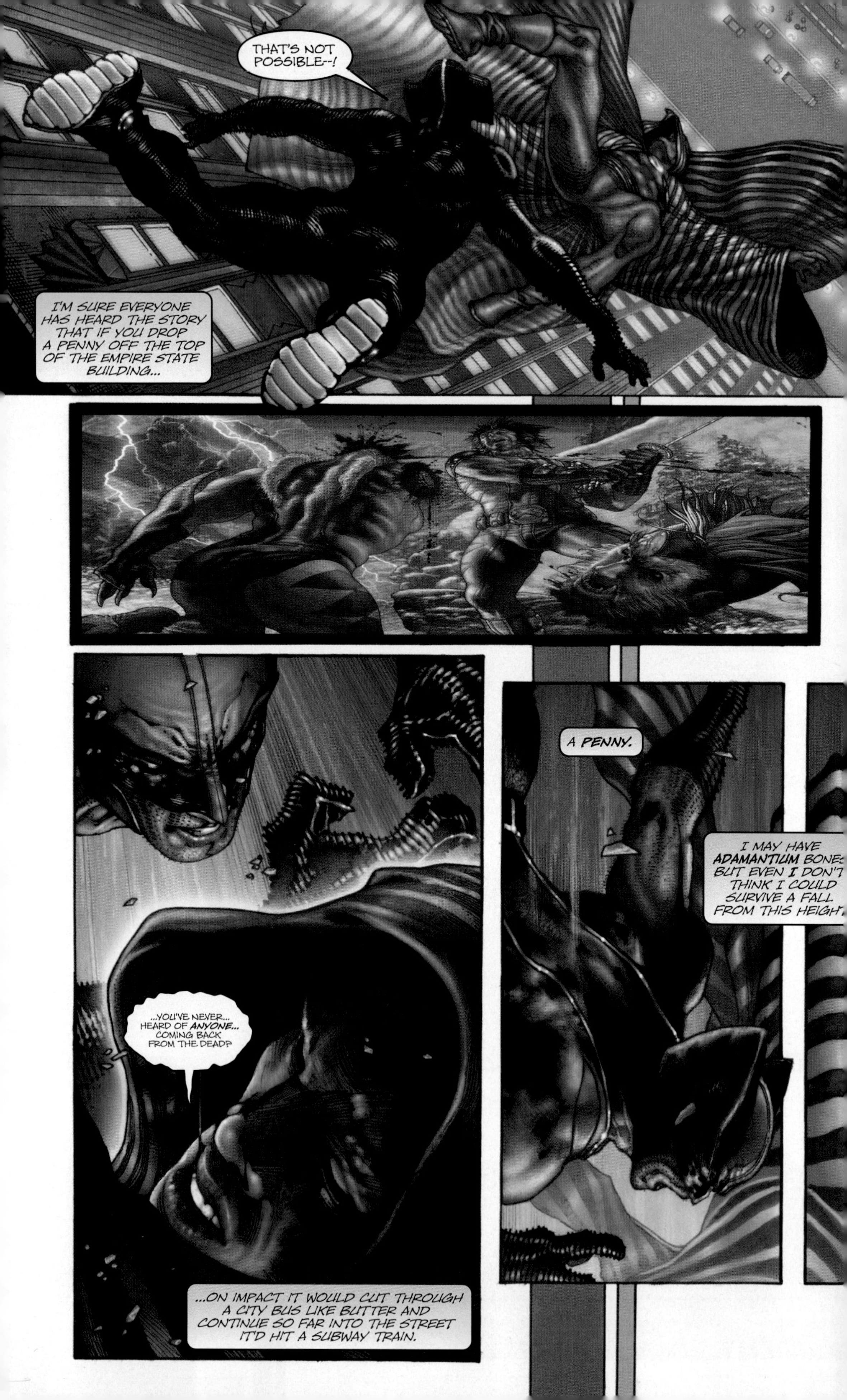
THAT'S NOT POSSIBLE--!
I'M SURE EVERYONE HAS HEARD THE STORY THAT IF YOU DROP A PENNY OFF THE TOP OF THE EMPIRE STATE BUILDING...
...YOU'VE NEVER... HEARD OF ANYONE... COMING BACK FROM THE DEAD?
...ON IMPACT IT WOULD CUT THROUGH A CITY BUS LIKE BUTTER AND CONTINUE SO FAR INTO THE STREET IT'D HIT A SUBWAY TRAIN.
A PENNY.
I MAY HAVE ADAMANTIUM BONE BUT EVEN I DON'T THINK I COULD SURVIVE A FALL FROM THIS HEIGHT

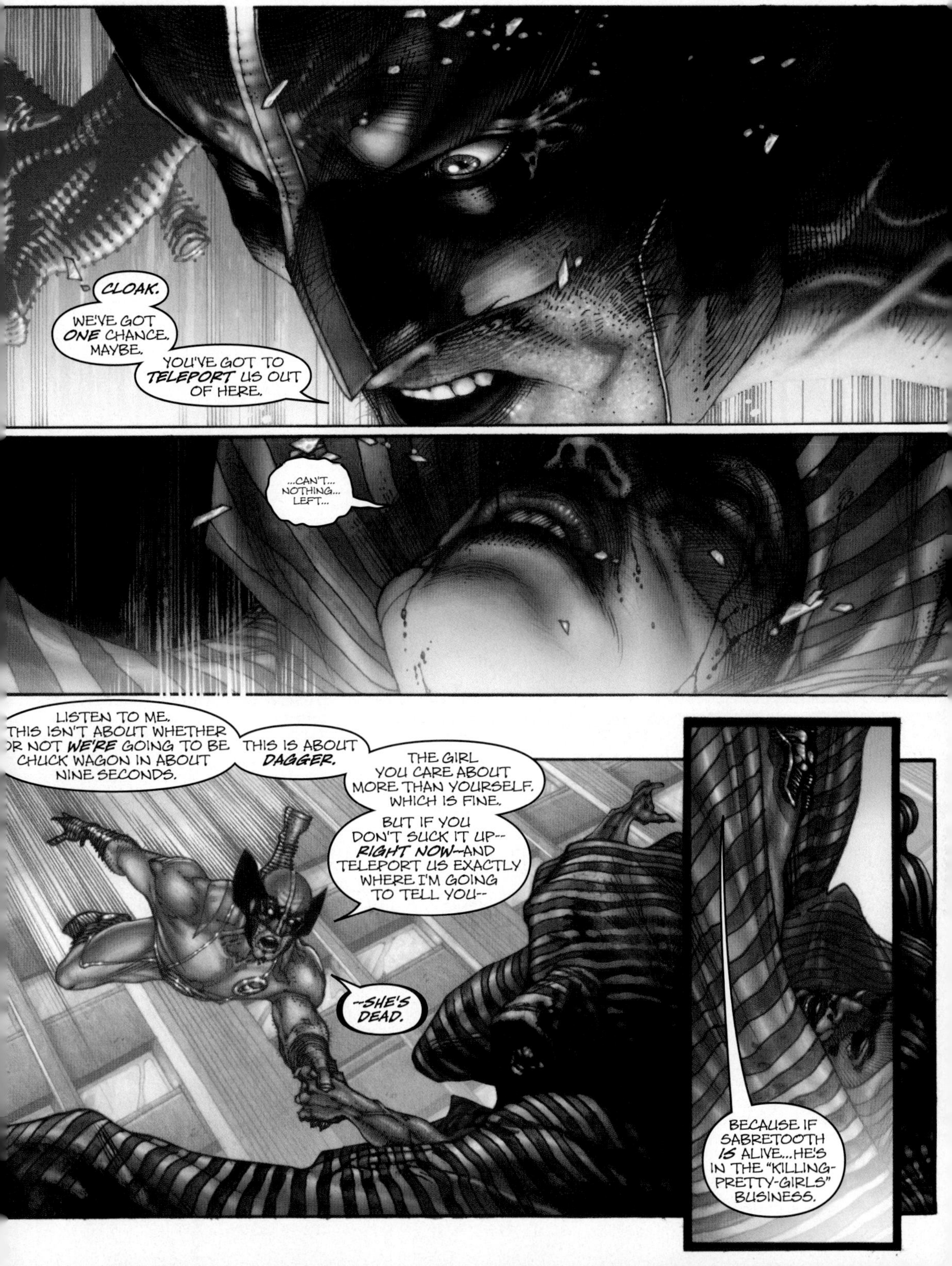
CLOAK.
WE'VE GOT ONE CHANCE. MAYBE.
YOU'VE GOT TO TELEPORT US OUT OF HERE.
...CAN'T... NOTHING... LEFT...
LISTEN TO ME. THIS ISN'T ABOUT WHETHER OR NOT WE'RE GOING TO BE CHUCK WAGON IN ABOUT NINE SECONDS.
THIS IS ABOUT DAGGER.
THE GIRL YOU CARE ABOUT MORE THAN YOURSELF. WHICH IS FINE.
BUT IF YOU DON'T SUCK IT UP-- RIGHT NOW--AND TELEPORT US EXACTLY WHERE I'M GOING TO TELL YOU--
--SHE'S DEAD.
BECAUSE IF SABRETOOTH IS ALIVE...HE'S IN THE "KILLING-PRETTY-GIRLS" BUSINESS.

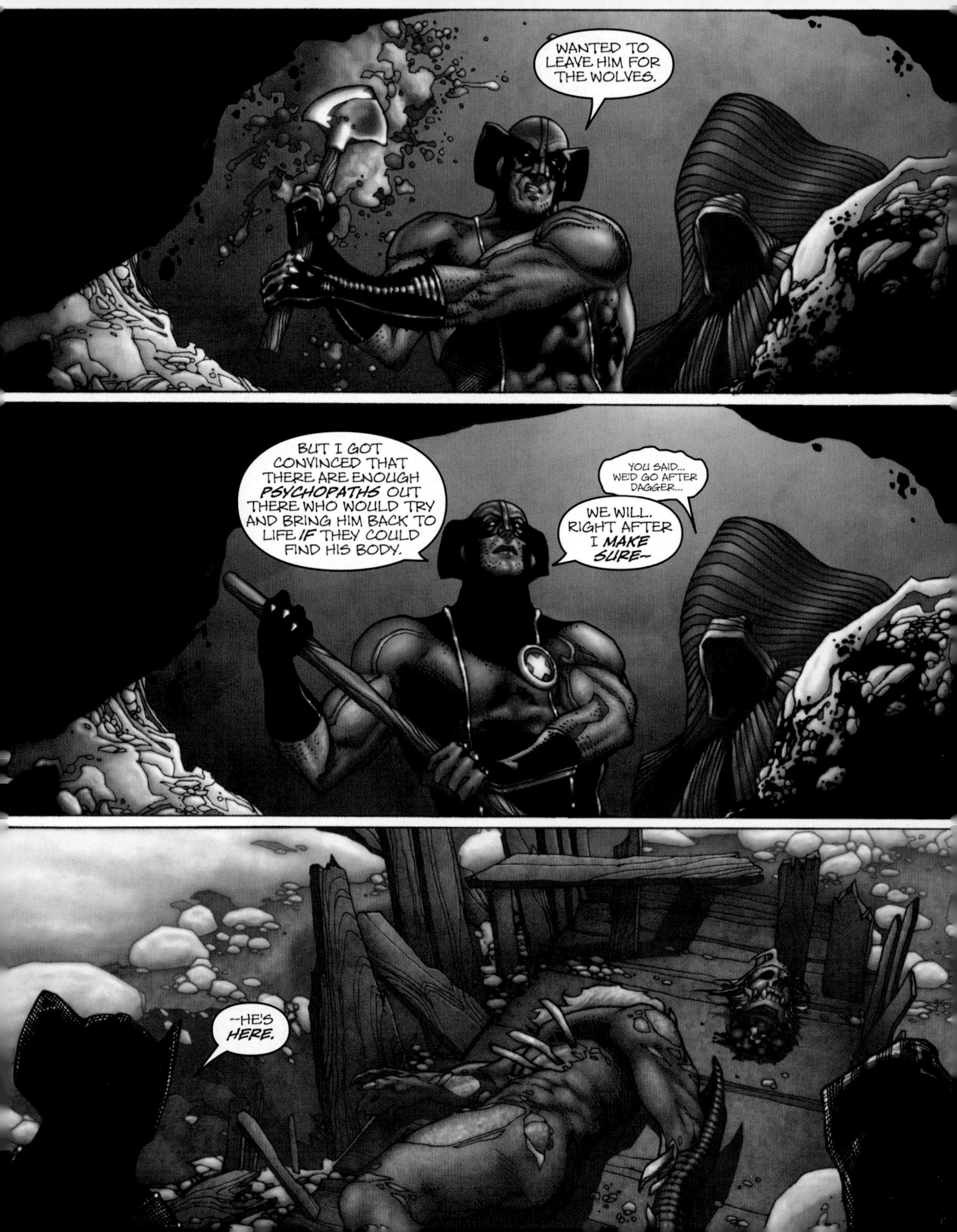
WANTED TO LEAVE HIM FOR THE WOLVES.
BUT I GOT CONVINCED THAT THERE ARE ENOUGH PSYCHOPATHS OUT THERE WHO WOULD TRY AND BRING HIM BACK TO LIFE IF THEY COULD FIND HIS BODY.
YOU SAID... WE'D GO AFTER DAGGER...
WE WILL. RIGHT AFTER I MAKE SURE--
--HE'S HERE.

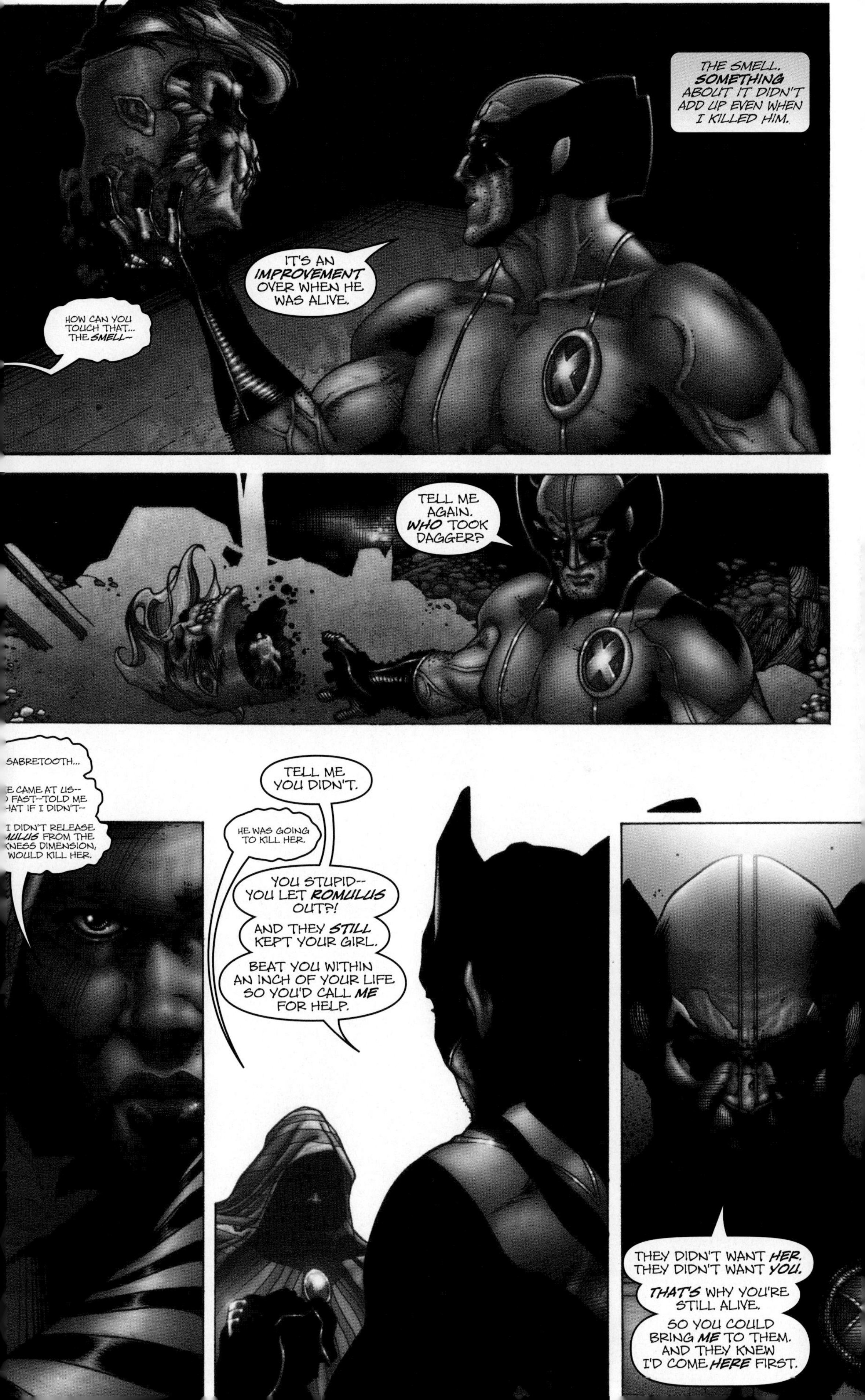
THE SMELL. **SOMETHING** ABOUT IT DIDN'T ADD UP EVEN WHEN I KILLED HIM.
HOW CAN YOU TOUCH THAT... THE **SMELL**--
IT'S AN **IMPROVEMENT** OVER WHEN HE WAS ALIVE.
TELL ME AGAIN. **WHO** TOOK DAGGER?
TELL ME YOU DIDN'T.
SABRETOOTH...
E CAME AT US-- FAST--TOLD ME HAT IF I DIDN'T--
I DIDN'T RELEASE **ULUS** FROM THE KNESS DIMENSION, WOULD KILL HER.
HE WAS GOING TO KILL HER.
YOU STUPID-- YOU LET **ROMULUS** OUT?!
AND THEY **STILL** KEPT YOUR GIRL.
BEAT YOU WITHIN AN INCH OF YOUR LIFE SO YOU'D CALL **ME** FOR HELP.
THEY DIDN'T WANT **HER**. THEY DIDN'T WANT **YOU**.
THAT'S WHY YOU'RE STILL ALIVE.
SO YOU COULD BRING **ME** TO THEM. AND THEY KNEW I'D COME **HERE** FIRST.

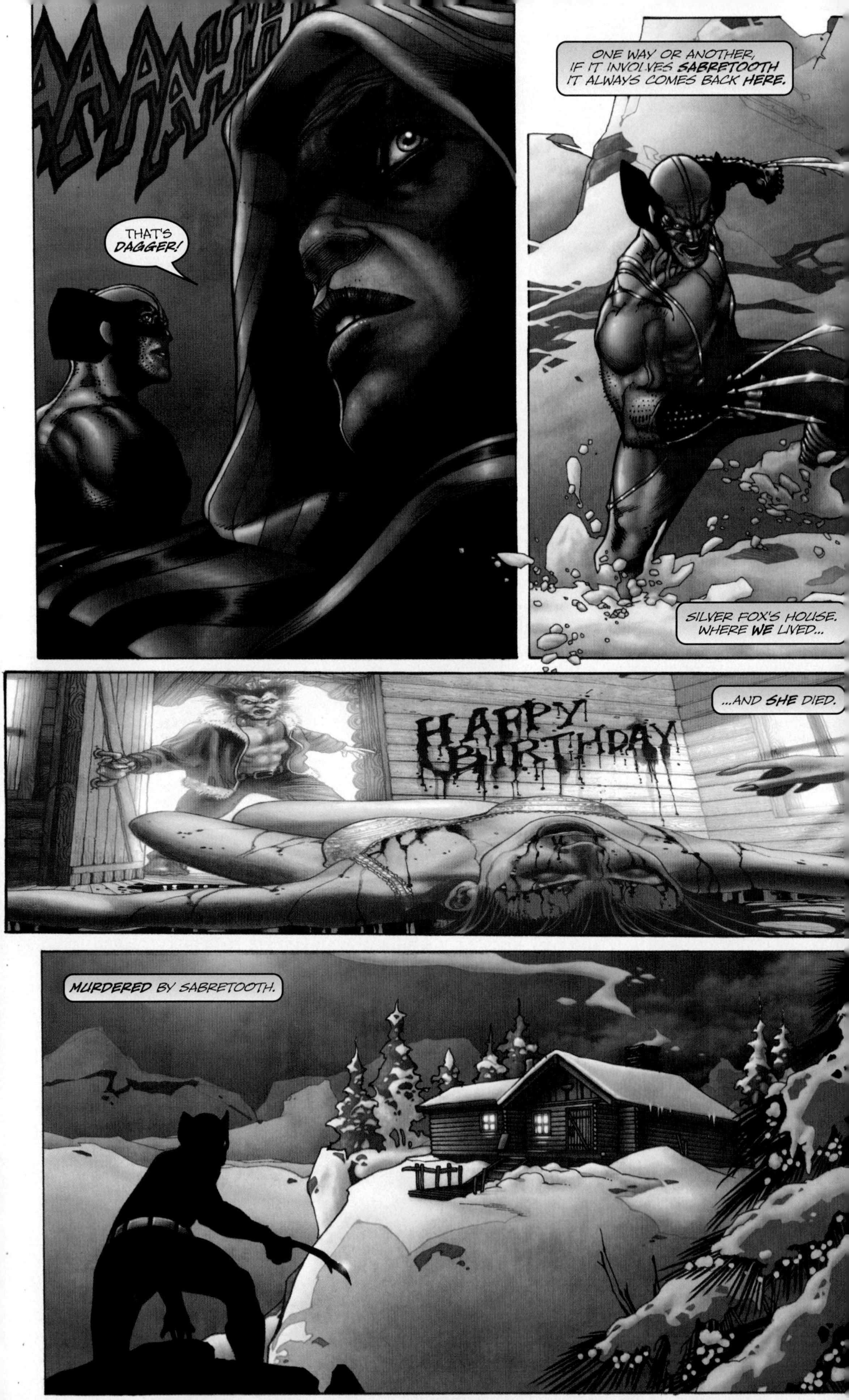
AAAAHH
THAT'S DAGGER!
ONE WAY OR ANOTHER, IF IT INVOLVES SABRETOOTH IT ALWAYS COMES BACK HERE.
SILVER FOX'S HOUSE. WHERE WE LIVED...
...AND SHE DIED.
HAPPY BIRTHDAY
MURDERED BY SABRETOOTH.

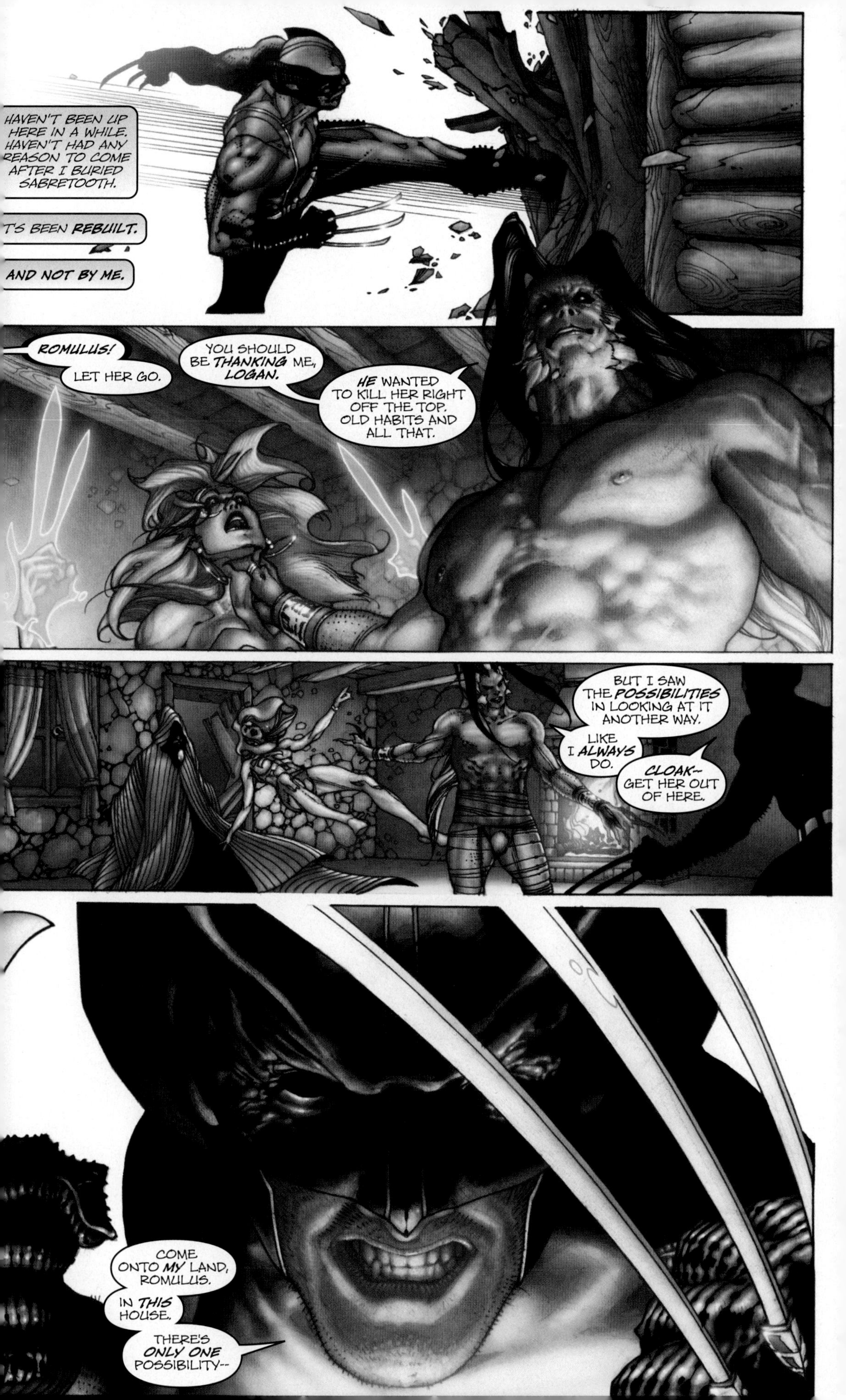
HAVEN'T BEEN UP HERE IN A WHILE. HAVEN'T HAD ANY REASON TO COME AFTER I BURIED SABRETOOTH.
T'S BEEN REBUILT.
AND NOT BY ME.
ROMULUS!
LET HER GO.
YOU SHOULD BE THANKING ME, LOGAN.
HE WANTED TO KILL HER RIGHT OFF THE TOP. OLD HABITS AND ALL THAT.
BUT I SAW THE POSSIBILITIES IN LOOKING AT IT ANOTHER WAY.
LIKE I ALWAYS DO.
CLOAK-- GET HER OUT OF HERE.
COME ONTO MY LAND, ROMULUS.
IN THIS HOUSE.
THERE'S ONLY ONE POSSIBILITY--

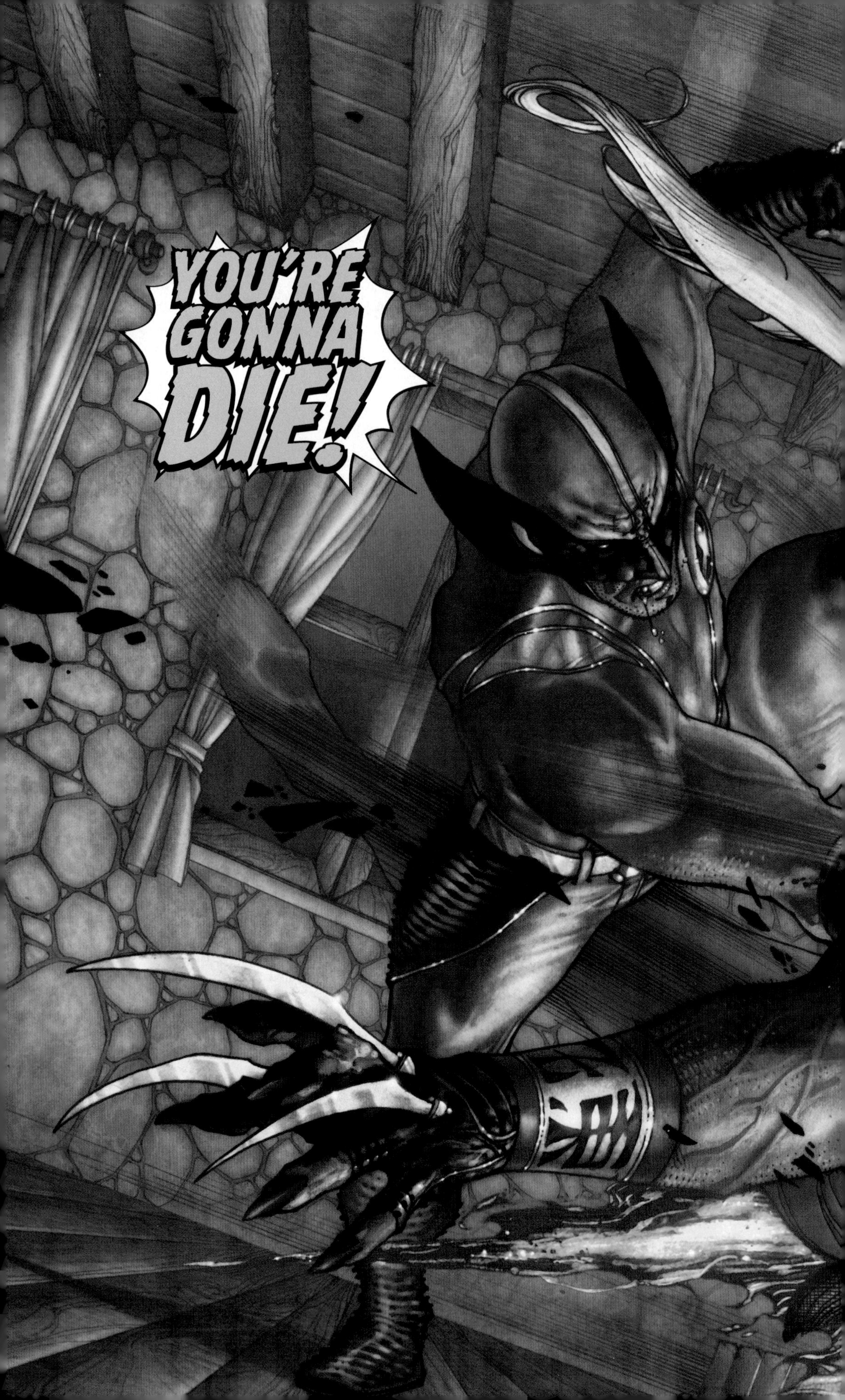
YOU'RE GONNA DIE!

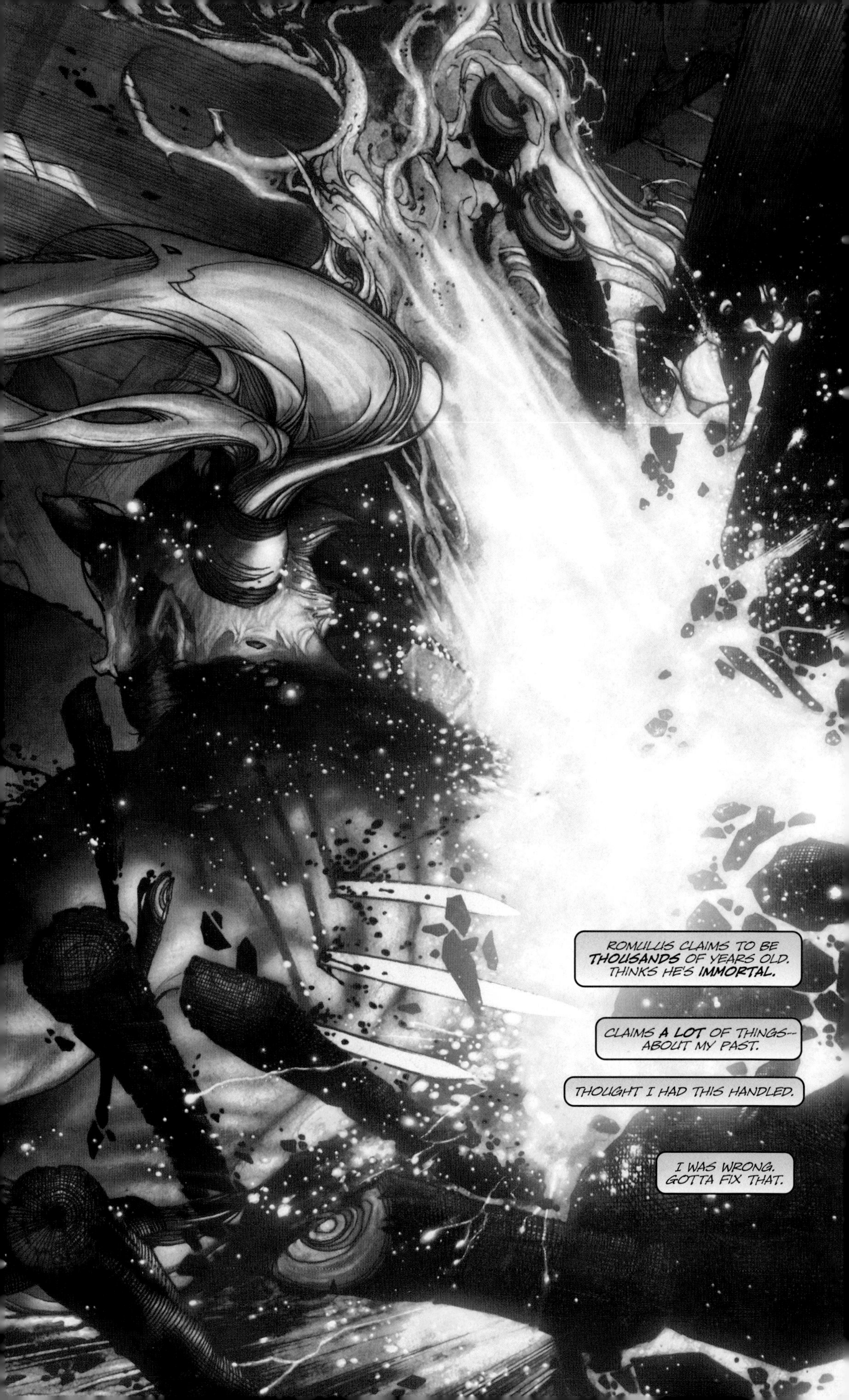
ROMULUS CLAIMS TO BE **THOUSANDS** OF YEARS OLD. THINKS HE'S **IMMORTAL.**
CLAIMS **A LOT** OF THINGS-- ABOUT MY PAST.
THOUGHT I HAD THIS HANDLED.
I WAS WRONG. GOTTA FIX THAT.

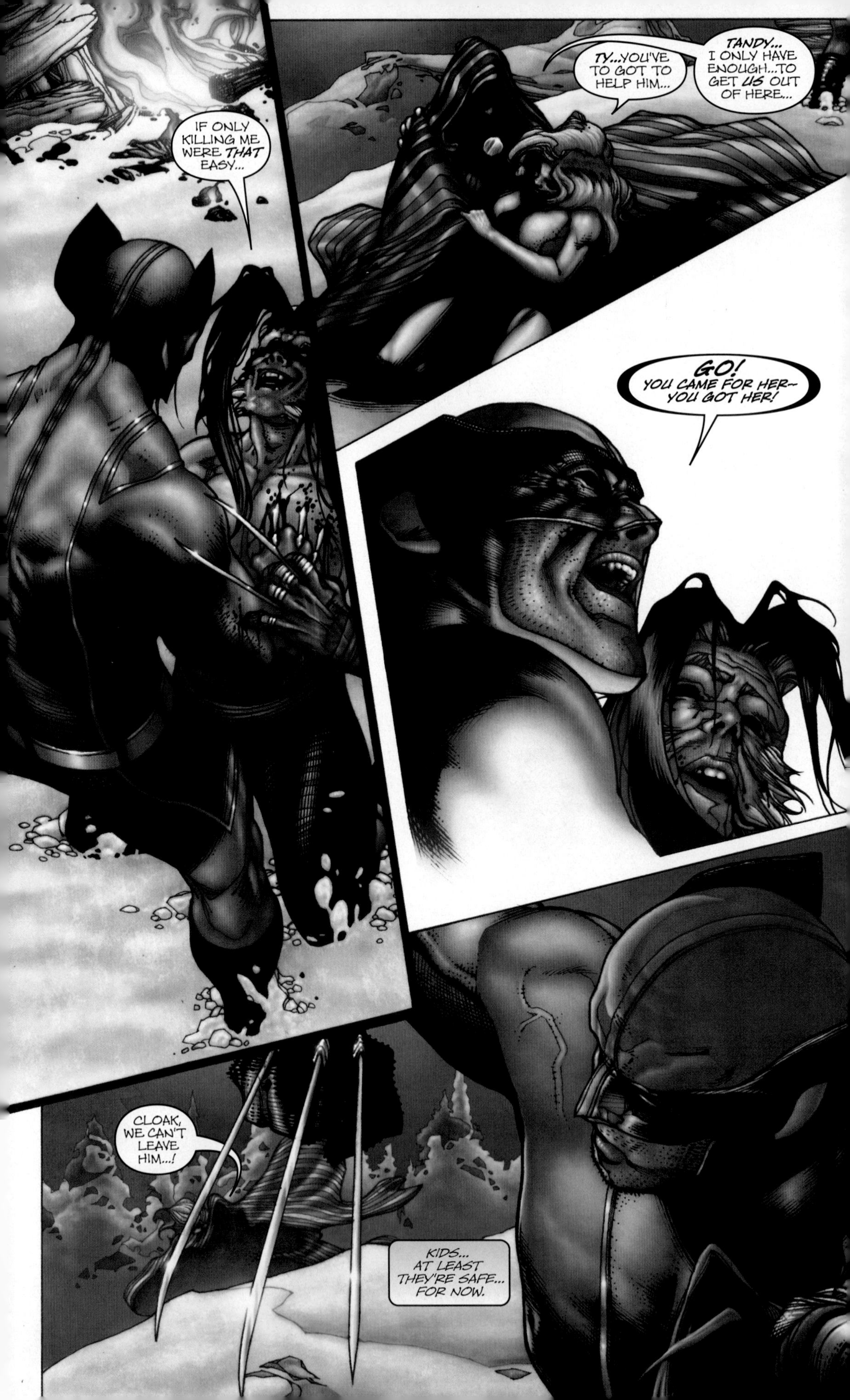

IF ONLY KILLING ME WERE *THAT* EASY...
TY...YOU'VE TO GOT TO HELP HIM...
TANDY... I ONLY HAVE ENOUGH...TO GET *US* OUT OF HERE...
GO! YOU CAME FOR HER-- YOU GOT HER!
CLOAK, WE CAN'T LEAVE HIM...!
KIDS... AT LEAST THEY'RE SAFE... FOR NOW.

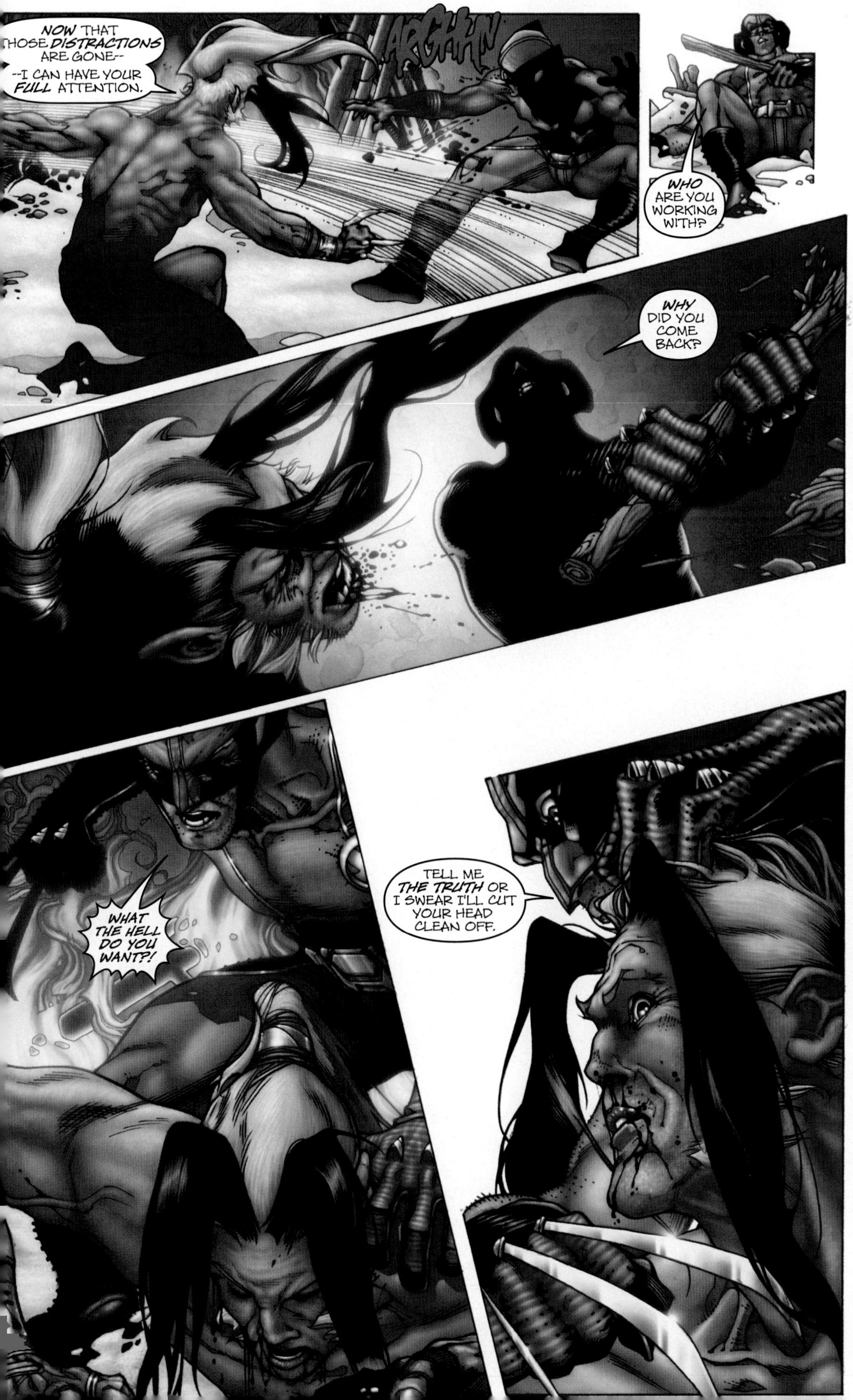
NOW THAT THOSE DISTRACTIONS ARE GONE--
--I CAN HAVE YOUR FULL ATTENTION.
ARGHHN
WHO ARE YOU WORKING WITH?
WHY DID YOU COME BACK?
WHAT THE HELL DO YOU WANT?!
TELL ME THE TRUTH OR I SWEAR I'LL CUT YOUR HEAD CLEAN OFF.

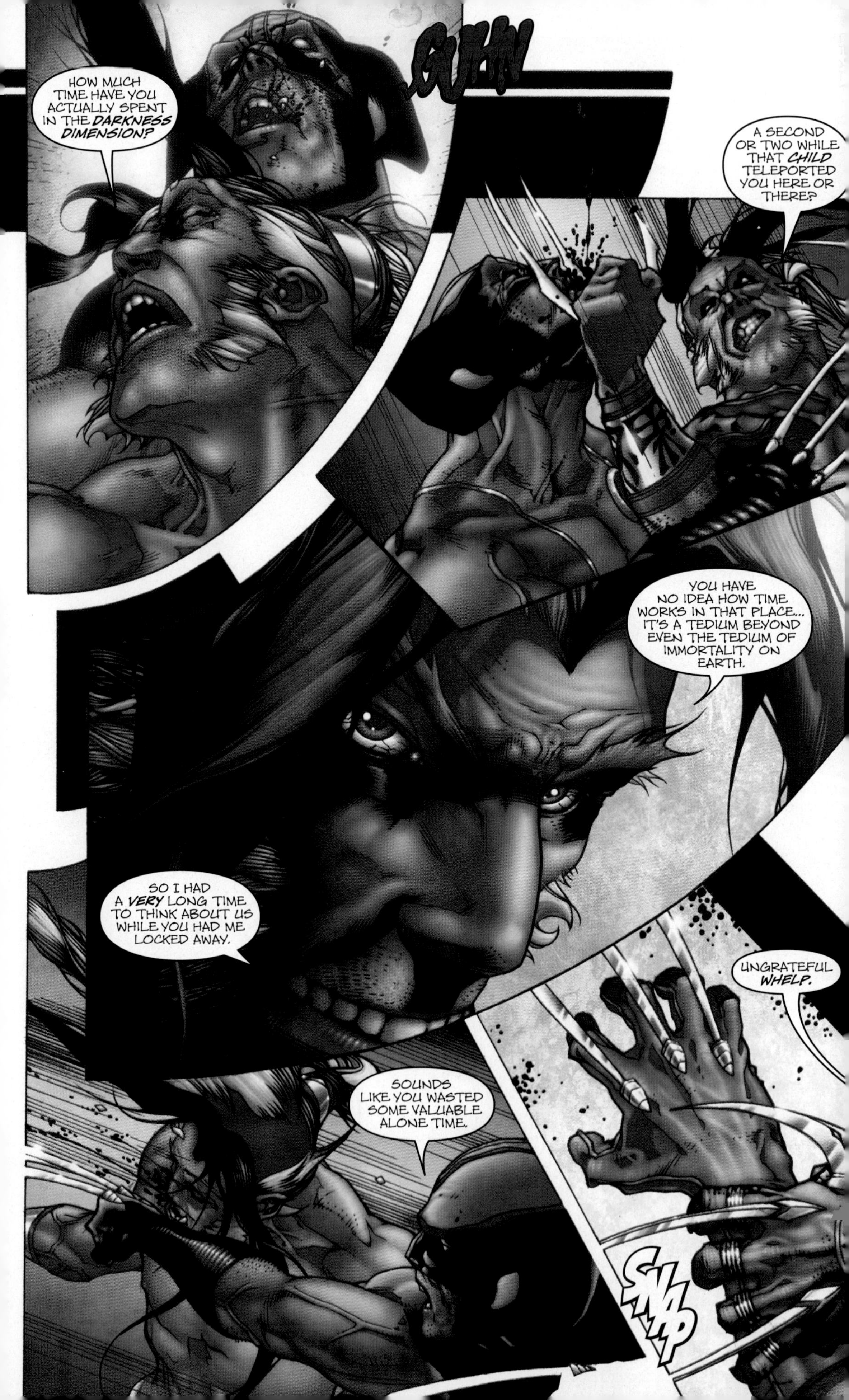

GUHN
HOW MUCH TIME HAVE YOU ACTUALLY SPENT IN THE DARKNESS DIMENSION?
A SECOND OR TWO WHILE THAT CHILD TELEPORTED YOU HERE OR THERE?
YOU HAVE NO IDEA HOW TIME WORKS IN THAT PLACE... IT'S A TEDIUM BEYOND EVEN THE TEDIUM OF IMMORTALITY ON EARTH.
SO I HAD A VERY LONG TIME TO THINK ABOUT US WHILE YOU HAD ME LOCKED AWAY.
UNGRATEFUL WHELP.
SOUNDS LIKE YOU WASTED SOME VALUABLE ALONE TIME.
SNAP

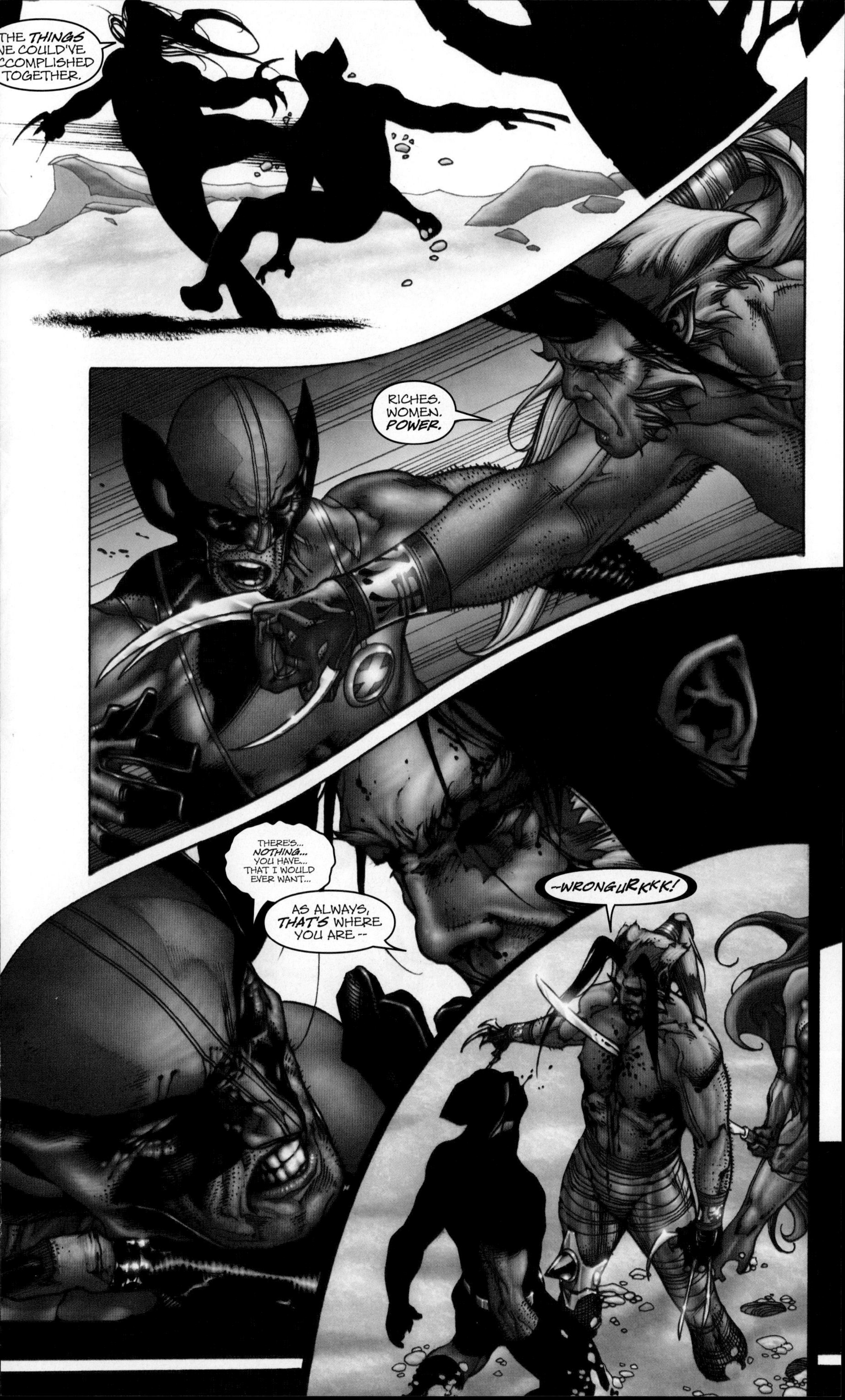
THE THINGS WE COULD'VE ACCOMPLISHED TOGETHER.
RICHES. WOMEN. POWER.
THERE'S... NOTHING... YOU HAVE... THAT I WOULD EVER WANT...
AS ALWAYS, THAT'S WHERE YOU ARE --
--WRONGURKKK!

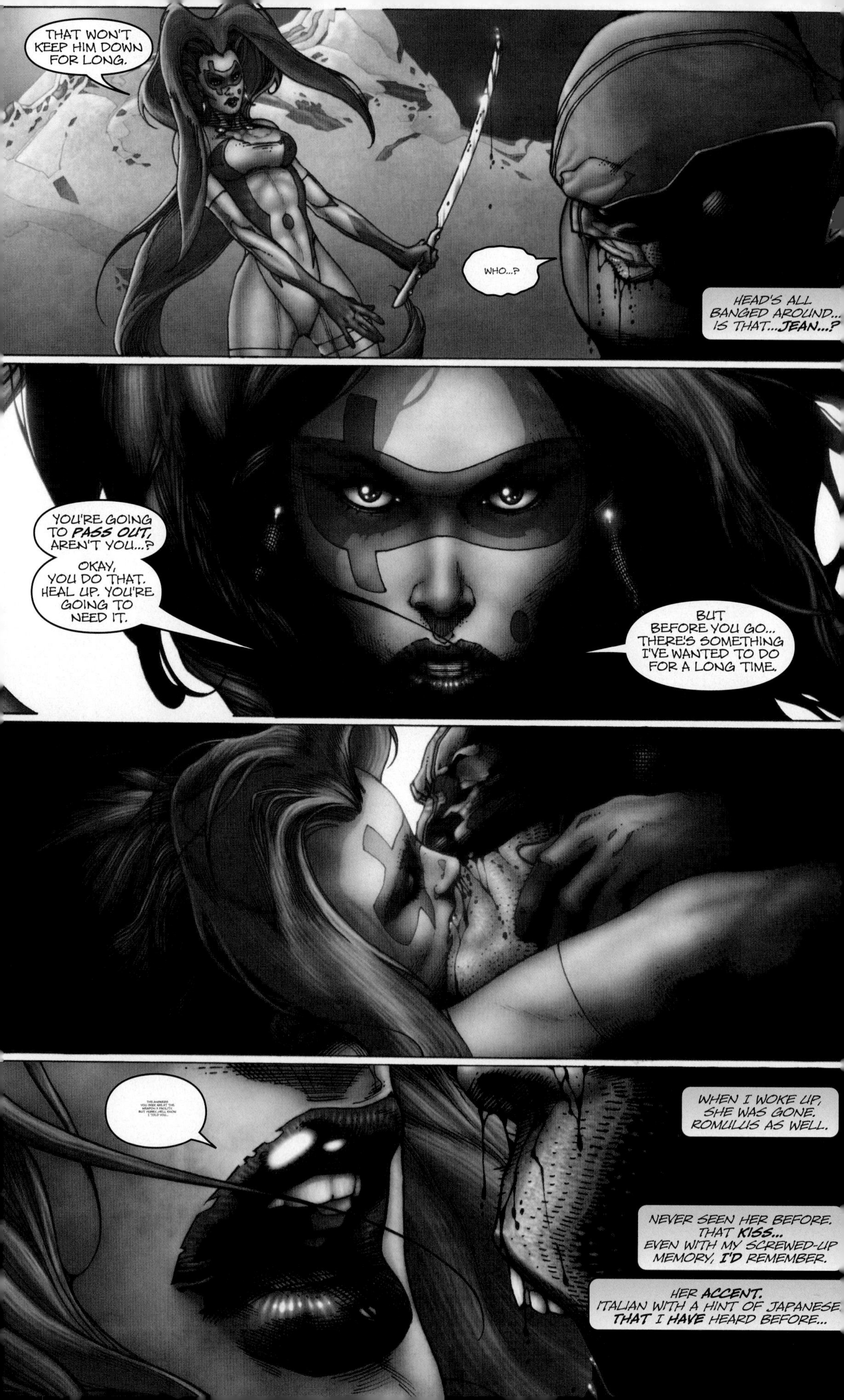
THAT WON'T KEEP HIM DOWN FOR LONG.
WHO...?
HEAD'S ALL BANGED AROUND... IS THAT...JEAN...?
YOU'RE GOING TO PASS OUT, AREN'T YOU...?
OKAY, YOU DO THAT. HEAL UP. YOU'RE GOING TO NEED IT.
BUT BEFORE YOU GO... THERE'S SOMETHING I'VE WANTED TO DO FOR A LONG TIME.
THE ANSWERS YOU SEEK ARE AT THE WEAPON X FACILITY. BUT HURRY...HE'LL KNOW I TOLD YOU...
WHEN I WOKE UP, SHE WAS GONE. ROMULUS AS WELL.
NEVER SEEN HER BEFORE. THAT KISS... EVEN WITH MY SCREWED-UP MEMORY, I'D REMEMBER.
HER ACCENT. ITALIAN WITH A HINT OF JAPANESE. THAT I HAVE HEARD BEFORE...

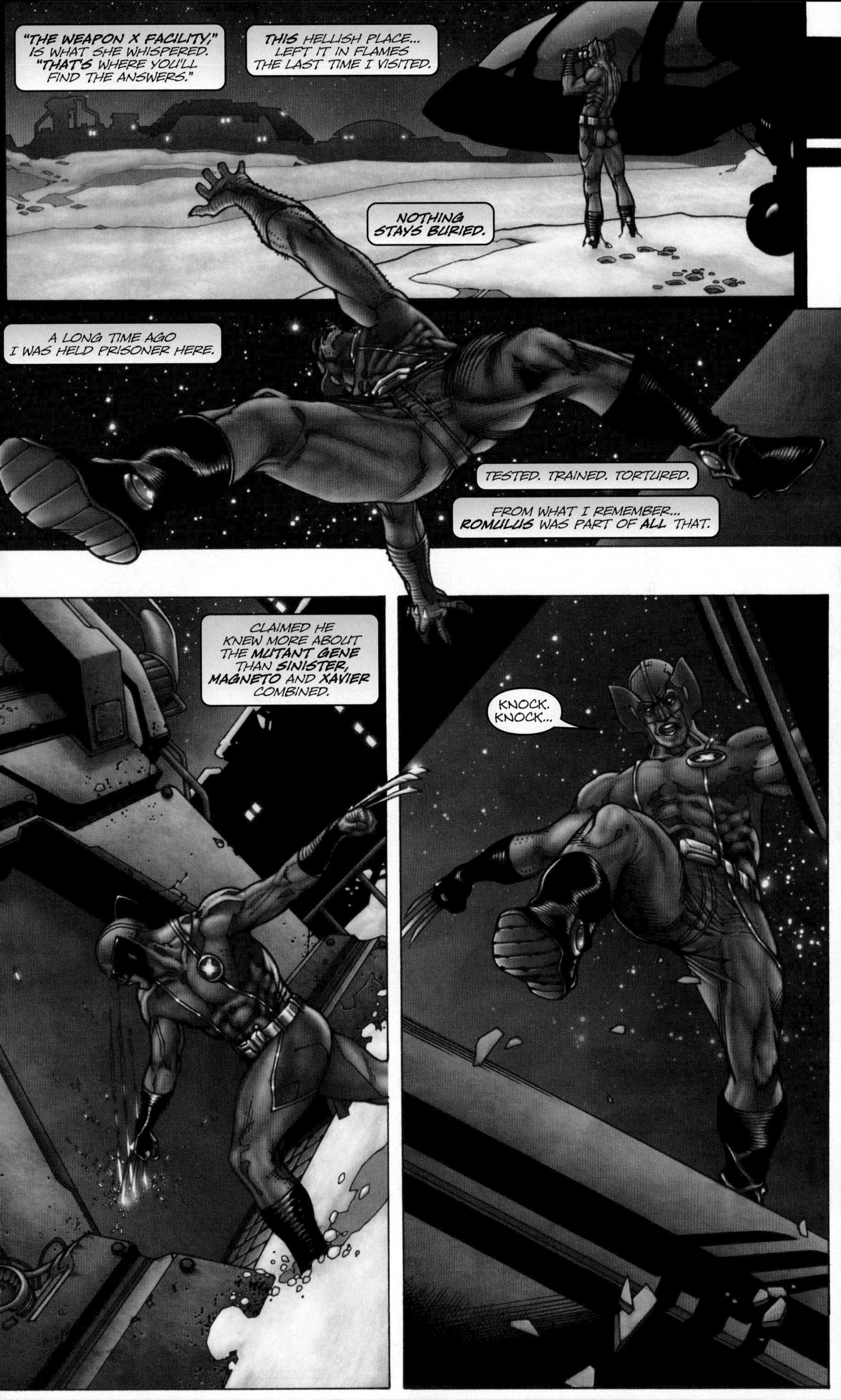

"THE WEAPON X FACILITY," IS WHAT SHE WHISPERED. "THAT'S WHERE YOU'LL FIND THE ANSWERS."
THIS HELLISH PLACE... LEFT IT IN FLAMES THE LAST TIME I VISITED.
NOTHING STAYS BURIED.
A LONG TIME AGO I WAS HELD PRISONER HERE.
TESTED. TRAINED. TORTURED.
FROM WHAT I REMEMBER... ROMULUS WAS PART OF ALL THAT.
CLAIMED HE KNEW MORE ABOUT THE MUTANT GENE THAN SINISTER, MAGNETO AND XAVIER COMBINED.
KNOCK. KNOCK...

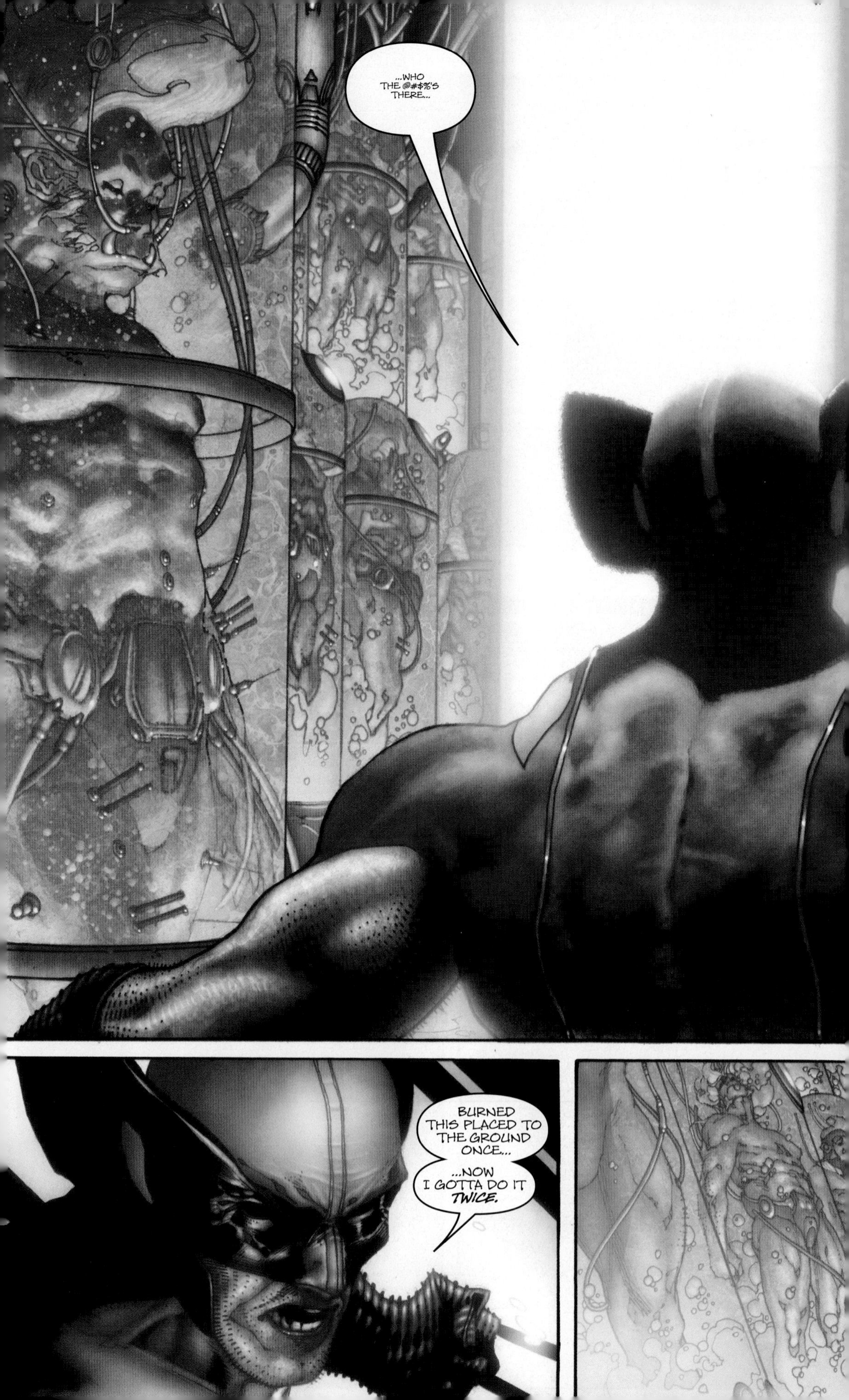
...WHO THE @#$%'S THERE...
BURNED THIS PLACED TO THE GROUND ONCE...
...NOW I GOTTA DO IT *TWICE.*

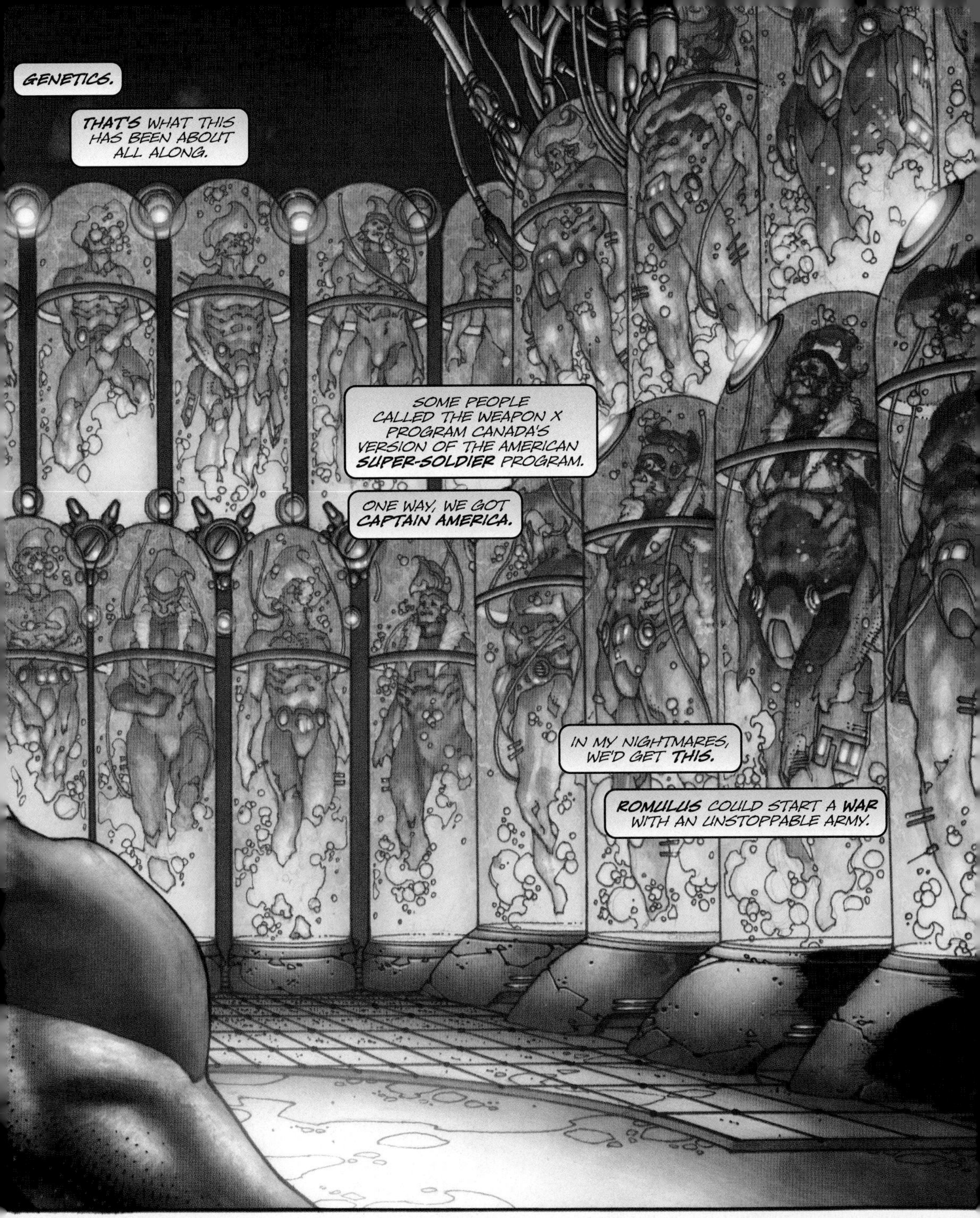
GENETICS.
THAT'S WHAT THIS HAS BEEN ABOUT ALL ALONG.
SOME PEOPLE CALLED THE WEAPON X PROGRAM CANADA'S VERSION OF THE AMERICAN SUPER-SOLDIER PROGRAM.
ONE WAY, WE GOT CAPTAIN AMERICA.
IN MY NIGHTMARES, WE'D GET THIS.
ROMULUS COULD START A WAR WITH AN UNSTOPPABLE ARMY.

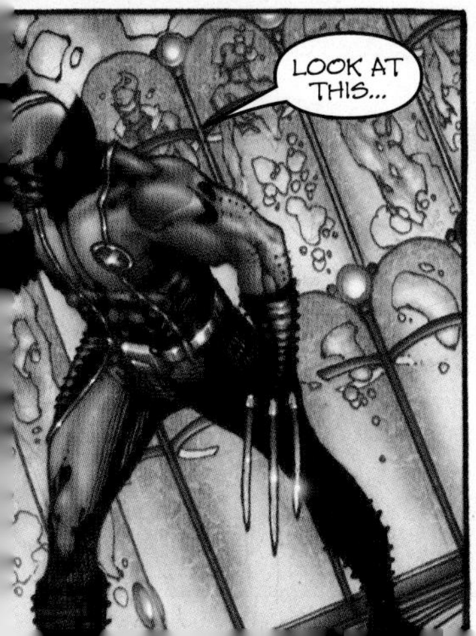
LOOK AT THIS...

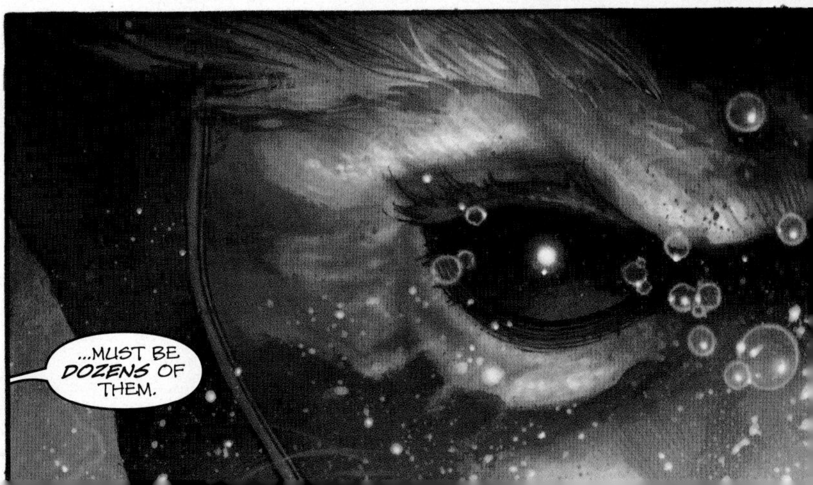
...MUST BE DOZENS OF THEM.

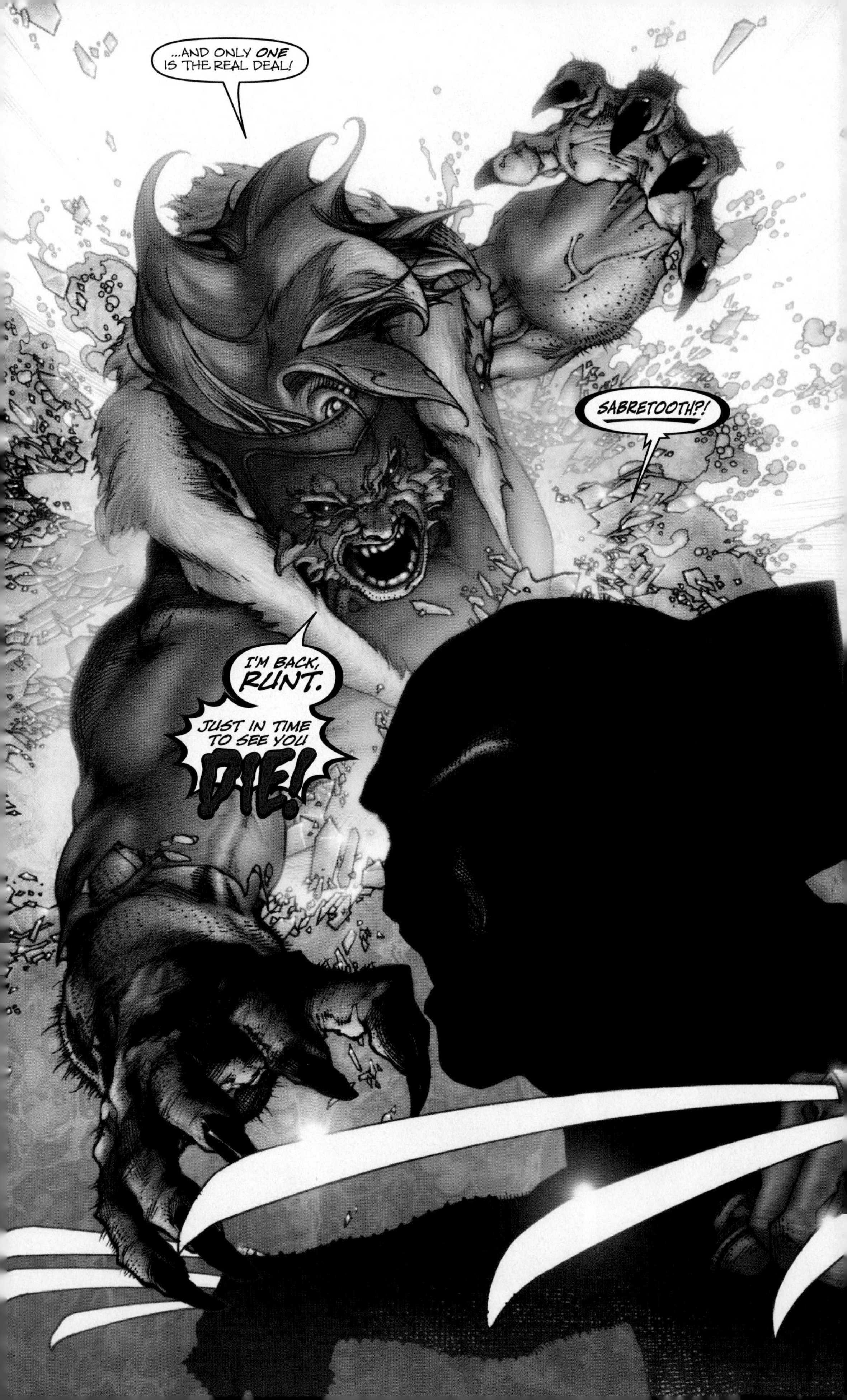
...AND ONLY ONE IS THE REAL DEAL!
SABRETOOTH?!
I'M BACK, RUNT.
JUST IN TIME TO SEE YOU DIE!

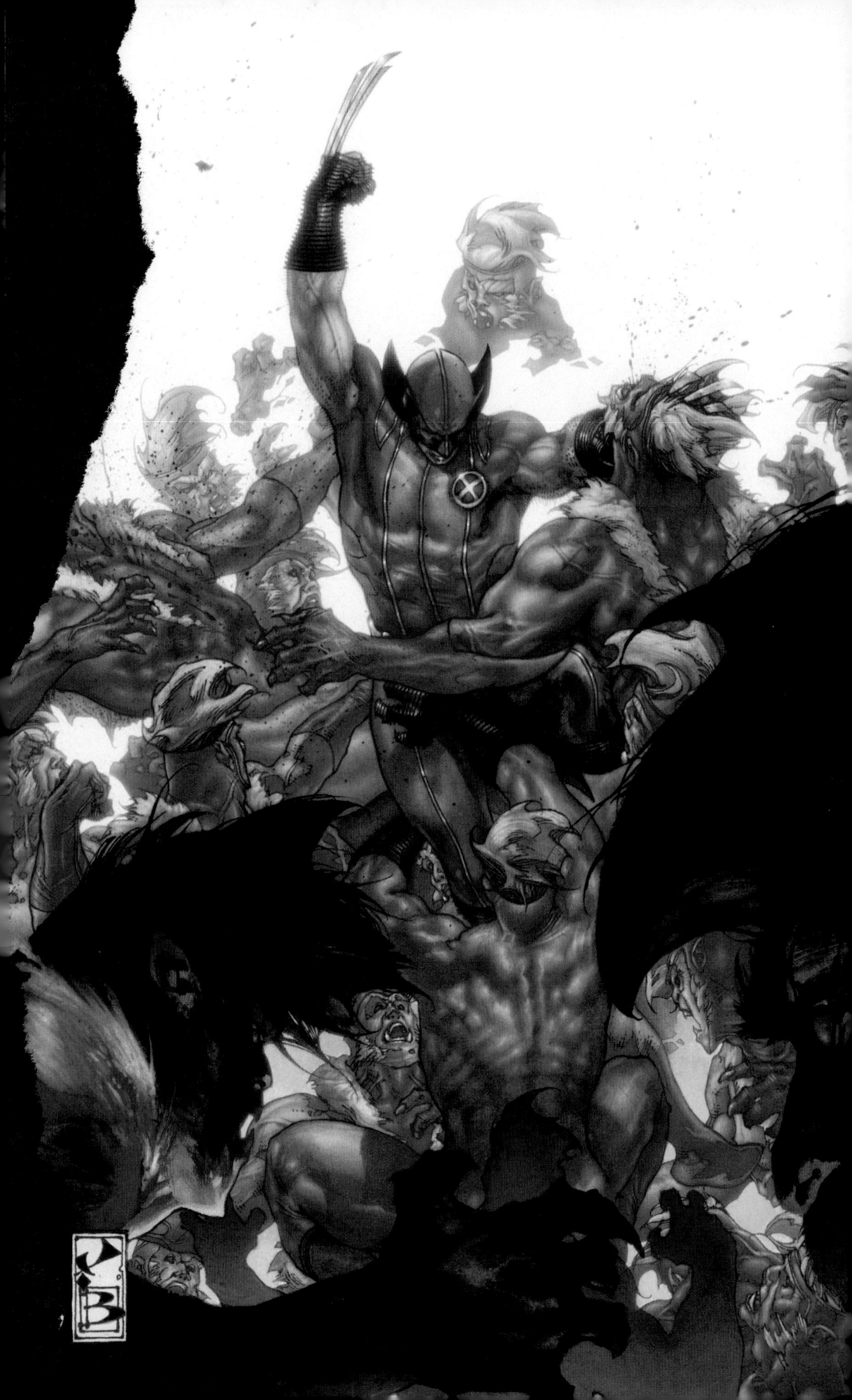

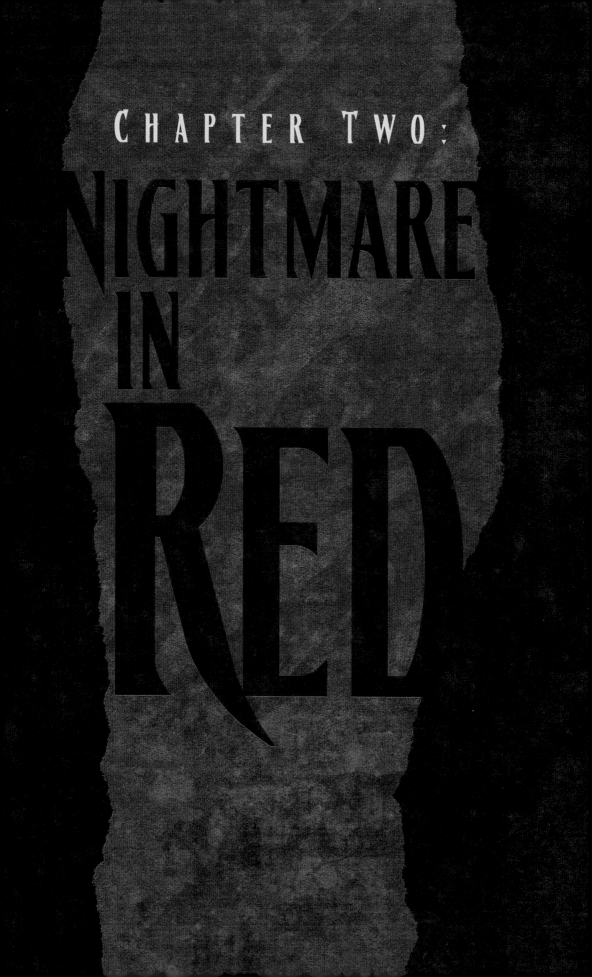

CHAPTER TWO:
NIGHTMARE IN RED

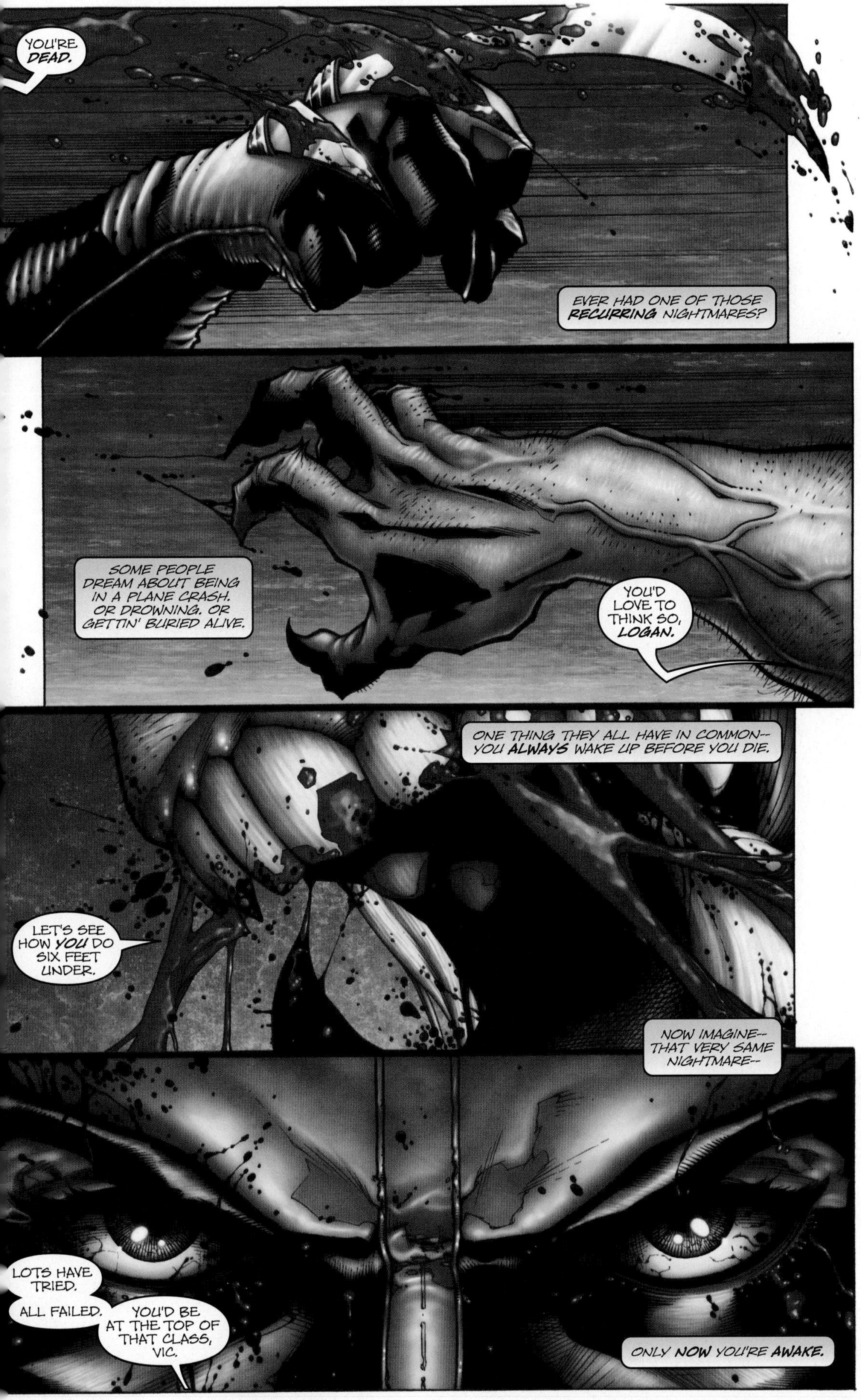
YOU'RE DEAD.
EVER HAD ONE OF THOSE RECURRING NIGHTMARES?
SOME PEOPLE DREAM ABOUT BEING IN A PLANE CRASH. OR DROWNING. OR GETTIN' BURIED ALIVE.
YOU'D LOVE TO THINK SO, LOGAN.
ONE THING THEY ALL HAVE IN COMMON-- YOU ALWAYS WAKE UP BEFORE YOU DIE.
LET'S SEE HOW YOU DO SIX FEET UNDER.
NOW IMAGINE-- THAT VERY SAME NIGHTMARE--
LOTS HAVE TRIED.
ALL FAILED.
YOU'D BE AT THE TOP OF THAT CLASS, VIC.
ONLY NOW YOU'RE AWAKE.

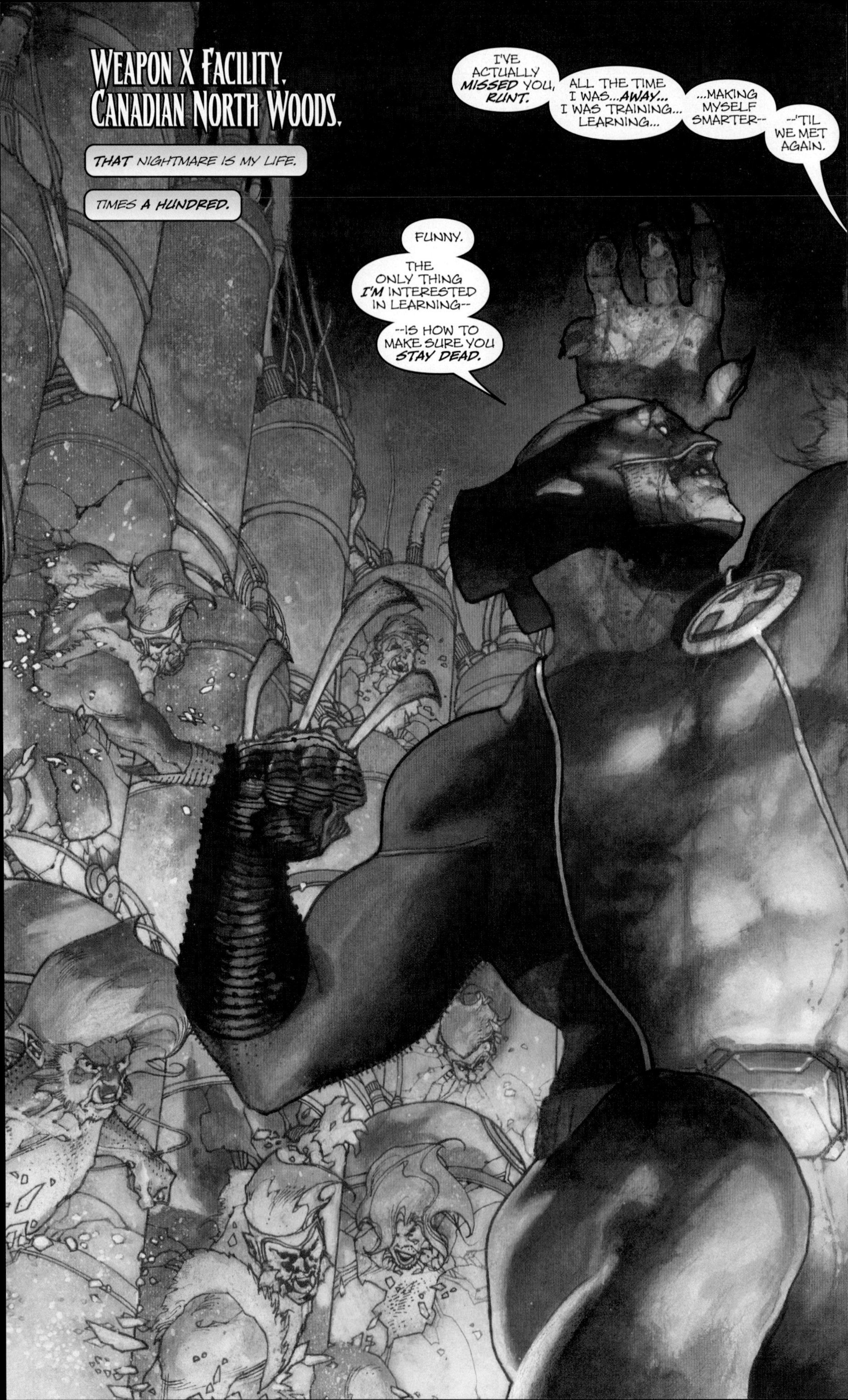
WEAPON X FACILITY.
CANADIAN NORTH WOODS.
THAT NIGHTMARE IS MY LIFE.
TIMES A HUNDRED.
I'VE ACTUALLY MISSED YOU, RUNT.
ALL THE TIME I WAS...AWAY... I WAS TRAINING... LEARNING...
...MAKING MYSELF SMARTER--
--'TIL WE MET AGAIN.
FUNNY.
THE ONLY THING I'M INTERESTED IN LEARNING--
--IS HOW TO MAKE SURE YOU STAY DEAD.

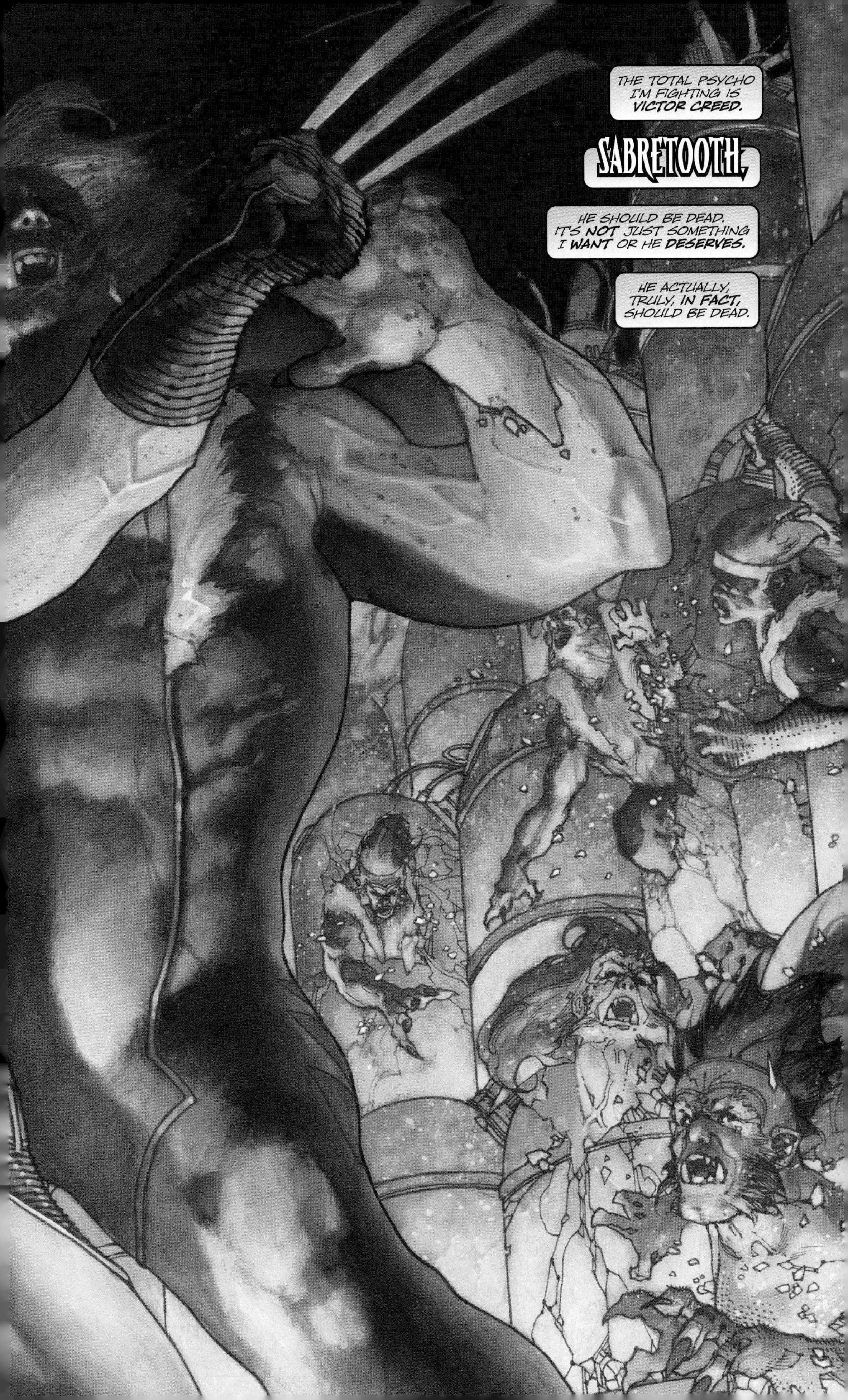

THE TOTAL PSYCHO I'M FIGHTING IS VICTOR CREED.
SABRETOOTH.
HE SHOULD BE DEAD. IT'S NOT JUST SOMETHING I WANT OR HE DESERVES.
HE ACTUALLY, TRULY, IN FACT, SHOULD BE DEAD.

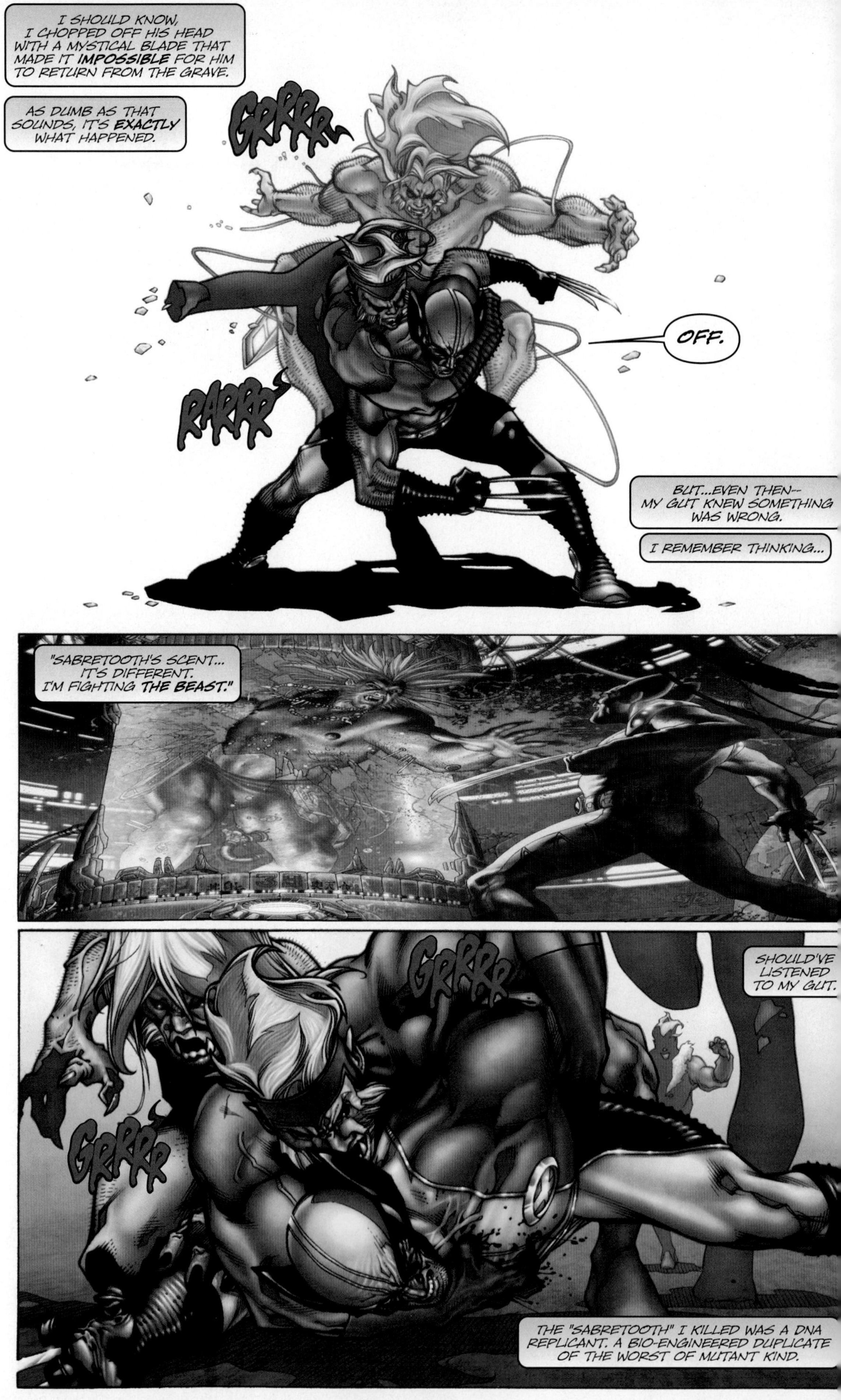

I SHOULD KNOW, I CHOPPED OFF HIS HEAD WITH A MYSTICAL BLADE THAT MADE IT IMPOSSIBLE FOR HIM TO RETURN FROM THE GRAVE.
AS DUMB AS THAT SOUNDS, IT'S EXACTLY WHAT HAPPENED.
GRRRR
OFF.
RARRR
BUT...EVEN THEN-- MY GUT KNEW SOMETHING WAS WRONG.
I REMEMBER THINKING...
"SABRETOOTH'S SCENT... IT'S DIFFERENT. I'M FIGHTING THE BEAST."
GRRRR
SHOULD'VE LISTENED TO MY GUT.
GRRRR
THE "SABRETOOTH" I KILLED WAS A DNA REPLICANT. A BIO-ENGINEERED DUPLICATE OF THE WORST OF MUTANT KIND.

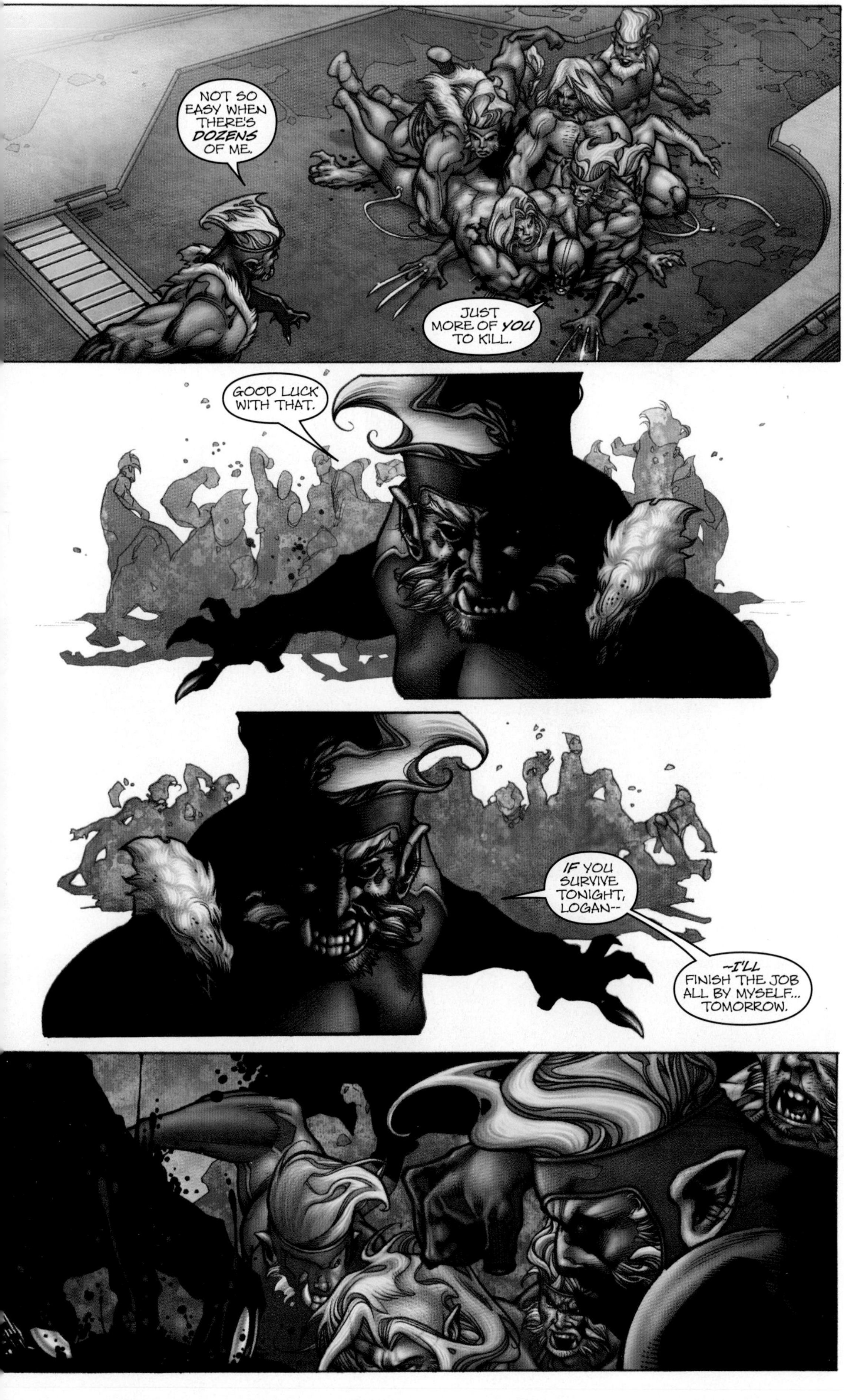
NOT SO EASY WHEN THERE'S DOZENS OF ME.
JUST MORE OF YOU TO KILL.
GOOD LUCK WITH THAT.
IF YOU SURVIVE TONIGHT, LOGAN--
--I'LL FINISH THE JOB ALL BY MYSELF... TOMORROW.

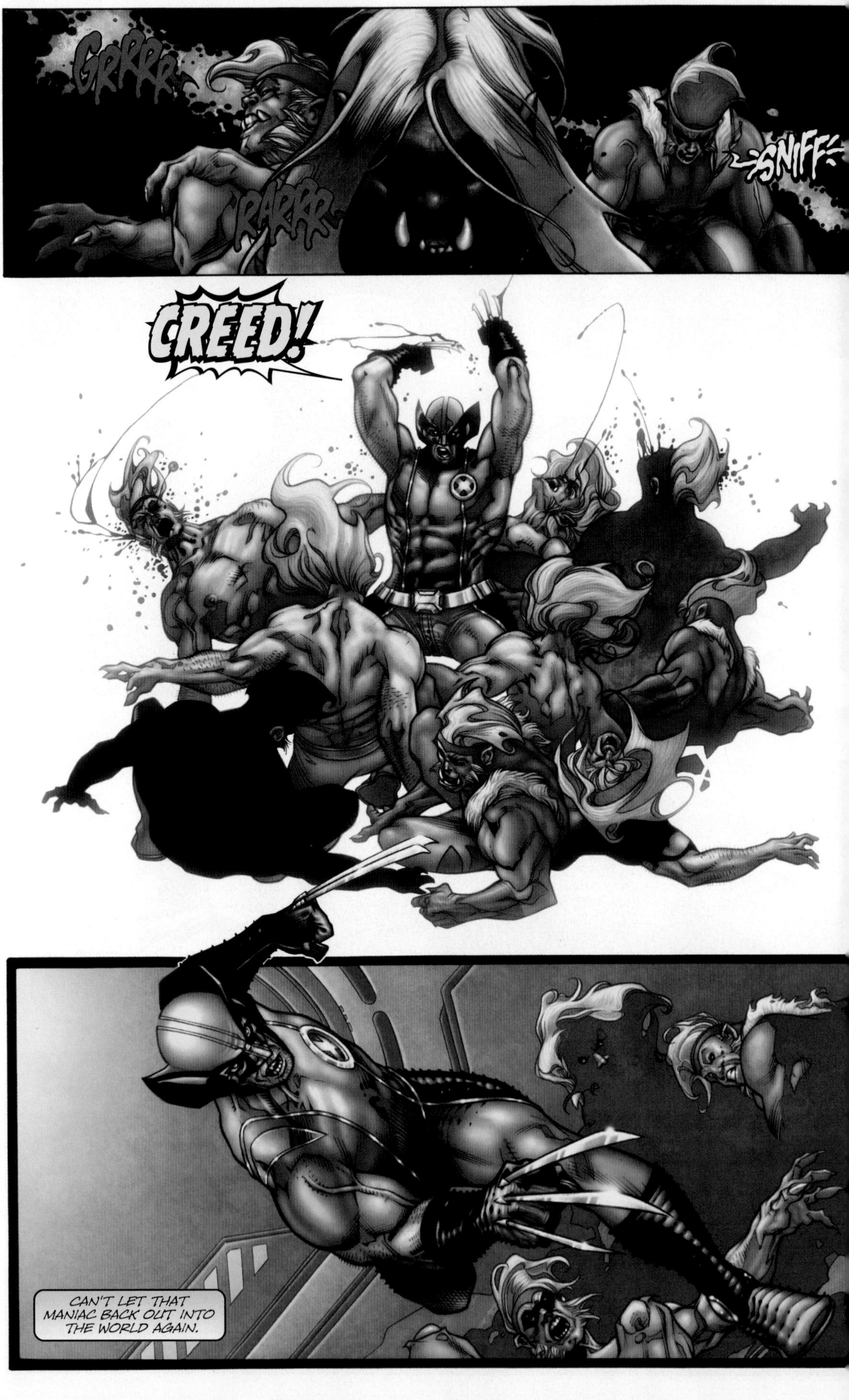
GRRRR
RARRR
SNIFF
CREED!
CAN'T LET THAT MANIAC BACK OUT INTO THE WORLD AGAIN.

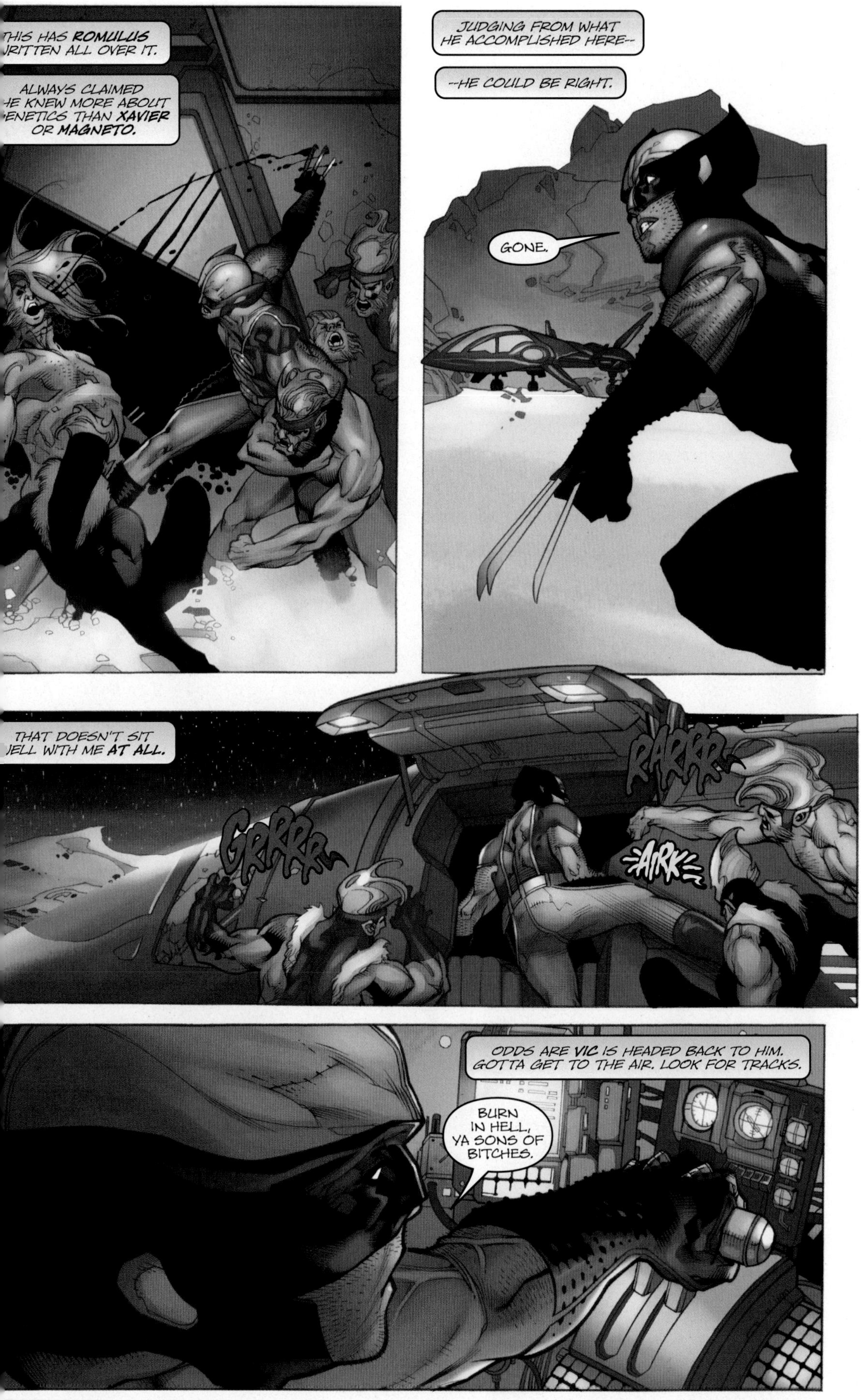
THIS HAS ROMULUS
RITTEN ALL OVER IT.
ALWAYS CLAIMED HE KNEW MORE ABOUT ENETICS THAN XAVIER OR MAGNETO.
JUDGING FROM WHAT HE ACCOMPLISHED HERE--
--HE COULD BE RIGHT.
GONE.
THAT DOESN'T SIT ELL WITH ME AT ALL.
RARRR
GRRRR
AIRK
ODDS ARE VIC IS HEADED BACK TO HIM. GOTTA GET TO THE AIR. LOOK FOR TRACKS.
BURN IN HELL, YA SONS OF BITCHES.

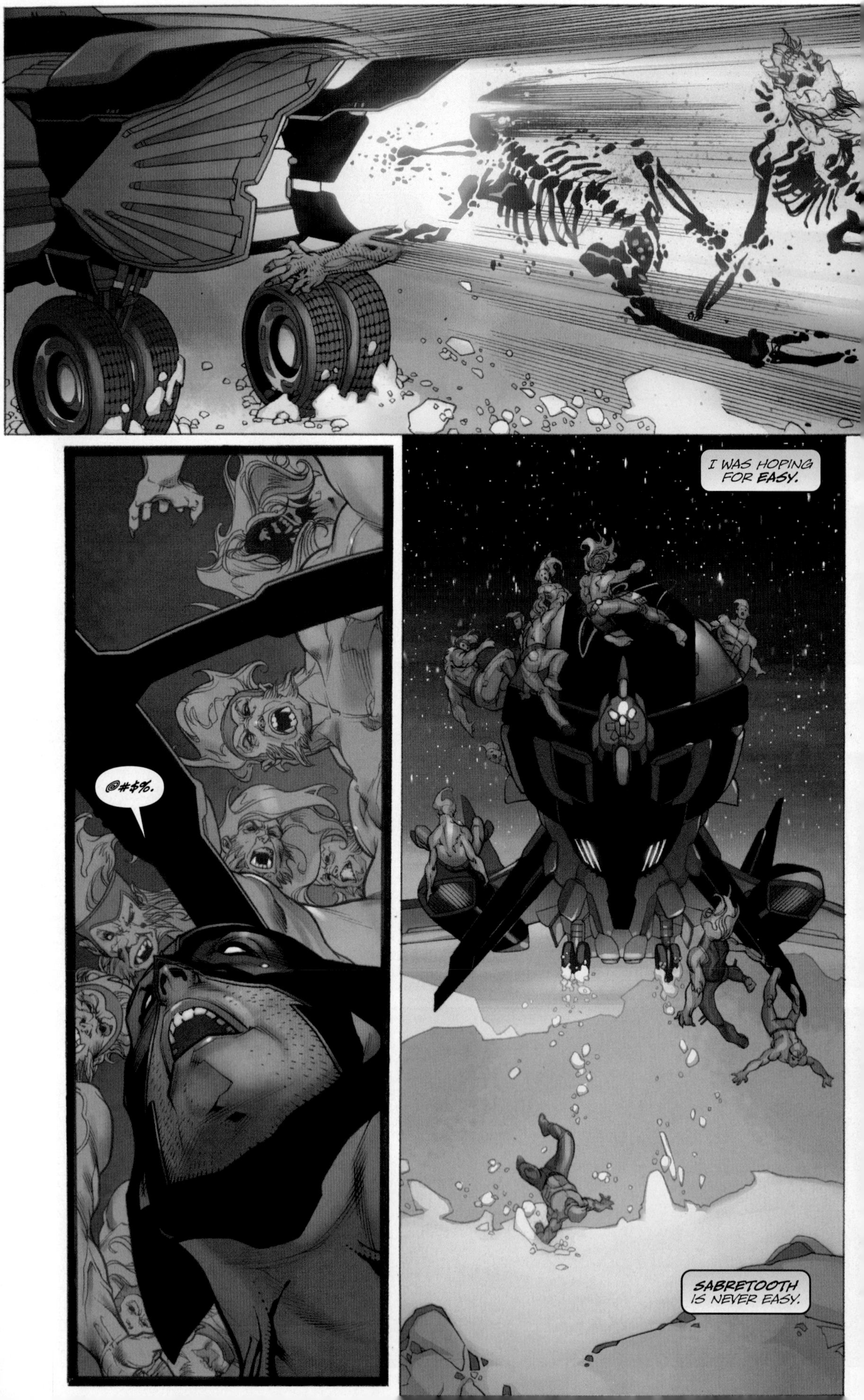
@#$%.
I WAS HOPING FOR EASY.
SABRETOOTH IS NEVER EASY.

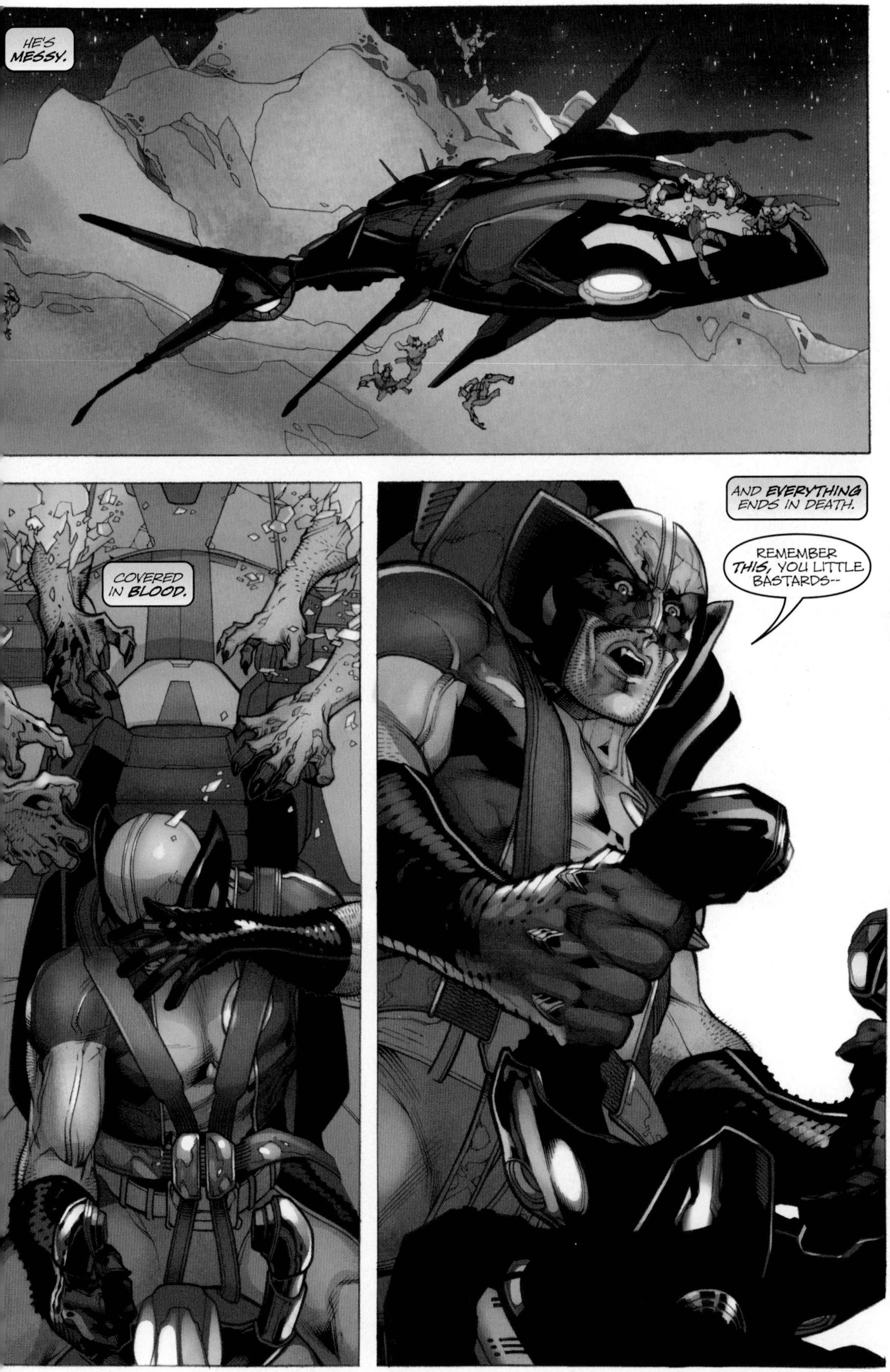
HE'S MESSY.
COVERED IN BLOOD.
AND EVERYTHING ENDS IN DEATH.
REMEMBER THIS, YOU LITTLE BASTARDS--

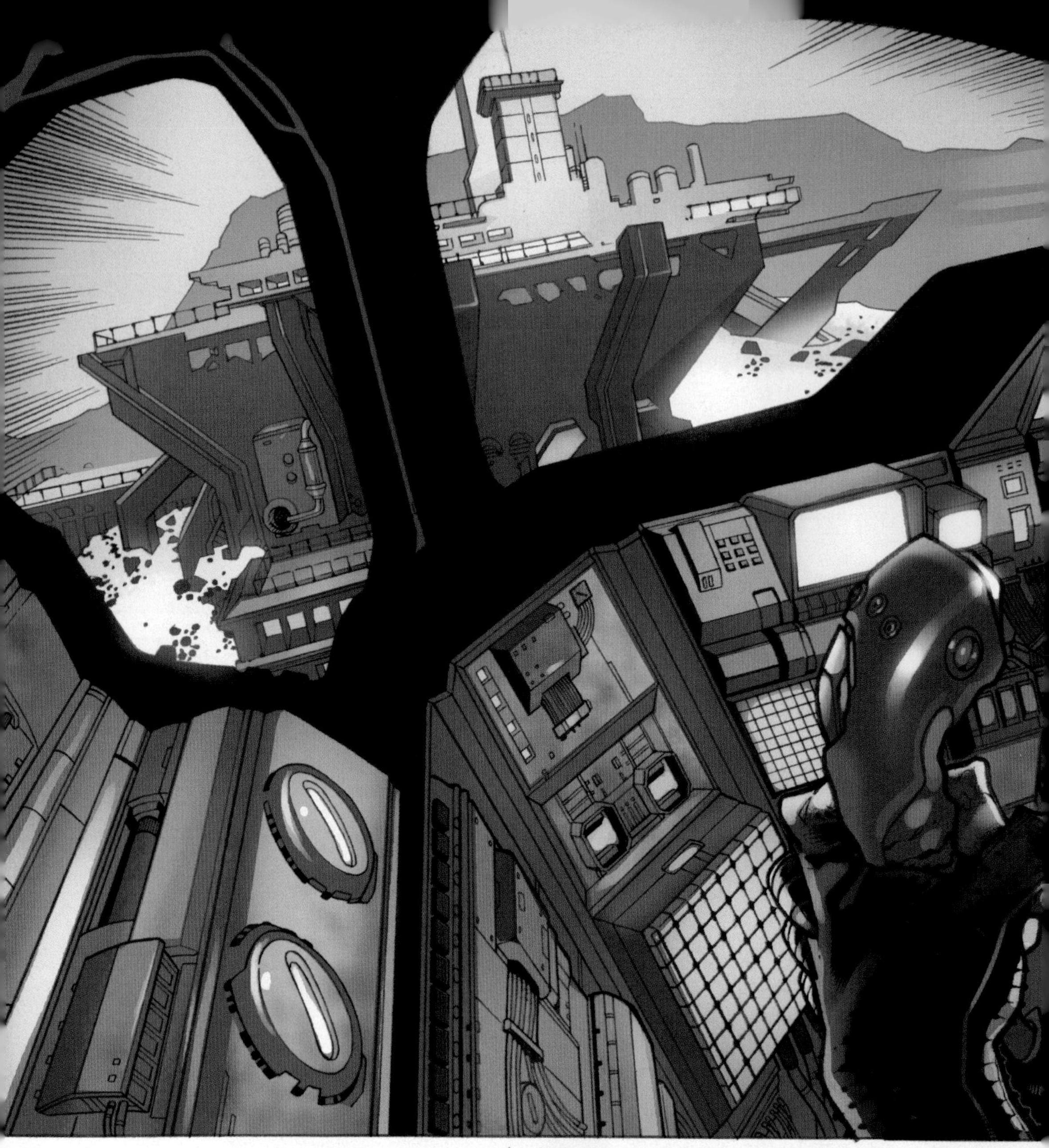
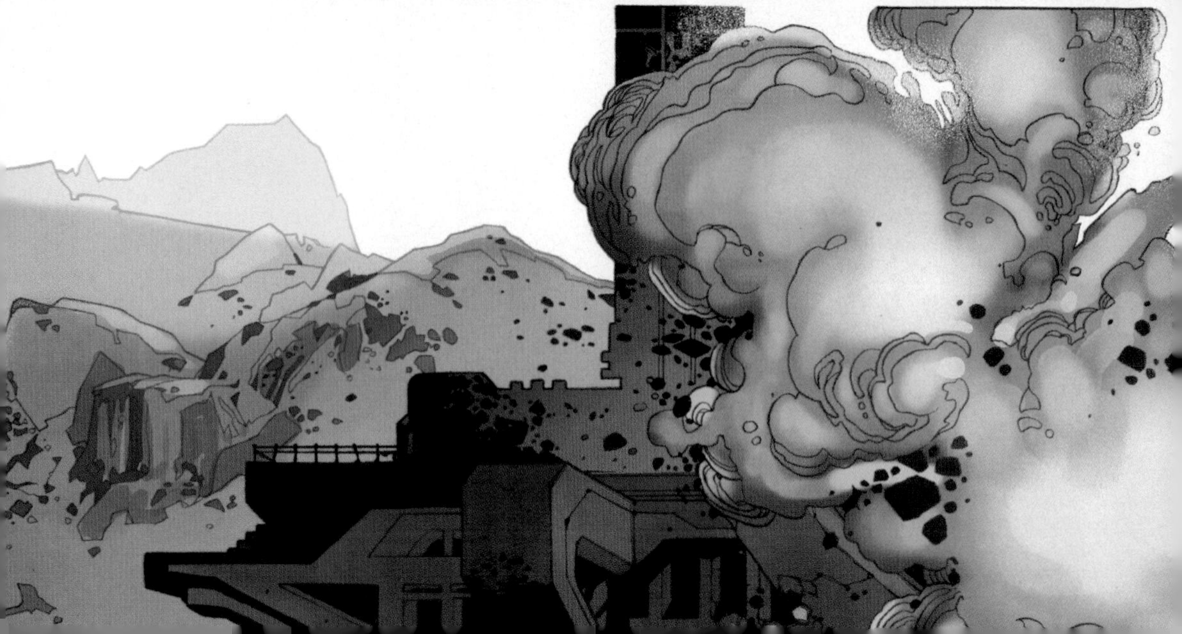

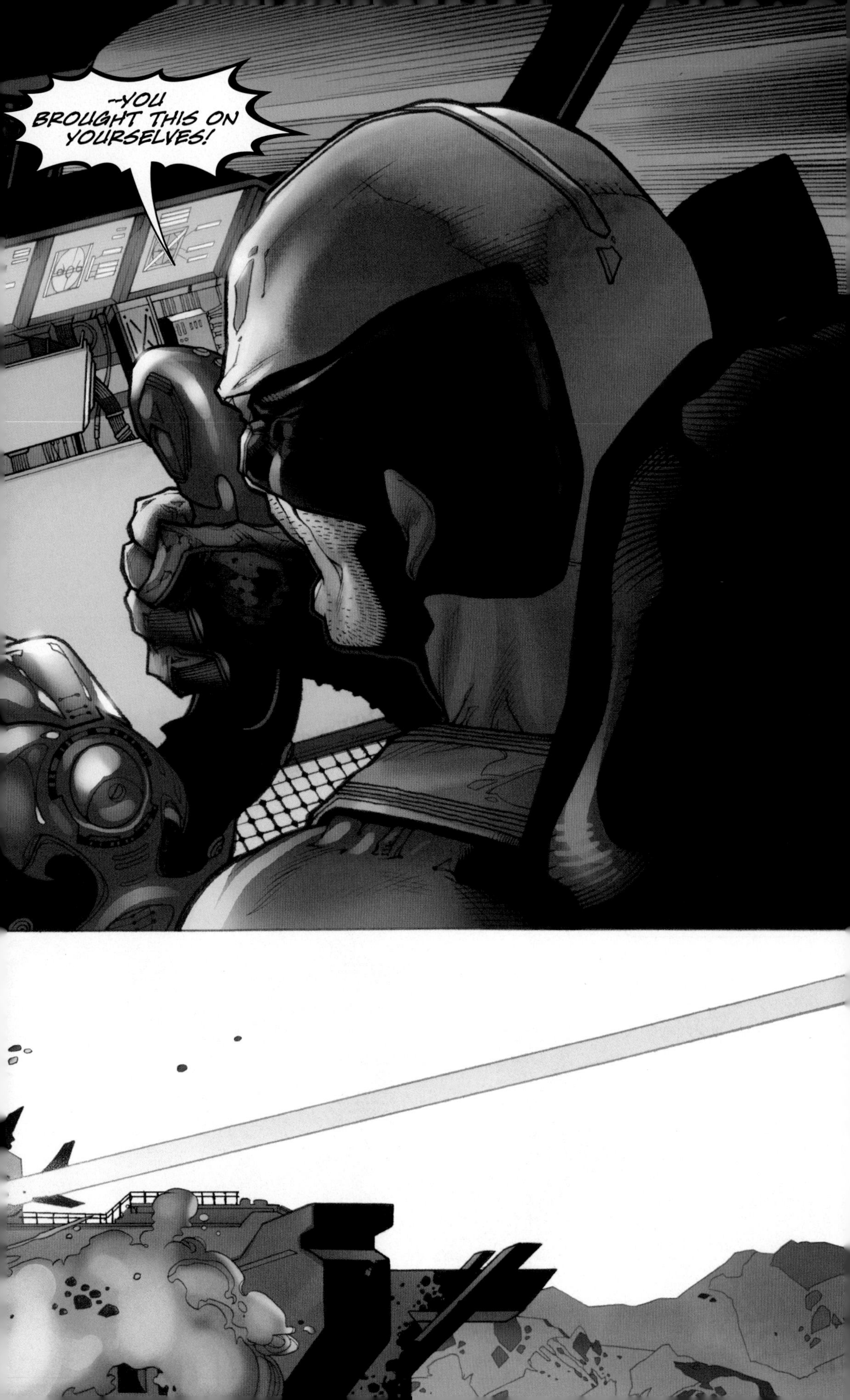
--YOU BROUGHT THIS ON YOURSELVES!

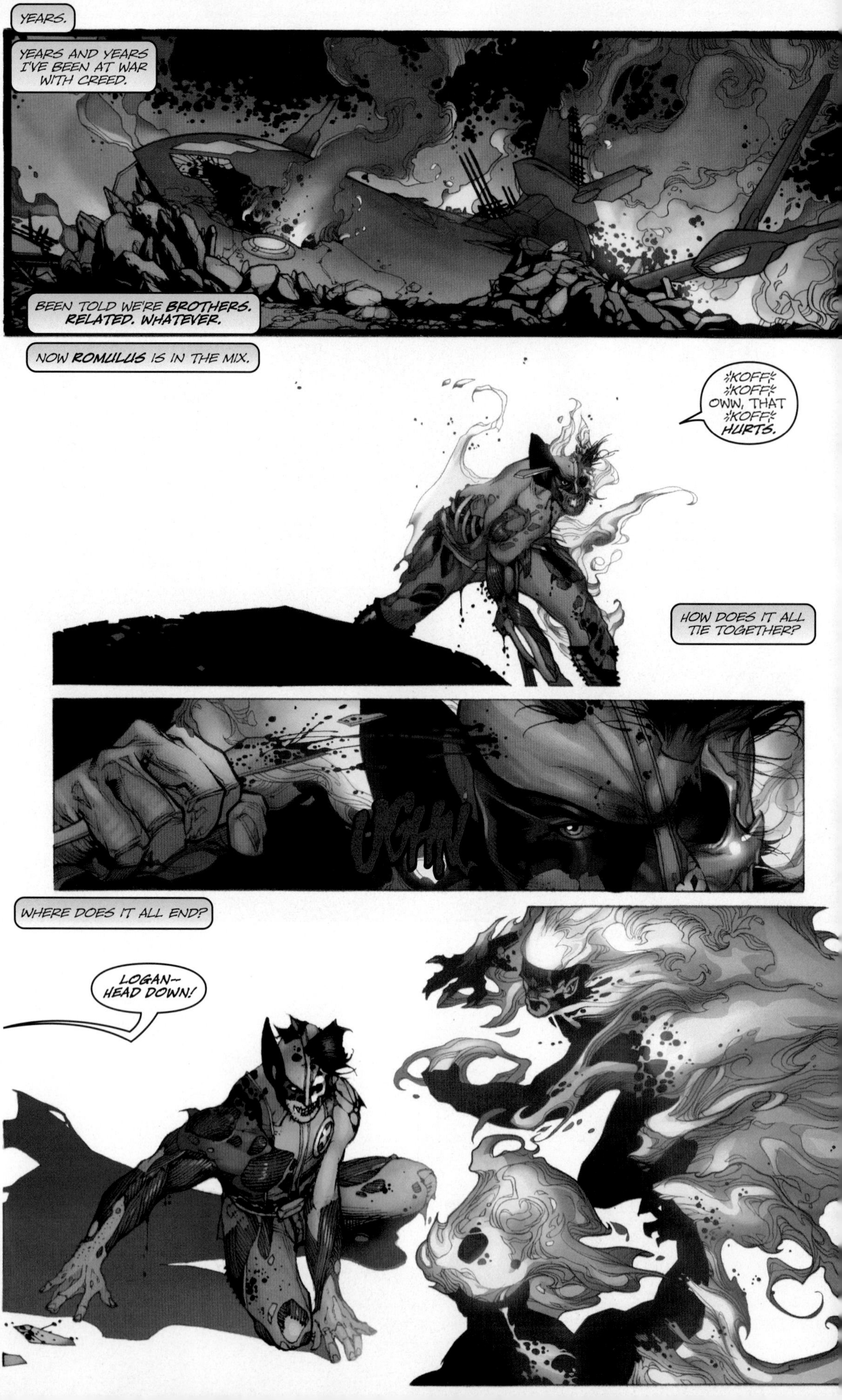
YEARS.
YEARS AND YEARS I'VE BEEN AT WAR WITH CREED.
BEEN TOLD WE'RE **BROTHERS. RELATED. WHATEVER.**
NOW **ROMULUS** IS IN THE MIX.
KOFF *KOFF* OWW, THAT *KOFF* **HURTS.**
HOW DOES IT ALL TIE TOGETHER?
UGHN
WHERE DOES IT ALL END?
LOGAN-- HEAD DOWN!

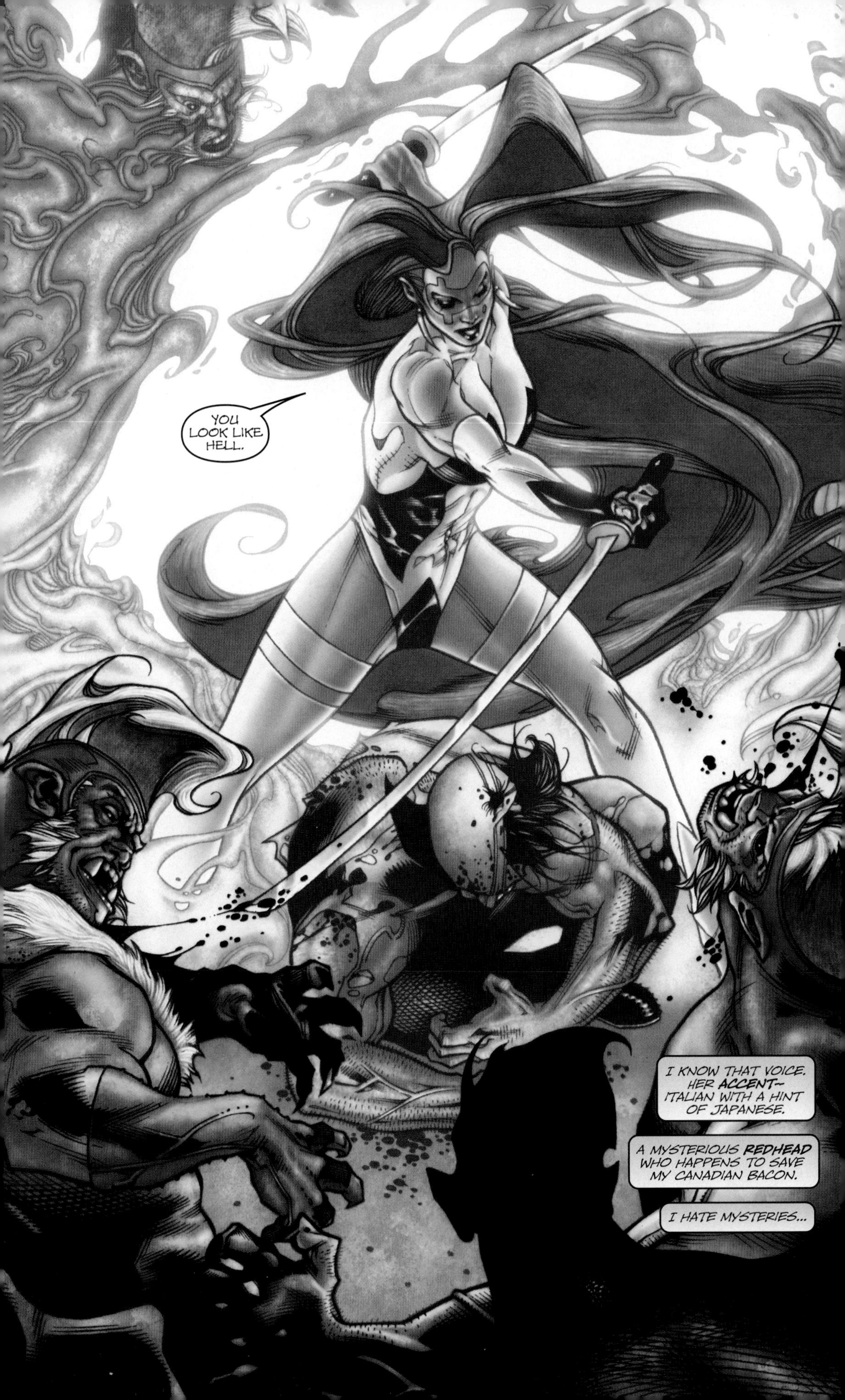

YOU LOOK LIKE HELL.
I KNOW THAT VOICE. HER ACCENT-- ITALIAN WITH A HINT OF JAPANESE.
A MYSTERIOUS REDHEAD WHO HAPPENS TO SAVE MY CANADIAN BACON.
I HATE MYSTERIES...

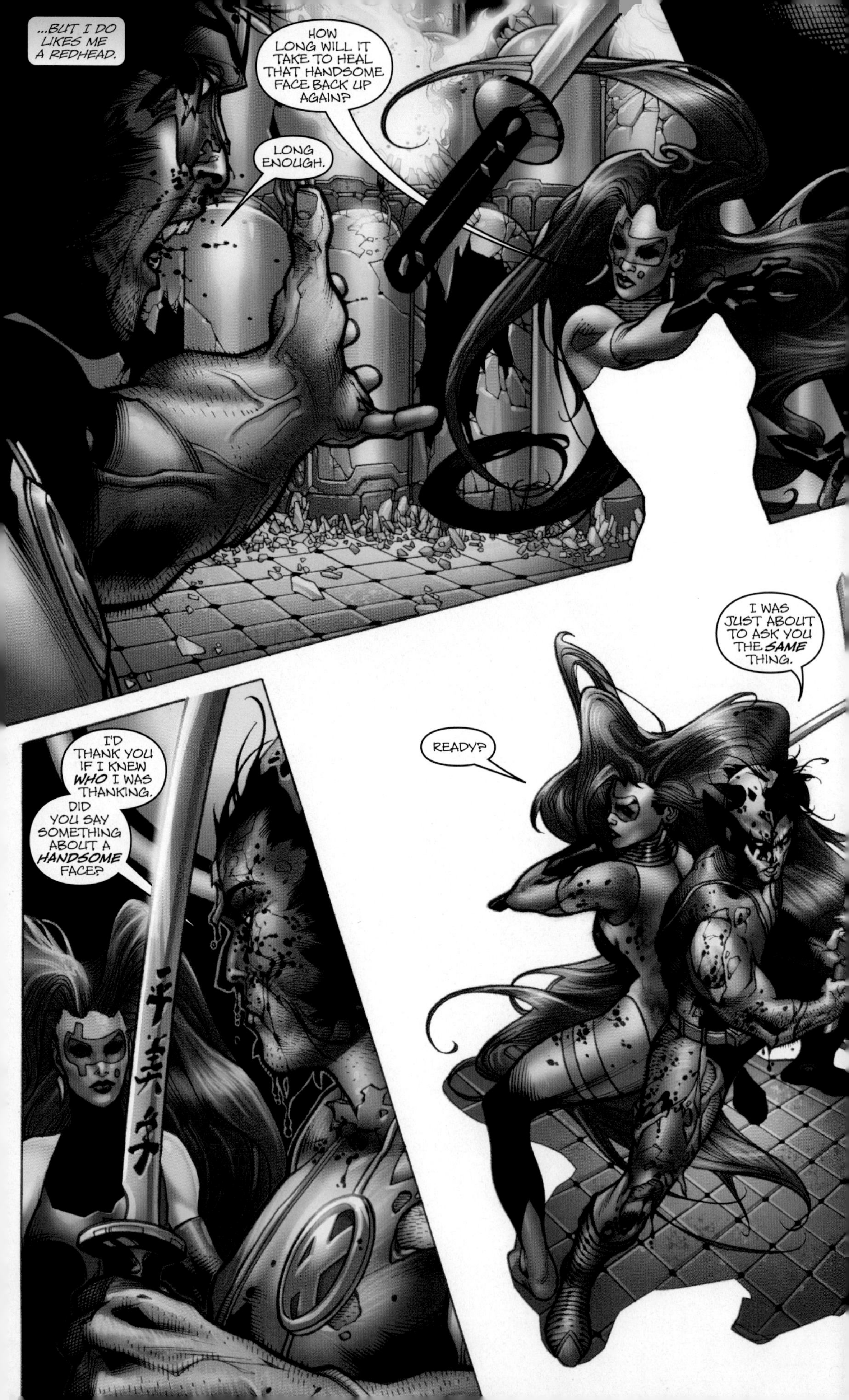
...BUT I DO LIKES ME A REDHEAD.
HOW LONG WILL IT TAKE TO HEAL THAT HANDSOME FACE BACK UP AGAIN?
LONG ENOUGH.
I'D THANK YOU IF I KNEW WHO I WAS THANKING.
DID YOU SAY SOMETHING ABOUT A HANDSOME FACE?
READY?
I WAS JUST ABOUT TO ASK YOU THE SAME THING.

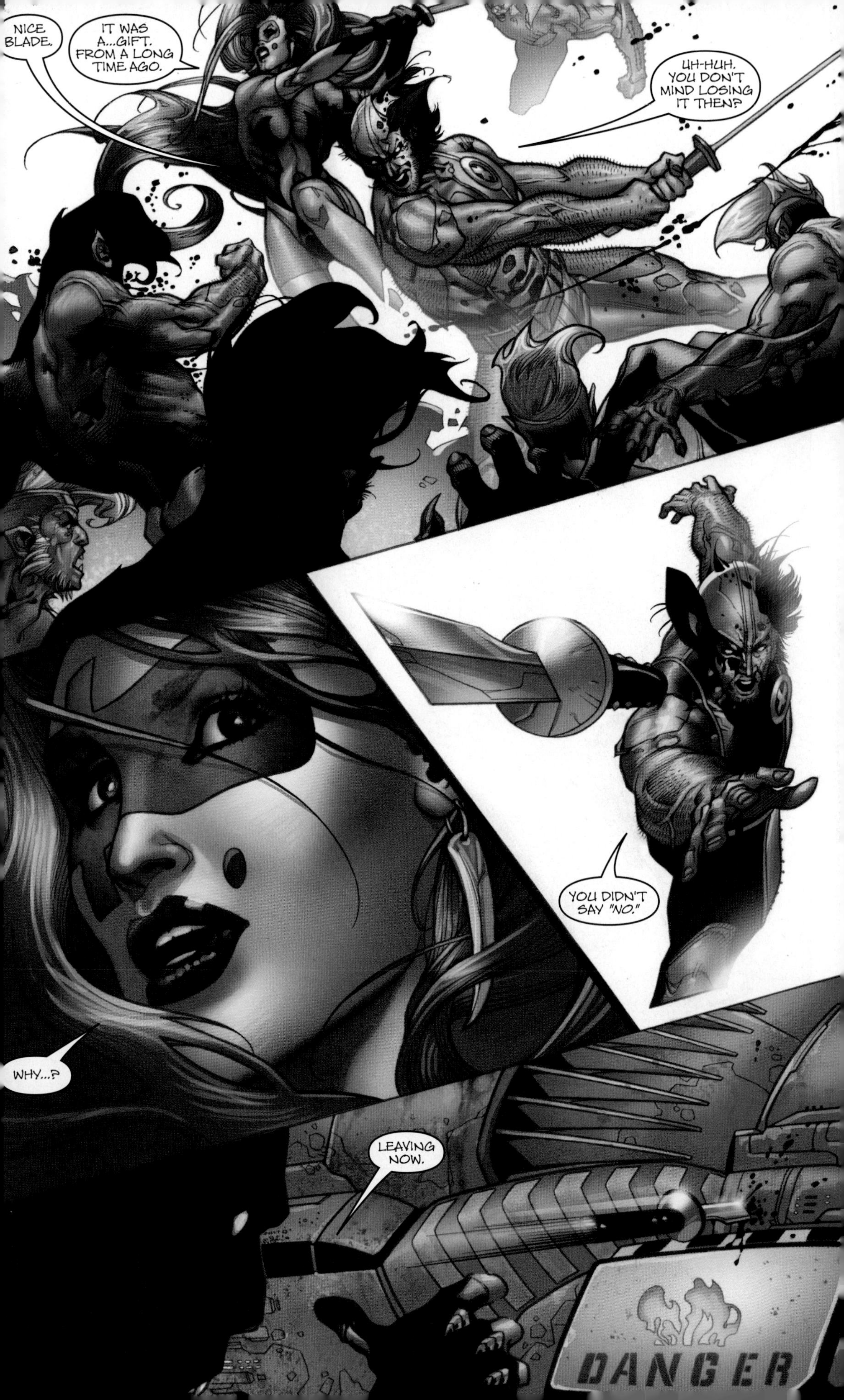
NICE BLADE.
IT WAS A...GIFT. FROM A LONG TIME AGO.
UH-HUH. YOU DON'T MIND LOSING IT THEN?
YOU DIDN'T SAY "NO."
WHY...?
LEAVING NOW.
DANGER

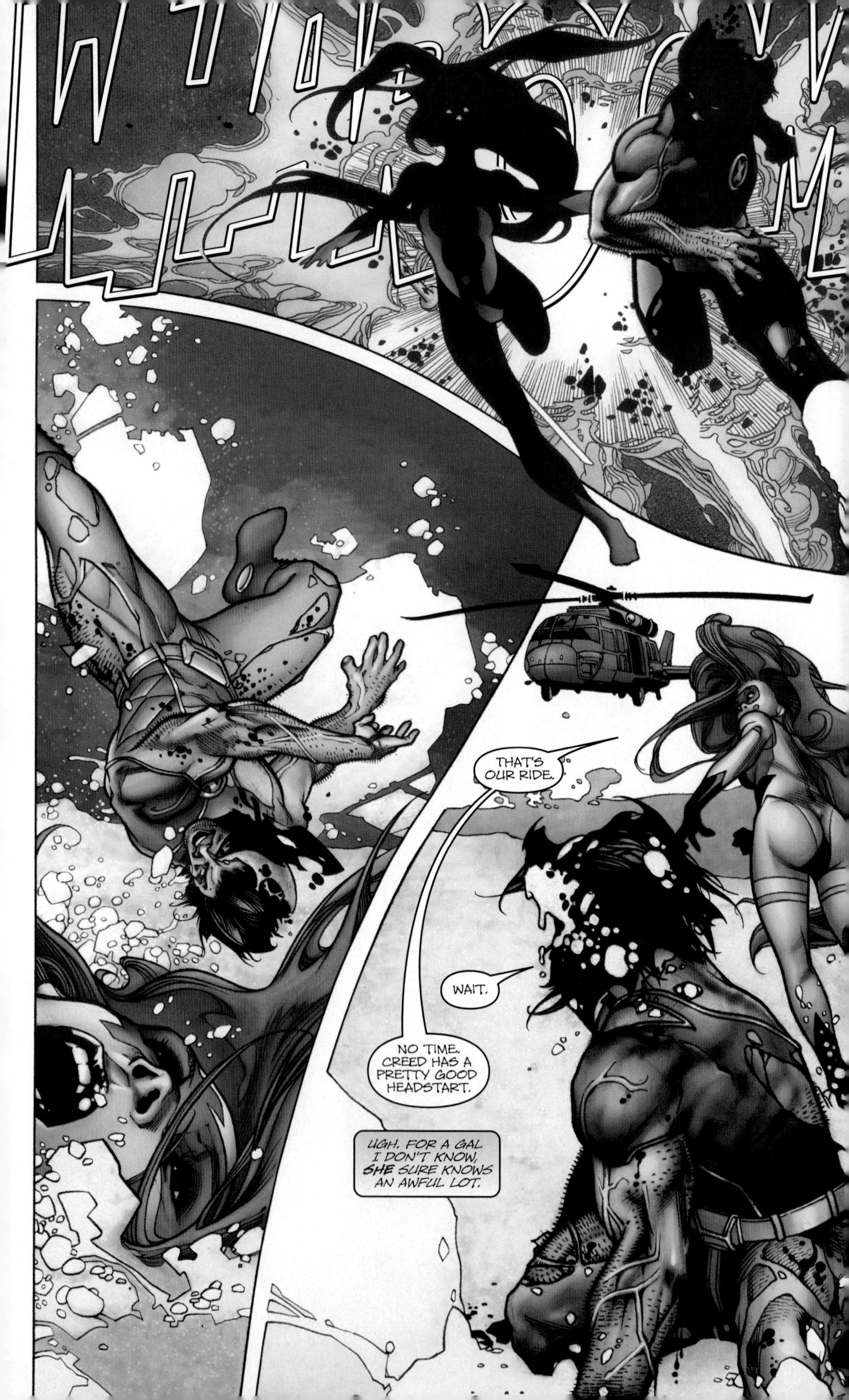
WHOOOM
THAT'S OUR RIDE.
WAIT.
NO TIME. CREED HAS A PRETTY GOOD HEADSTART.
UGH. FOR A GAL I DON'T KNOW, SHE SURE KNOWS AN AWFUL LOT.

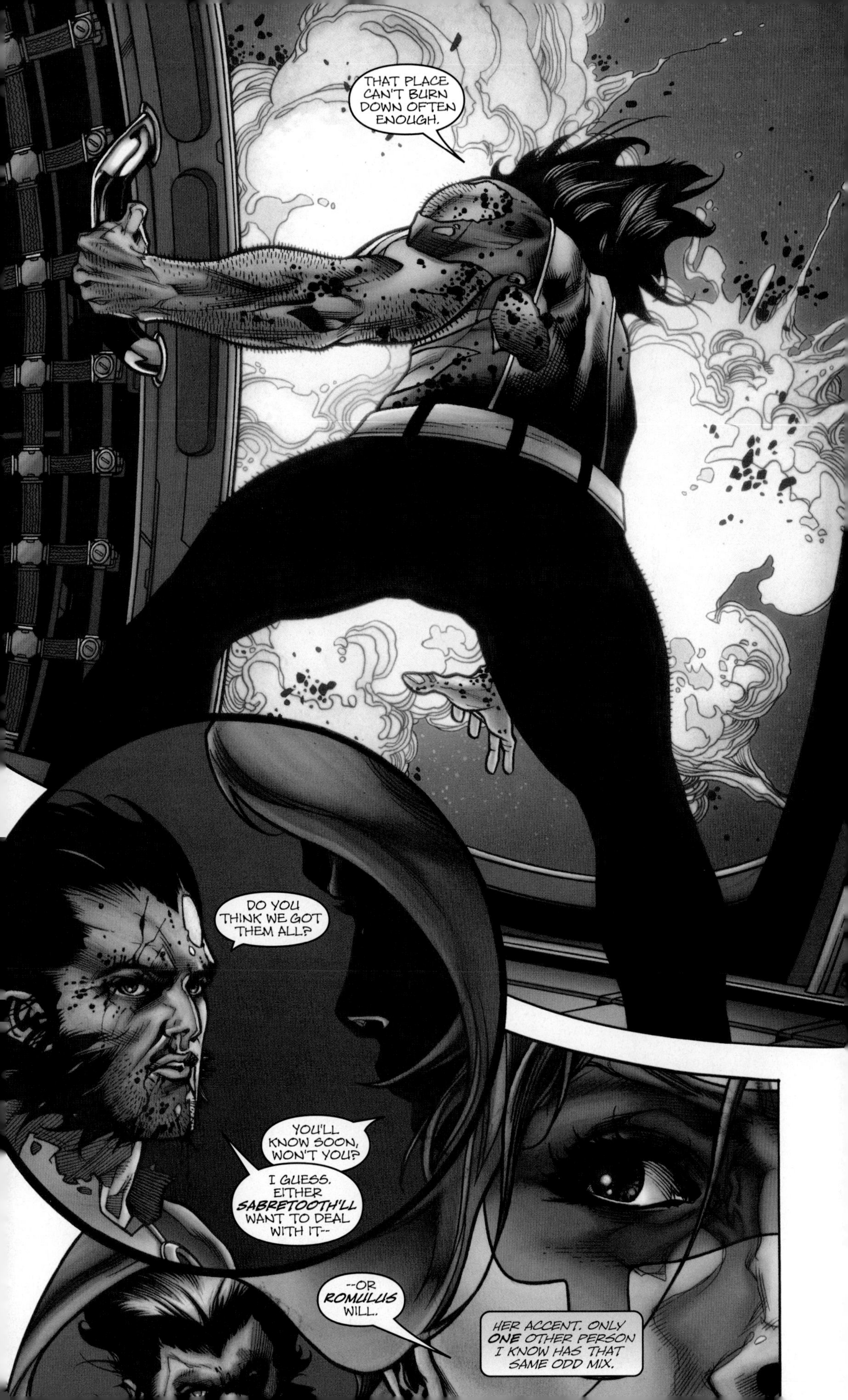
THAT PLACE CAN'T BURN DOWN OFTEN ENOUGH.
DO YOU THINK WE GOT THEM ALL?
YOU'LL KNOW SOON, WON'T YOU?
I GUESS. EITHER SABRETOOTH'LL WANT TO DEAL WITH IT--
--OR ROMULUS WILL.
HER ACCENT. ONLY ONE OTHER PERSON I KNOW HAS THAT SAME ODD MIX.

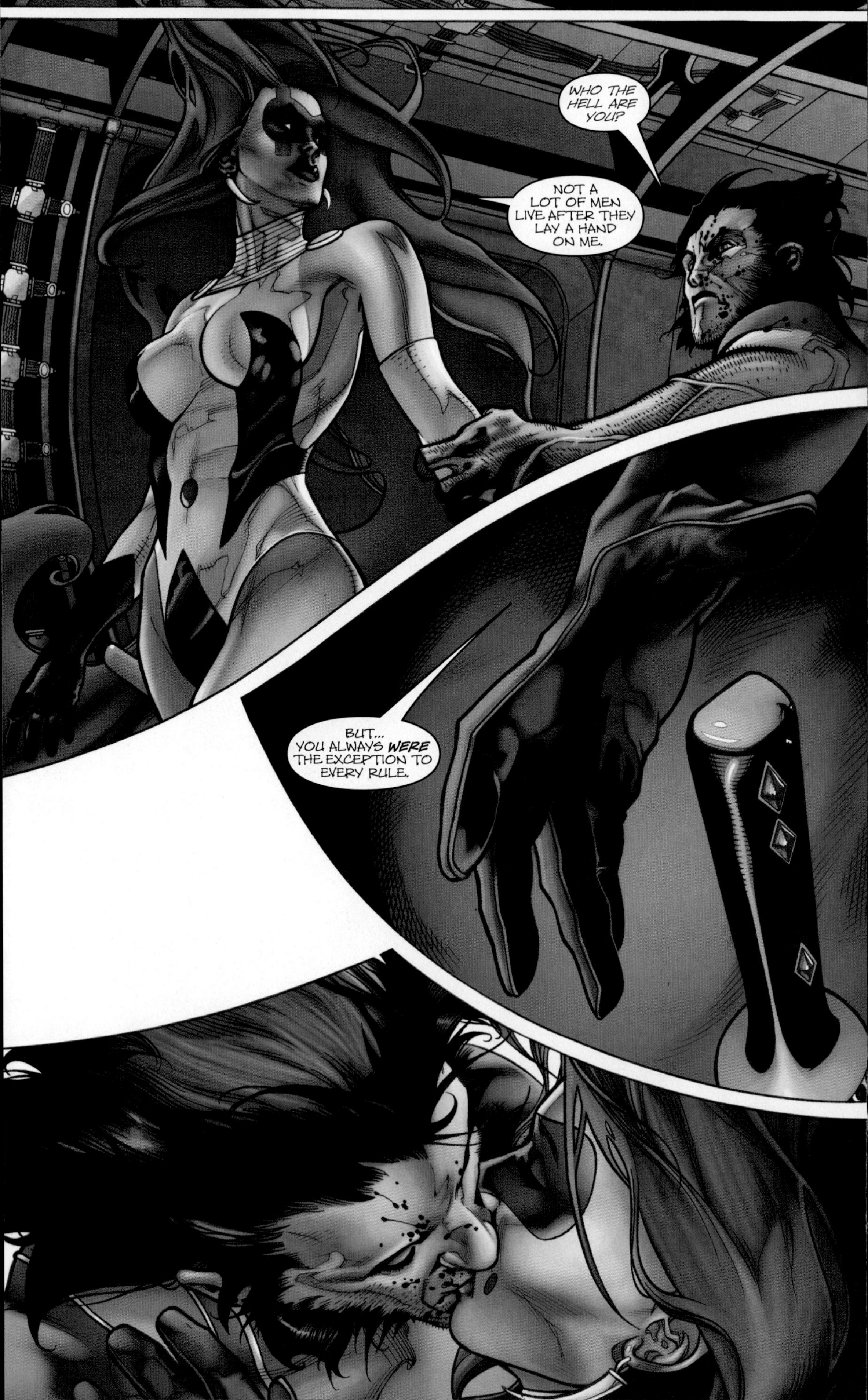
WHO THE HELL ARE YOU?
NOT A LOT OF MEN LIVE AFTER THEY LAY A HAND ON ME.
BUT... YOU ALWAYS *WERE* THE EXCEPTION TO EVERY RULE.

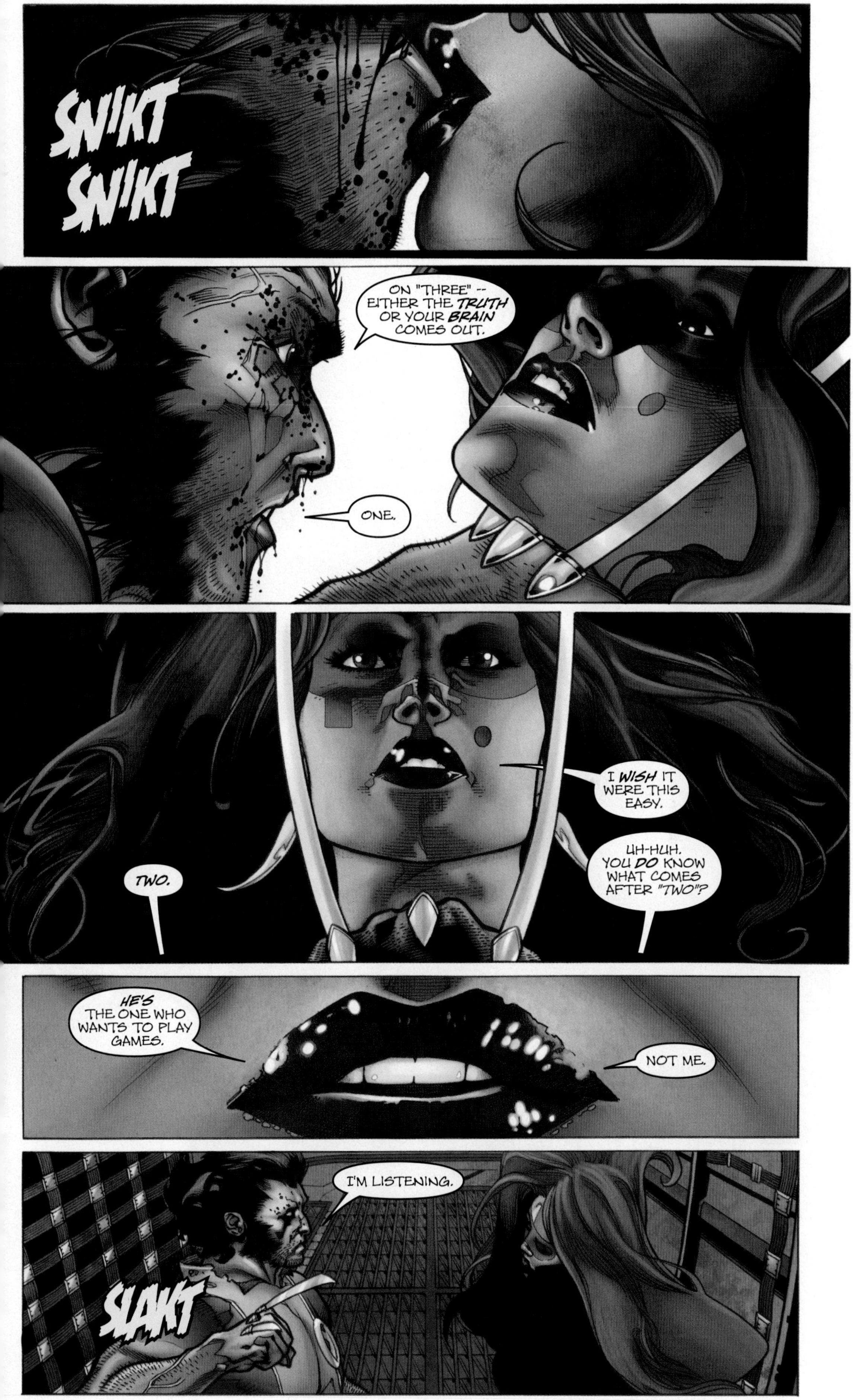
SNIKT
SNIKT
ON "THREE" -- EITHER THE TRUTH OR YOUR BRAIN COMES OUT.
ONE.
I WISH IT WERE THIS EASY.
TWO.
UH-HUH. YOU DO KNOW WHAT COMES AFTER "TWO"?
HE'S THE ONE WHO WANTS TO PLAY GAMES.
NOT ME.
I'M LISTENING.
SLAKT

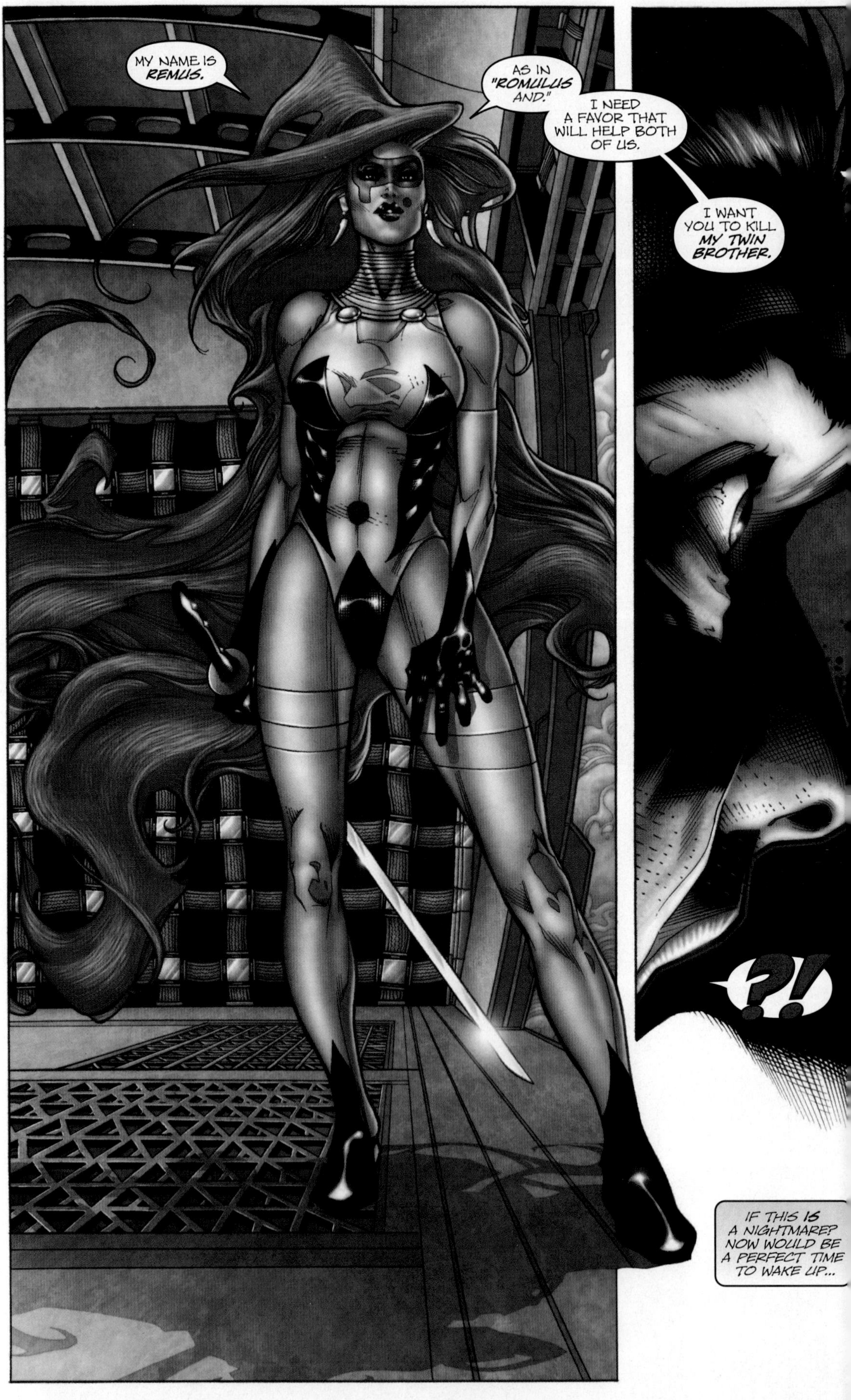
MY NAME IS REMUS.
AS IN "ROMULUS AND."
I NEED A FAVOR THAT WILL HELP BOTH OF US.
I WANT YOU TO KILL MY TWIN BROTHER.
?!
IF THIS IS A NIGHTMARE? NOW WOULD BE A PERFECT TIME TO WAKE UP...

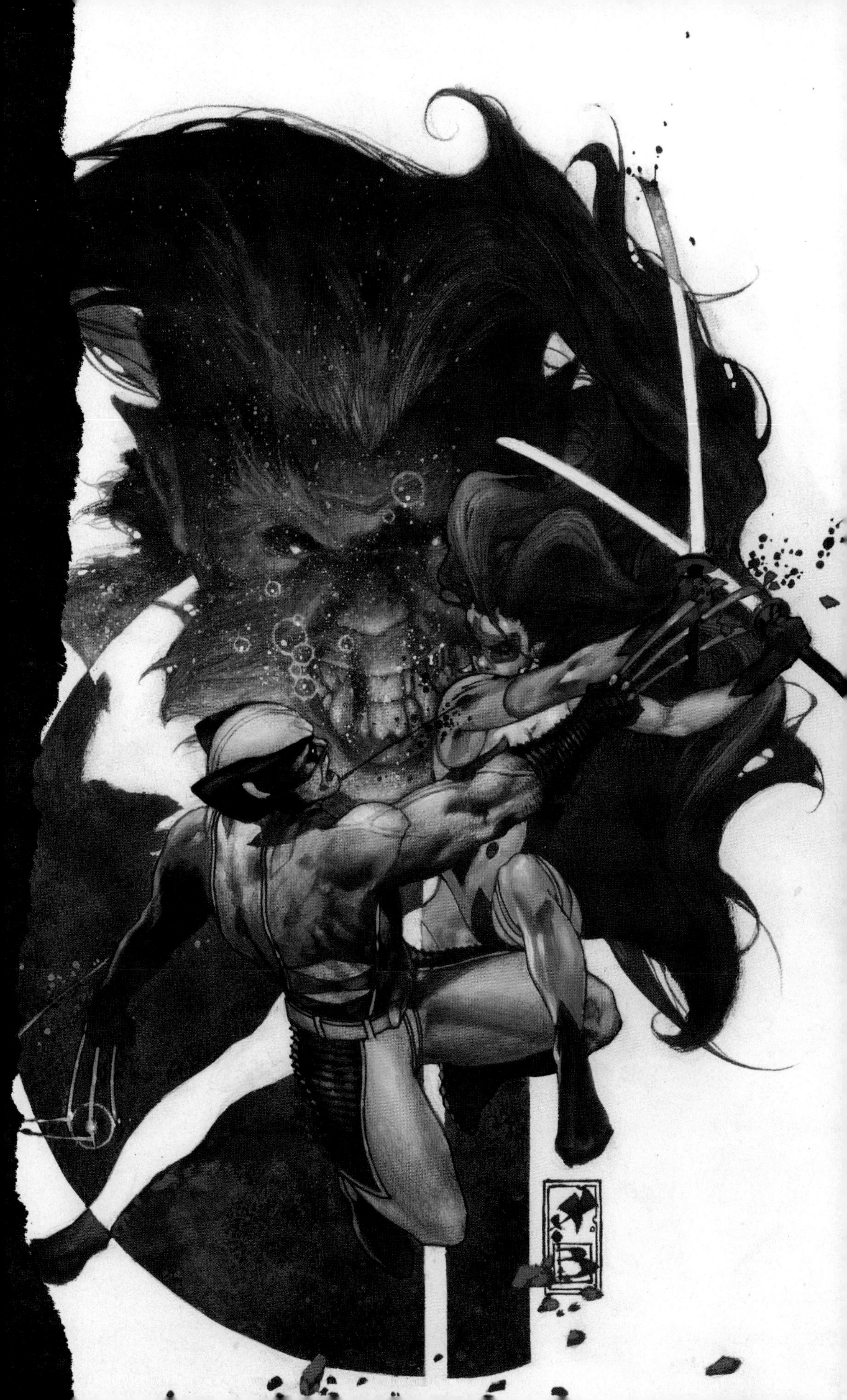

Chapter Three:

Remus

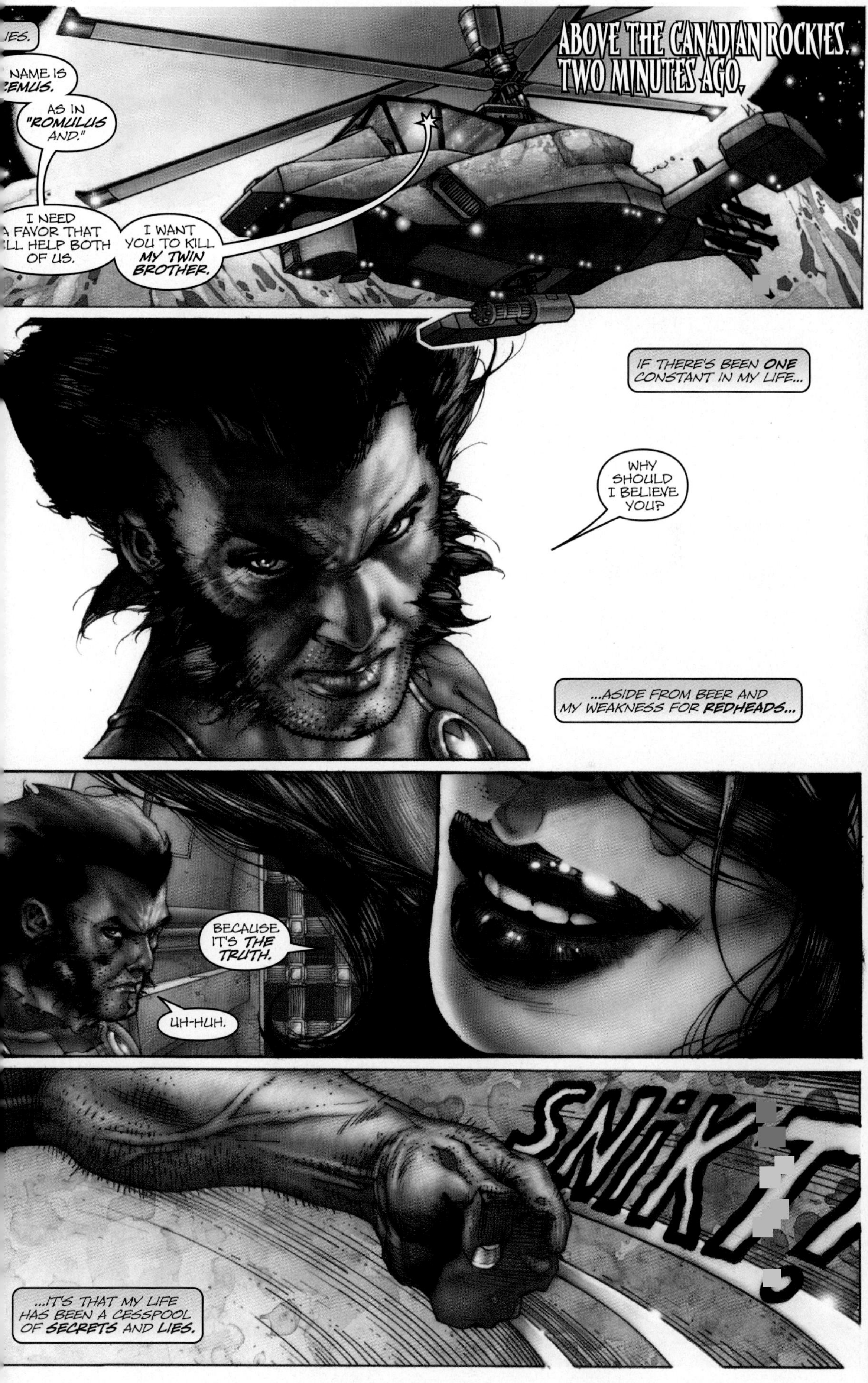

IES.
NAME IS EMUS.
AS IN "ROMULUS AND."
I NEED A FAVOR THAT LL HELP BOTH OF US.
I WANT YOU TO KILL MY TWIN BROTHER.
ABOVE THE CANADIAN ROCKIES. TWO MINUTES AGO.
IF THERE'S BEEN ONE CONSTANT IN MY LIFE...
WHY SHOULD I BELIEVE YOU?
...ASIDE FROM BEER AND MY WEAKNESS FOR REDHEADS...
BECAUSE IT'S THE TRUTH.
UH-HUH.
SNIKT
...IT'S THAT MY LIFE HAS BEEN A CESSPOOL OF SECRETS AND LIES.

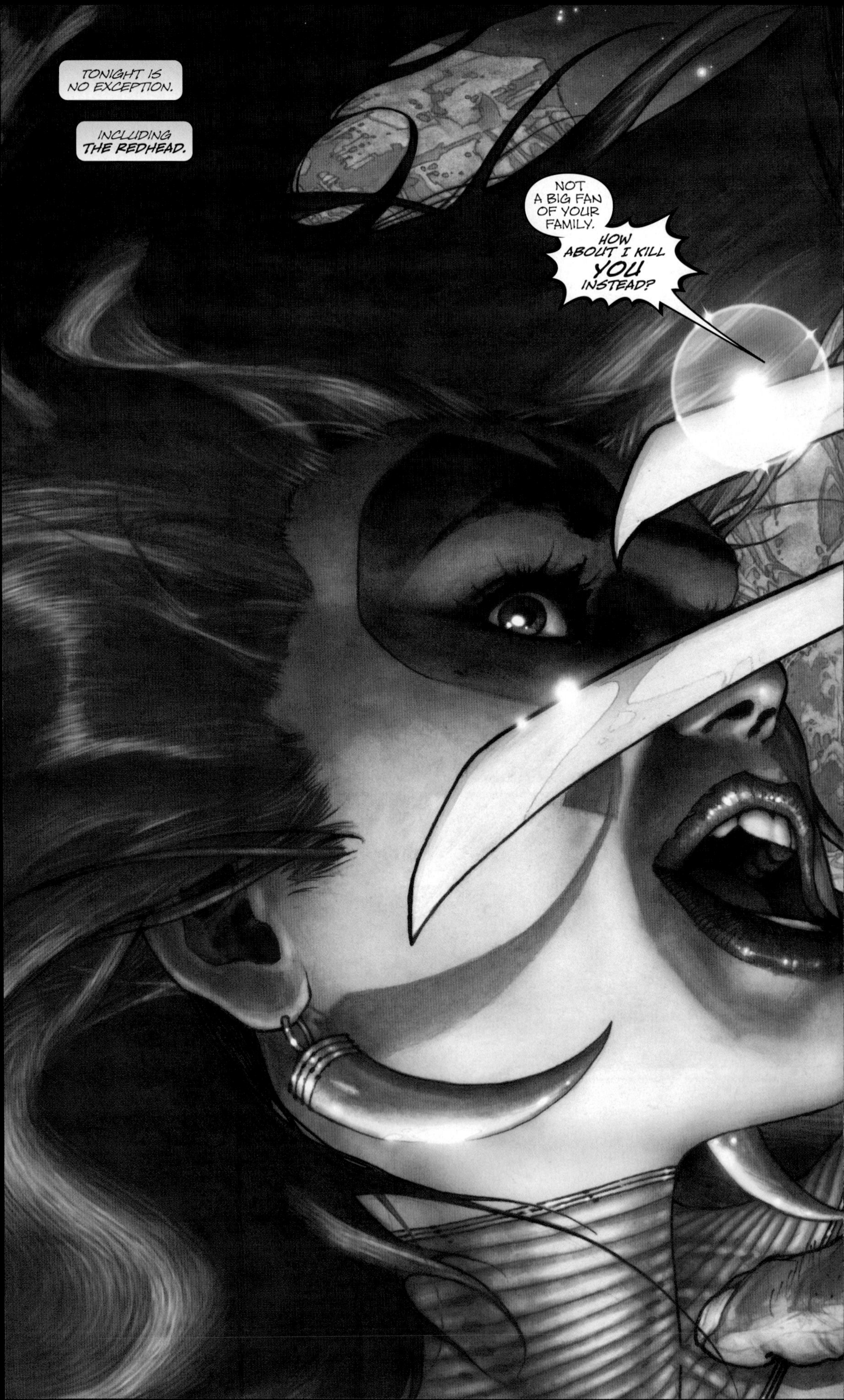
TONIGHT IS NO EXCEPTION.
INCLUDING THE REDHEAD.
NOT A BIG FAN OF YOUR FAMILY. HOW ABOUT I KILL YOU INSTEAD?

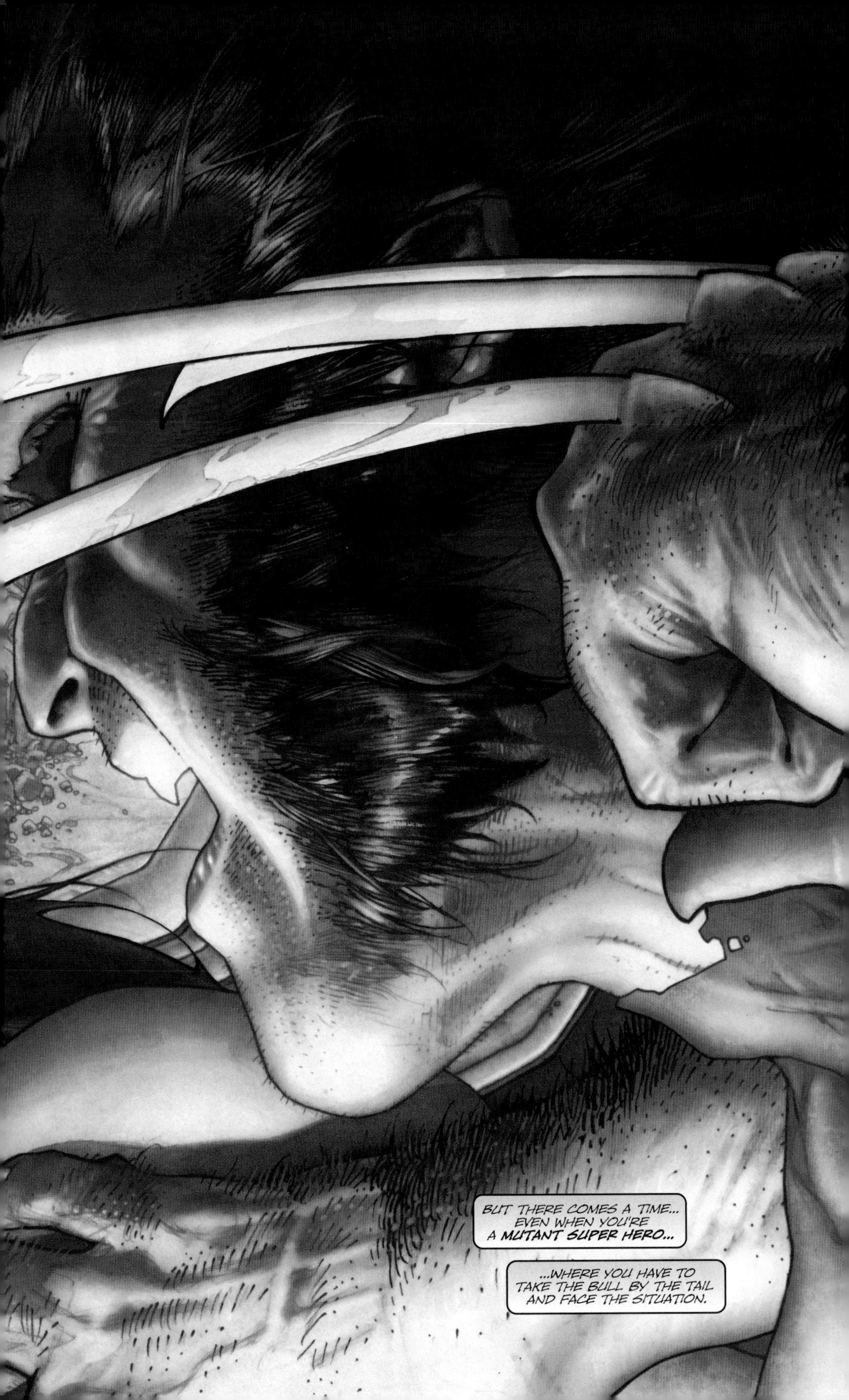
BUT THERE COMES A TIME... EVEN WHEN YOU'RE A MUTANT SUPER HERO...
...WHERE YOU HAVE TO TAKE THE BULL BY THE TAIL AND FACE THE SITUATION.

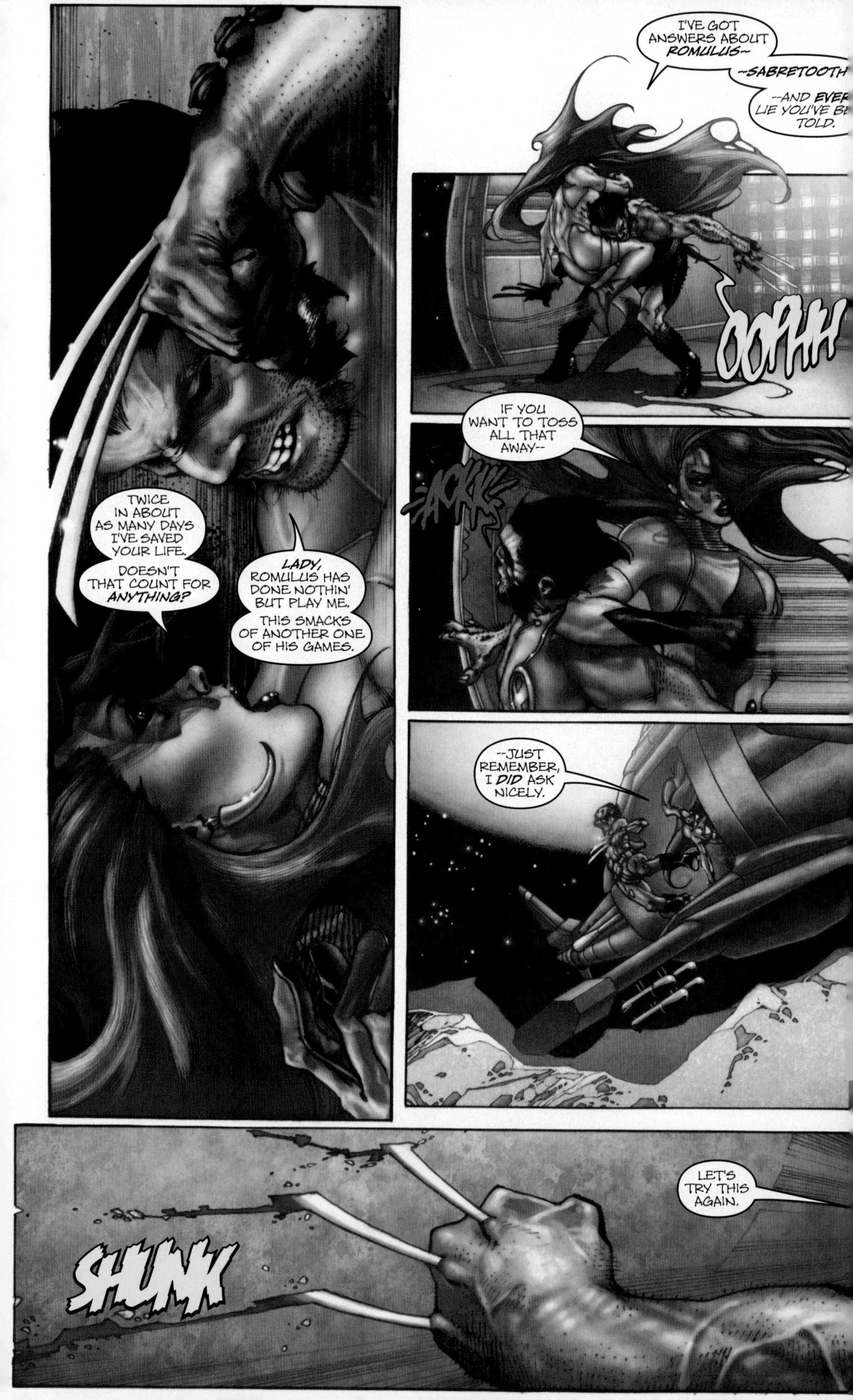

TWICE IN ABOUT AS MANY DAYS I'VE SAVED YOUR LIFE.
DOESN'T THAT COUNT FOR ANYTHING?
LADY, ROMULUS HAS DONE NOTHIN' BUT PLAY ME.
THIS SMACKS OF ANOTHER ONE OF HIS GAMES.
I'VE GOT ANSWERS ABOUT ROMULUS--
--SABRETOOTH
OOPHH
IF YOU WANT TO TOSS ALL THAT AWAY--
--JUST REMEMBER, I DID ASK NICELY.
LET'S TRY THIS AGAIN.
SHUNK

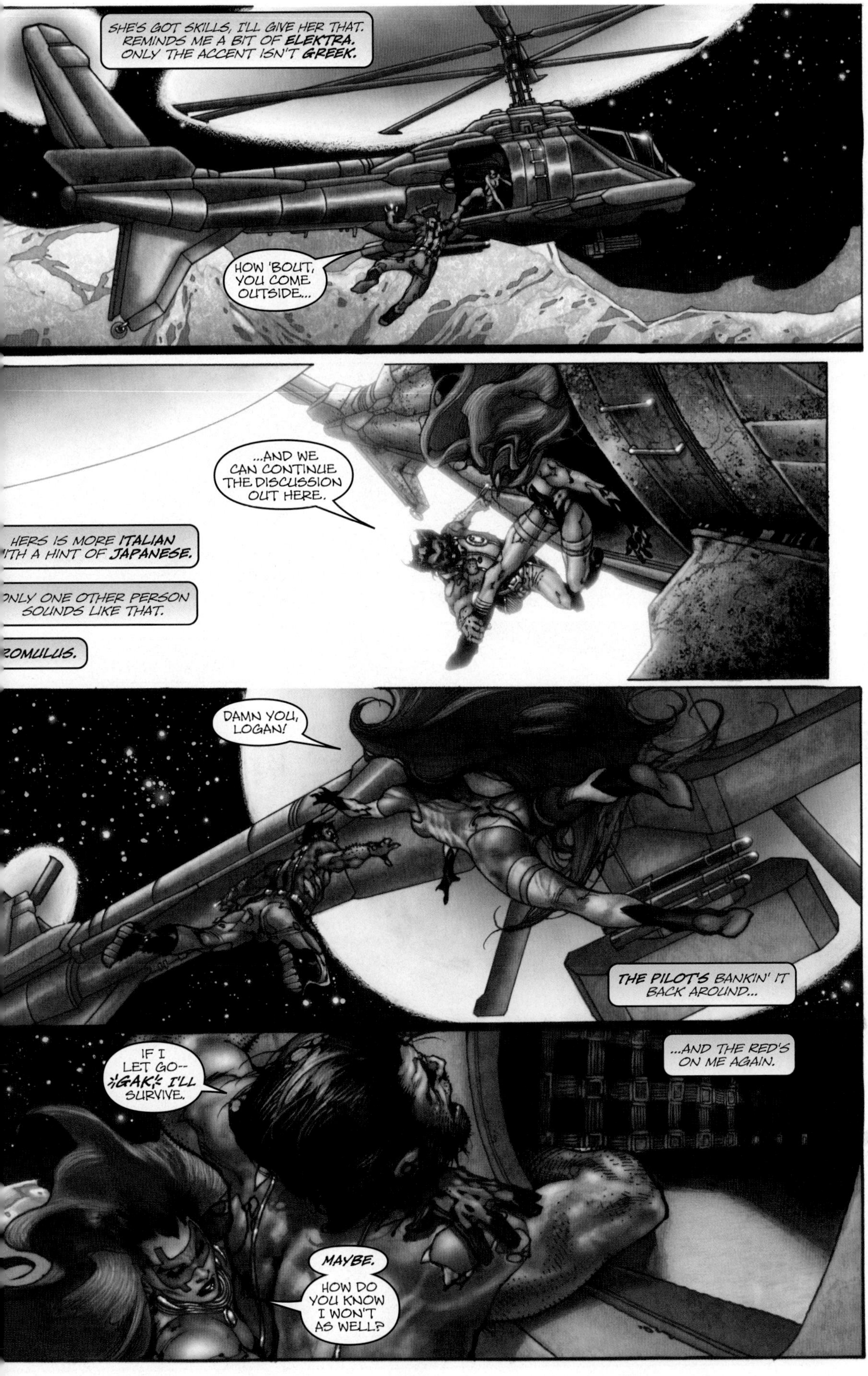
SHE'S GOT SKILLS, I'LL GIVE HER THAT. REMINDS ME A BIT OF **ELEKTRA.** ONLY THE ACCENT ISN'T **GREEK.**
HOW 'BOUT, YOU COME OUTSIDE...
...AND WE CAN CONTINUE THE DISCUSSION OUT HERE.
HERS IS MORE **ITALIAN** WITH A HINT OF **JAPANESE.**
ONLY ONE OTHER PERSON SOUNDS LIKE THAT.
ROMULUS.
DAMN YOU, LOGAN!
THE PILOT'S BANKIN' IT BACK AROUND...
...AND THE RED'S ON ME AGAIN.
IF I LET GO-- *GAK* I'LL SURVIVE.
MAYBE.
HOW DO YOU KNOW I WON'T AS WELL?

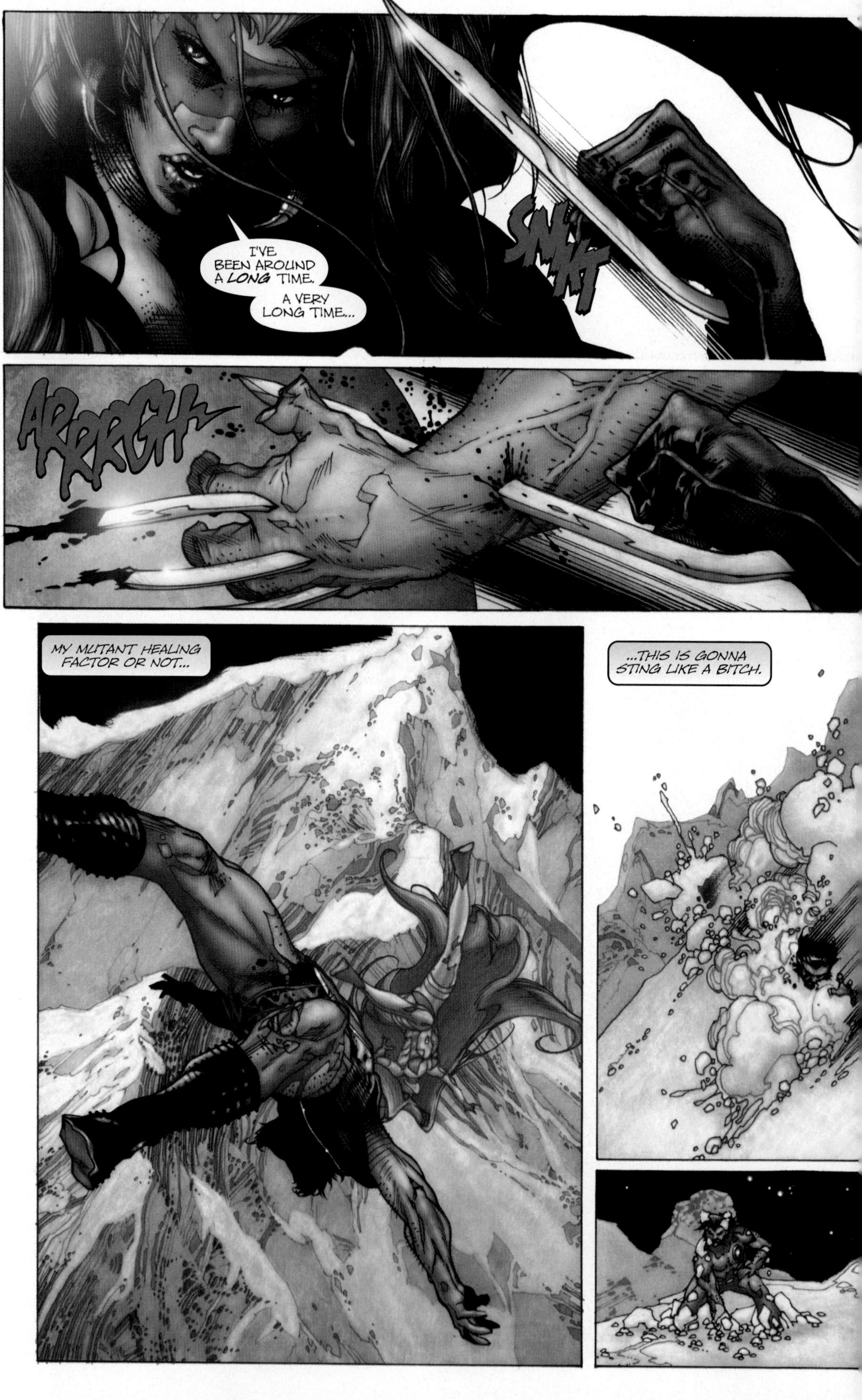
I'VE BEEN AROUND A LONG TIME.
A VERY LONG TIME...
SNIKT
ARRRGH
MY MUTANT HEALING FACTOR OR NOT...
...THIS IS GONNA STING LIKE A BITCH.

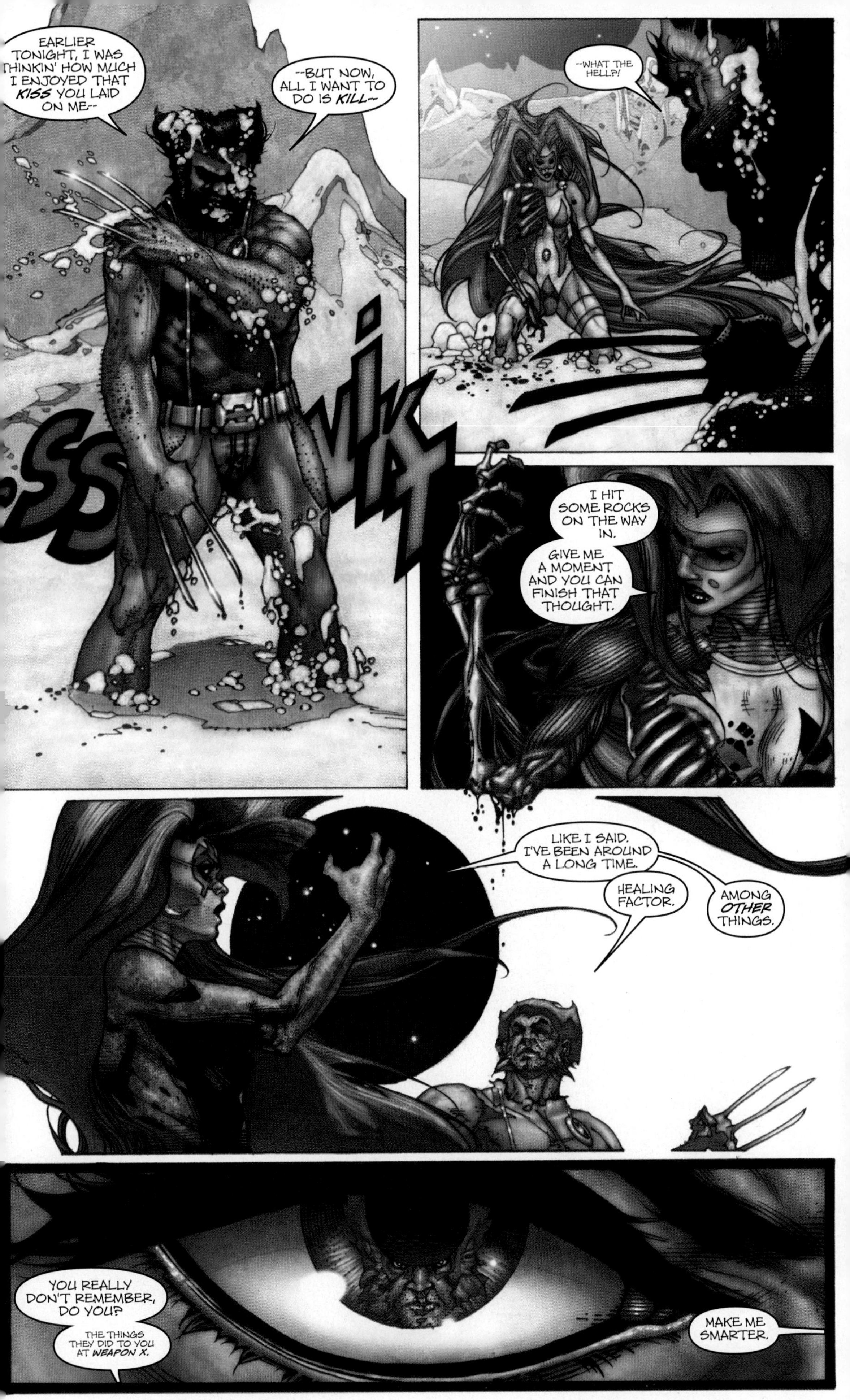
EARLIER TONIGHT, I WAS THINKIN' HOW MUCH I ENJOYED THAT KISS YOU LAID ON ME--
--BUT NOW, ALL I WANT TO DO IS KILL--
SSSNIKT
--WHAT THE HELL?!
I HIT SOME ROCKS ON THE WAY IN.
GIVE ME A MOMENT AND YOU CAN FINISH THAT THOUGHT.
LIKE I SAID. I'VE BEEN AROUND A LONG TIME.
HEALING FACTOR.
AMONG OTHER THINGS.
YOU REALLY DON'T REMEMBER, DO YOU?
THE THINGS THEY DID TO YOU AT WEAPON X.
MAKE ME SMARTER.

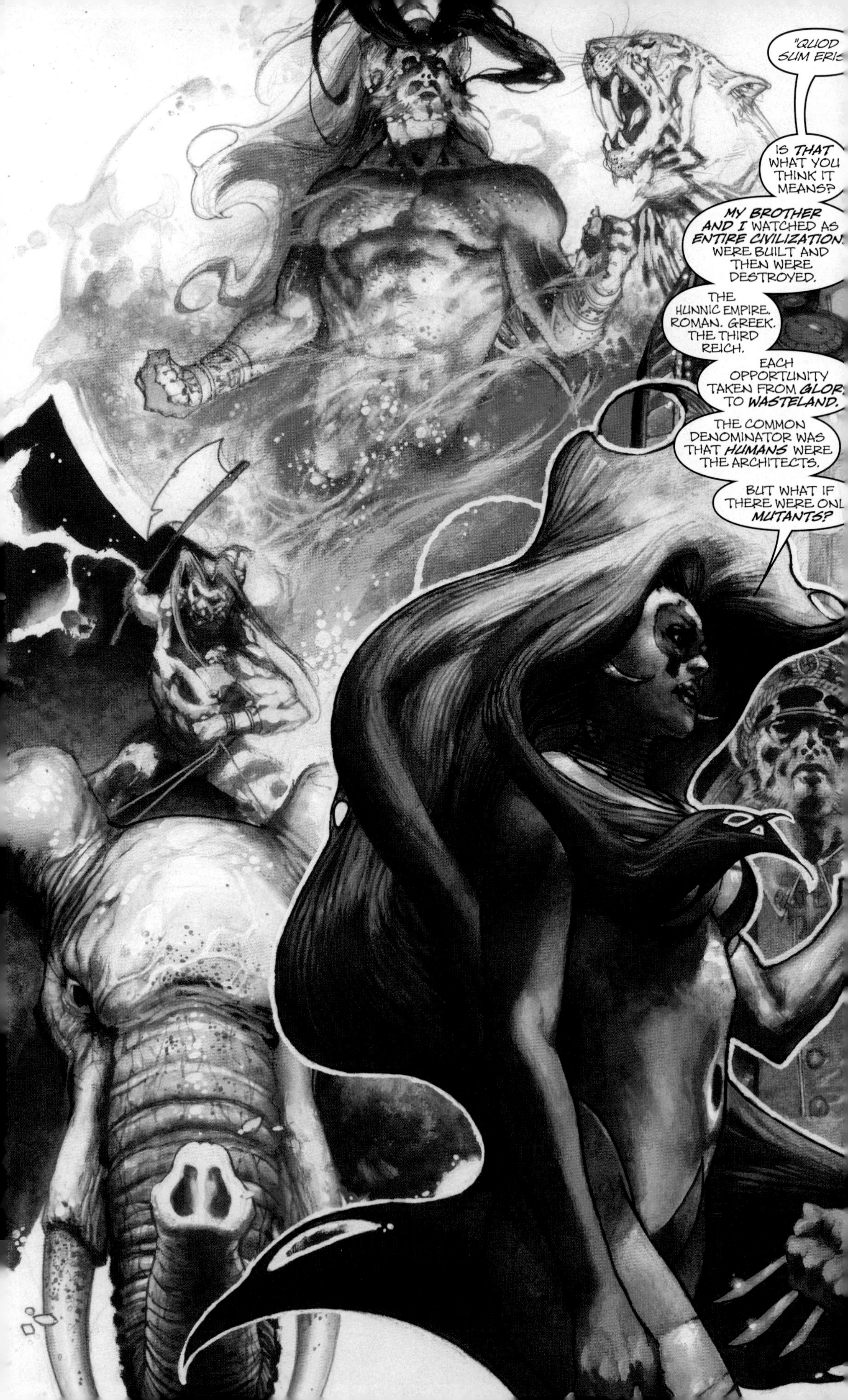
"QUOD SUM ERIS
IS THAT WHAT YOU THINK IT MEANS?
MY BROTHER AND I WATCHED AS ENTIRE CIVILIZATION WERE BUILT AND THEN WERE DESTROYED.
THE HUNNIC EMPIRE. ROMAN. GREEK. THE THIRD REICH.
EACH OPPORTUNITY TAKEN FROM GLOR TO WASTELAND.
THE COMMON DENOMINATOR WAS THAT HUMANS WERE THE ARCHITECTS.
BUT WHAT IF THERE WERE ONL MUTANTS?

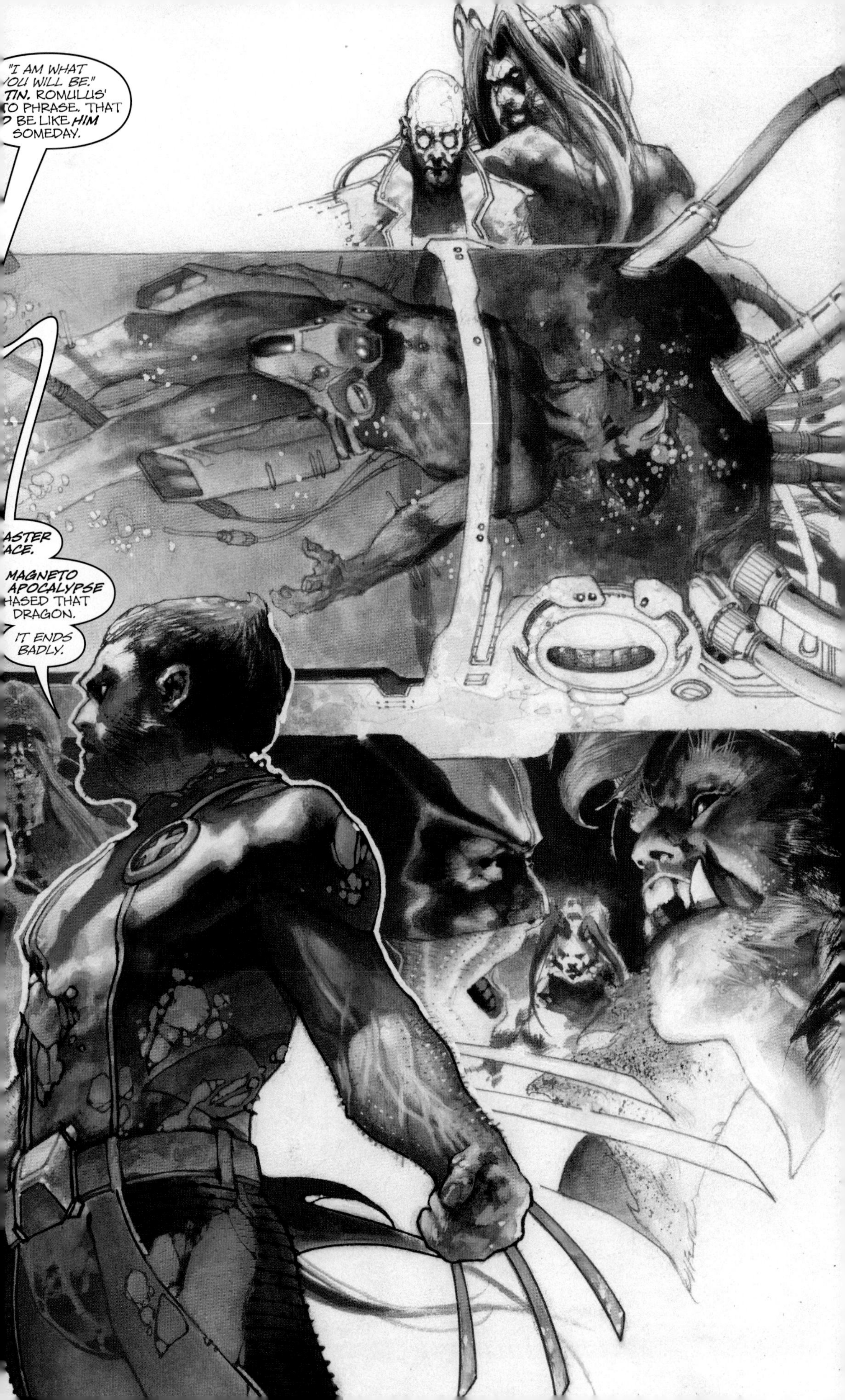
"I AM WHAT
OU WILL BE."
TIN. ROMULUS'
TO PHRASE. THAT
D BE LIKE HIM
SOMEDAY.
ASTER
ACE.
MAGNETO
APOCALYPSE
HASED THAT
DRAGON.
IT ENDS
BADLY.

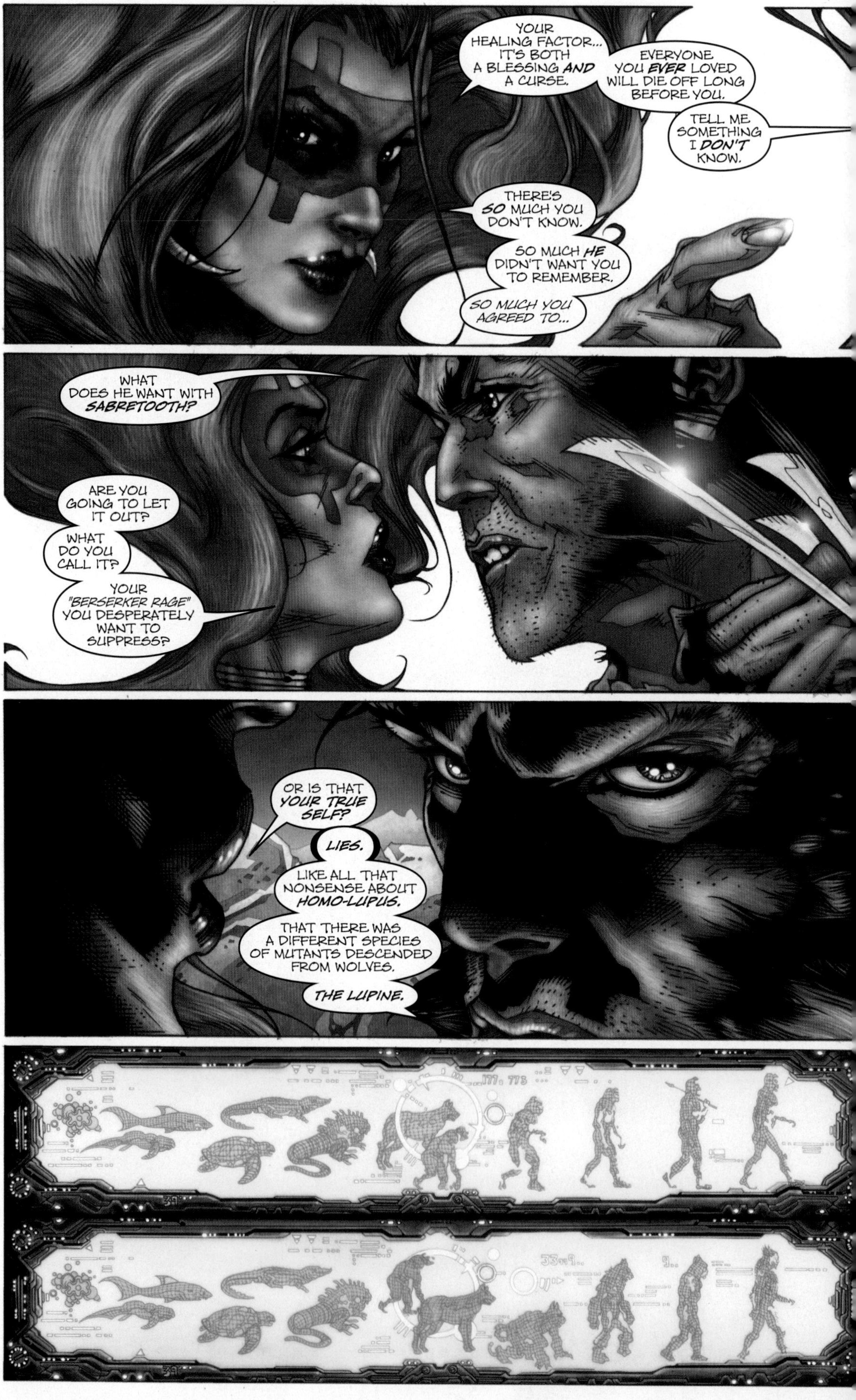
YOUR HEALING FACTOR... IT'S BOTH A BLESSING AND A CURSE.
EVERYONE YOU EVER LOVED WILL DIE OFF LONG BEFORE YOU.
TELL ME SOMETHING I DON'T KNOW.
THERE'S SO MUCH YOU DON'T KNOW.
SO MUCH HE DIDN'T WANT YOU TO REMEMBER.
SO MUCH YOU AGREED TO...
WHAT DOES HE WANT WITH SABRETOOTH?
ARE YOU GOING TO LET IT OUT?
WHAT DO YOU CALL IT?
YOUR "BERSERKER RAGE" YOU DESPERATELY WANT TO SUPPRESS?
OR IS THAT YOUR TRUE SELF?
LIES.
LIKE ALL THAT NONSENSE ABOUT HOMO-LUPUS.
THAT THERE WAS A DIFFERENT SPECIES OF MUTANTS DESCENDED FROM WOLVES.
THE LUPINE.

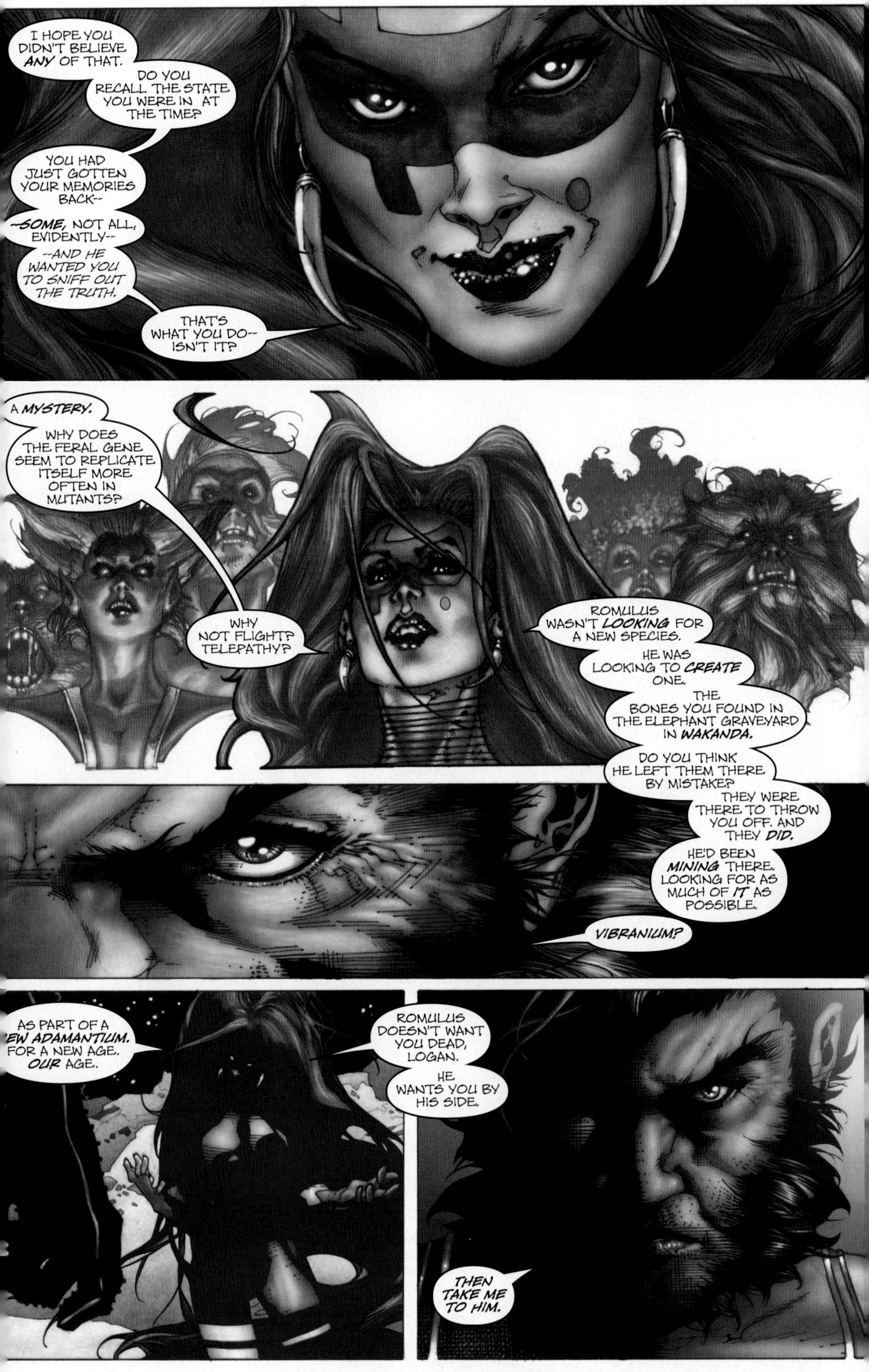
I HOPE YOU DIDN'T BELIEVE *ANY* OF THAT.
DO YOU RECALL THE STATE YOU WERE IN AT THE TIME?
YOU HAD JUST GOTTEN YOUR MEMORIES BACK--
--*SOME,* NOT ALL, EVIDENTLY--
--AND HE WANTED YOU TO SNIFF OUT THE TRUTH.
THAT'S WHAT YOU DO-- ISN'T IT?
A *MYSTERY.*
WHY DOES THE FERAL GENE SEEM TO REPLICATE ITSELF MORE OFTEN IN MUTANTS?
WHY NOT FLIGHT? TELEPATHY?
ROMULUS WASN'T *LOOKING* FOR A NEW SPECIES.
HE WAS LOOKING TO *CREATE* ONE.
THE BONES YOU FOUND IN THE ELEPHANT GRAVEYARD IN *WAKANDA.*
DO YOU THINK HE LEFT THEM THERE BY MISTAKE?
THEY WERE THERE TO THROW YOU OFF. AND THEY *DID.*
HE'D BEEN *MINING* THERE. LOOKING FOR AS MUCH OF *IT* AS POSSIBLE.
VIBRANIUM?
AS PART OF A EW ADAMANTIUM. FOR A NEW AGE. *OUR* AGE.
ROMULUS DOESN'T WANT YOU DEAD, LOGAN.
HE WANTS YOU BY HIS SIDE.
THEN TAKE ME TO HIM.

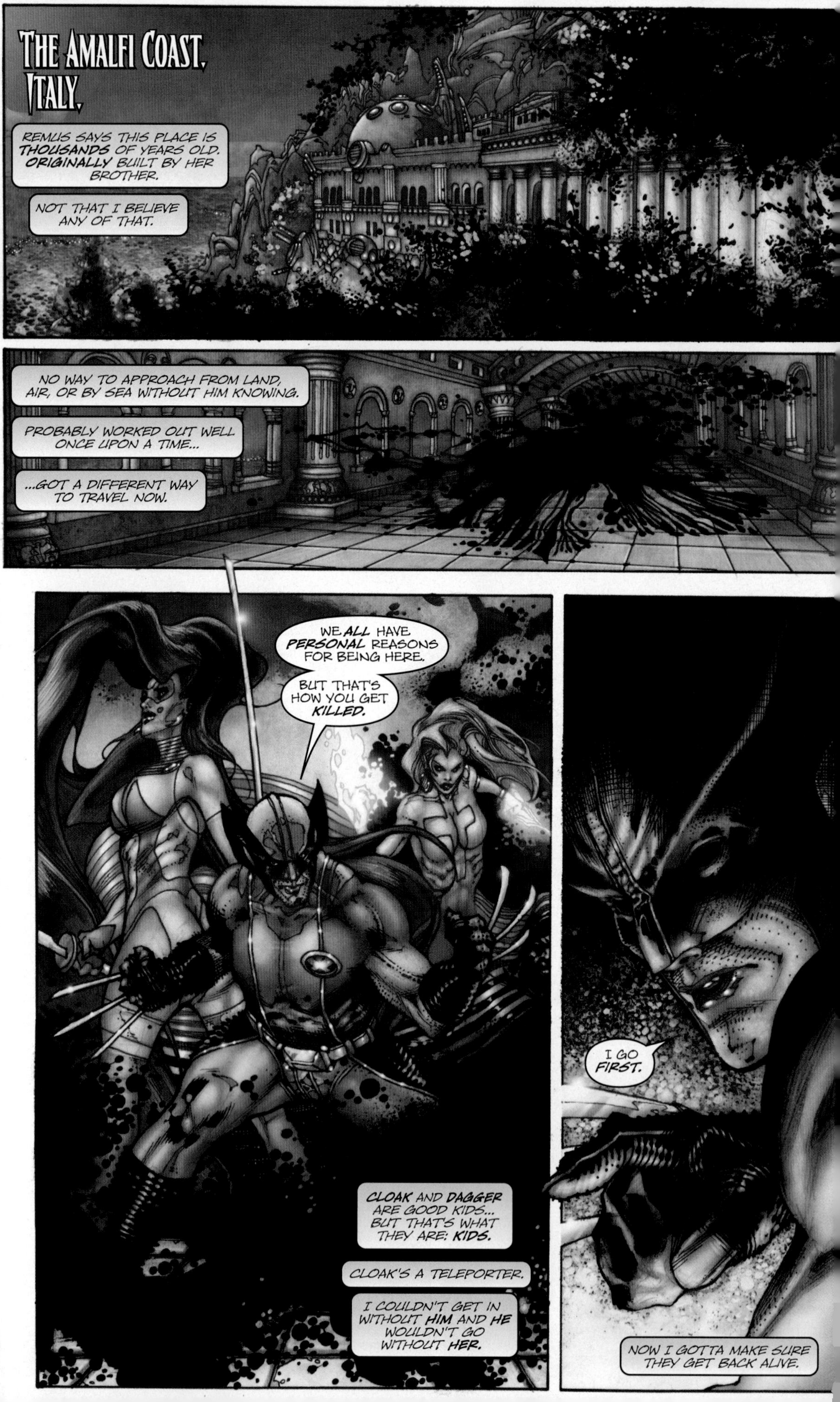

THE AMALFI COAST, ITALY.
REMUS SAYS THIS PLACE IS THOUSANDS OF YEARS OLD. ORIGINALLY BUILT BY HER BROTHER.
NOT THAT I BELIEVE ANY OF THAT.
NO WAY TO APPROACH FROM LAND, AIR, OR BY SEA WITHOUT HIM KNOWING.
PROBABLY WORKED OUT WELL ONCE UPON A TIME...
...GOT A DIFFERENT WAY TO TRAVEL NOW.
WE ALL HAVE PERSONAL REASONS FOR BEING HERE.
BUT THAT'S HOW YOU GET KILLED.
CLOAK AND DAGGER ARE GOOD KIDS... BUT THAT'S WHAT THEY ARE: KIDS.
CLOAK'S A TELEPORTER.
I COULDN'T GET IN WITHOUT HIM AND HE WOULDN'T GO WITHOUT HER.
I GO FIRST.
NOW I GOTTA MAKE SURE THEY GET BACK ALIVE.

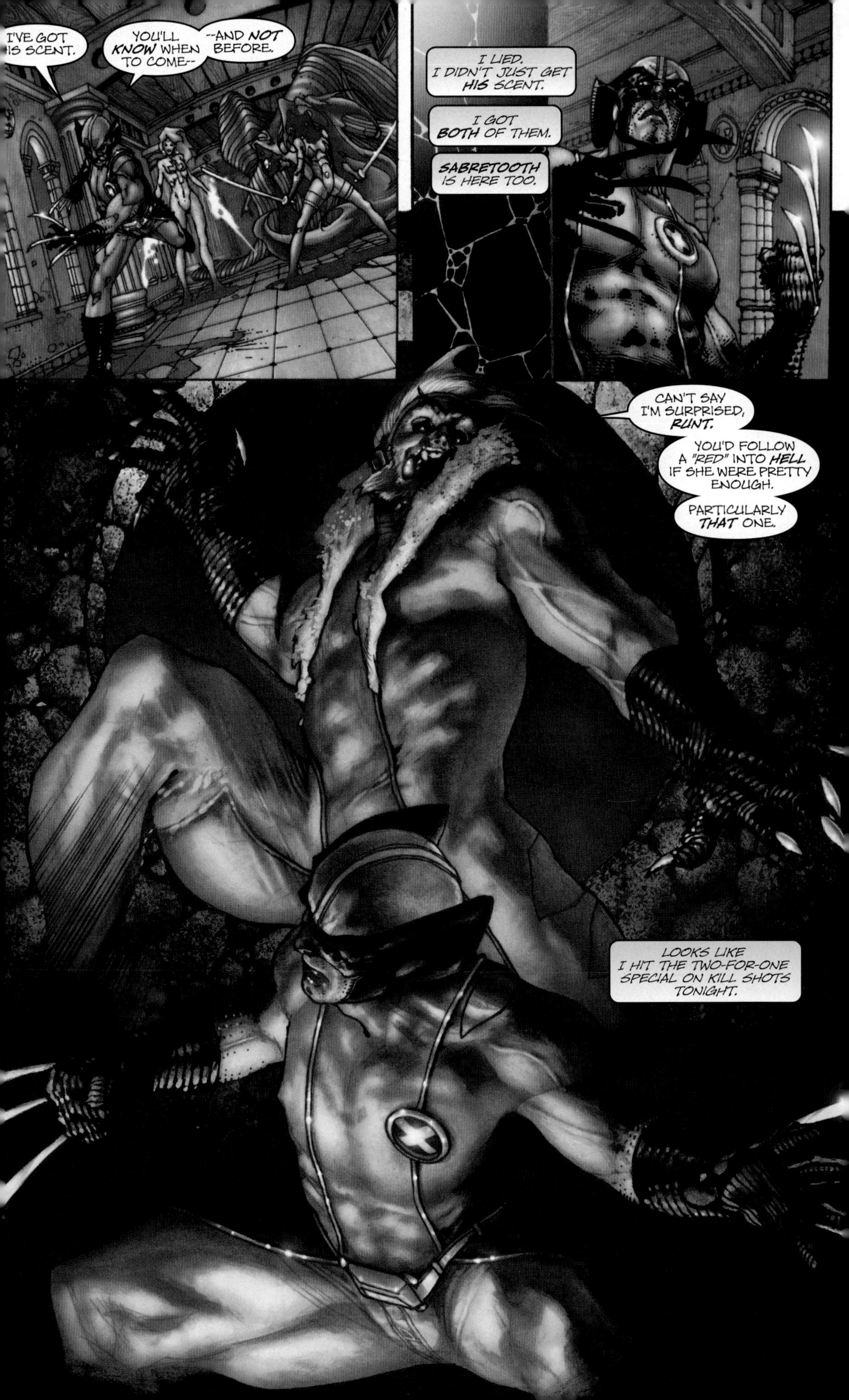
I'VE GOT HIS SCENT.
YOU'LL KNOW WHEN TO COME--
--AND NOT BEFORE.
I LIED. I DIDN'T JUST GET HIS SCENT.
I GOT BOTH OF THEM.
SABRETOOTH IS HERE TOO.
CAN'T SAY I'M SURPRISED, RUNT.
YOU'D FOLLOW A "RED" INTO HELL IF SHE WERE PRETTY ENOUGH.
PARTICULARLY THAT ONE.
LOOKS LIKE I HIT THE TWO-FOR-ONE SPECIAL ON KILL SHOTS TONIGHT.

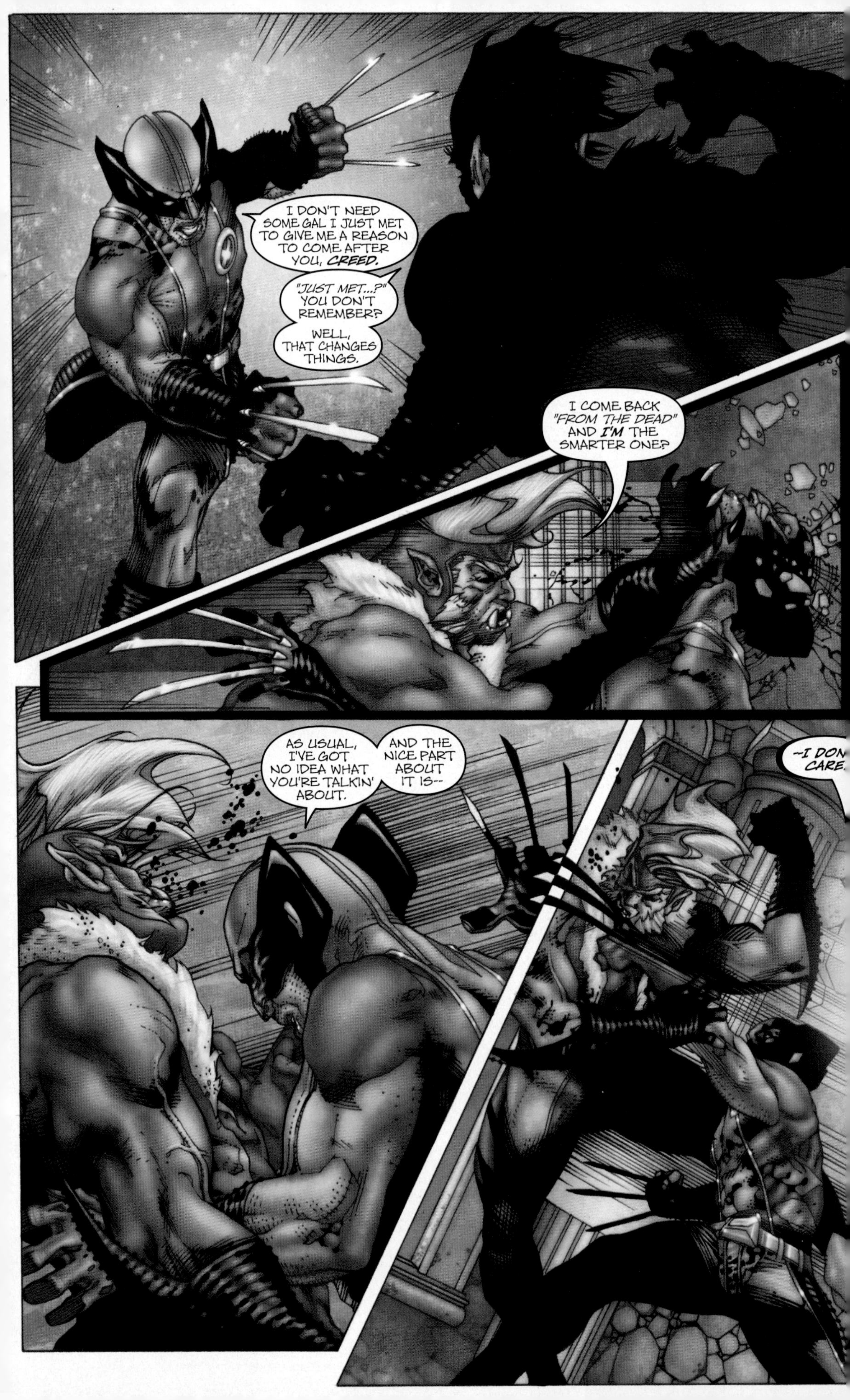
I DON'T NEED SOME GAL I JUST MET TO GIVE ME A REASON TO COME AFTER YOU, *CREED.*
"JUST MET...?" YOU DON'T REMEMBER?
WELL, THAT CHANGES THINGS.
I COME BACK "FROM THE DEAD" AND *I'M* THE SMARTER ONE?
AS USUAL, I'VE GOT NO IDEA WHAT YOU'RE TALKIN' ABOUT.
AND THE NICE PART ABOUT IT IS--
--I DON CARE.

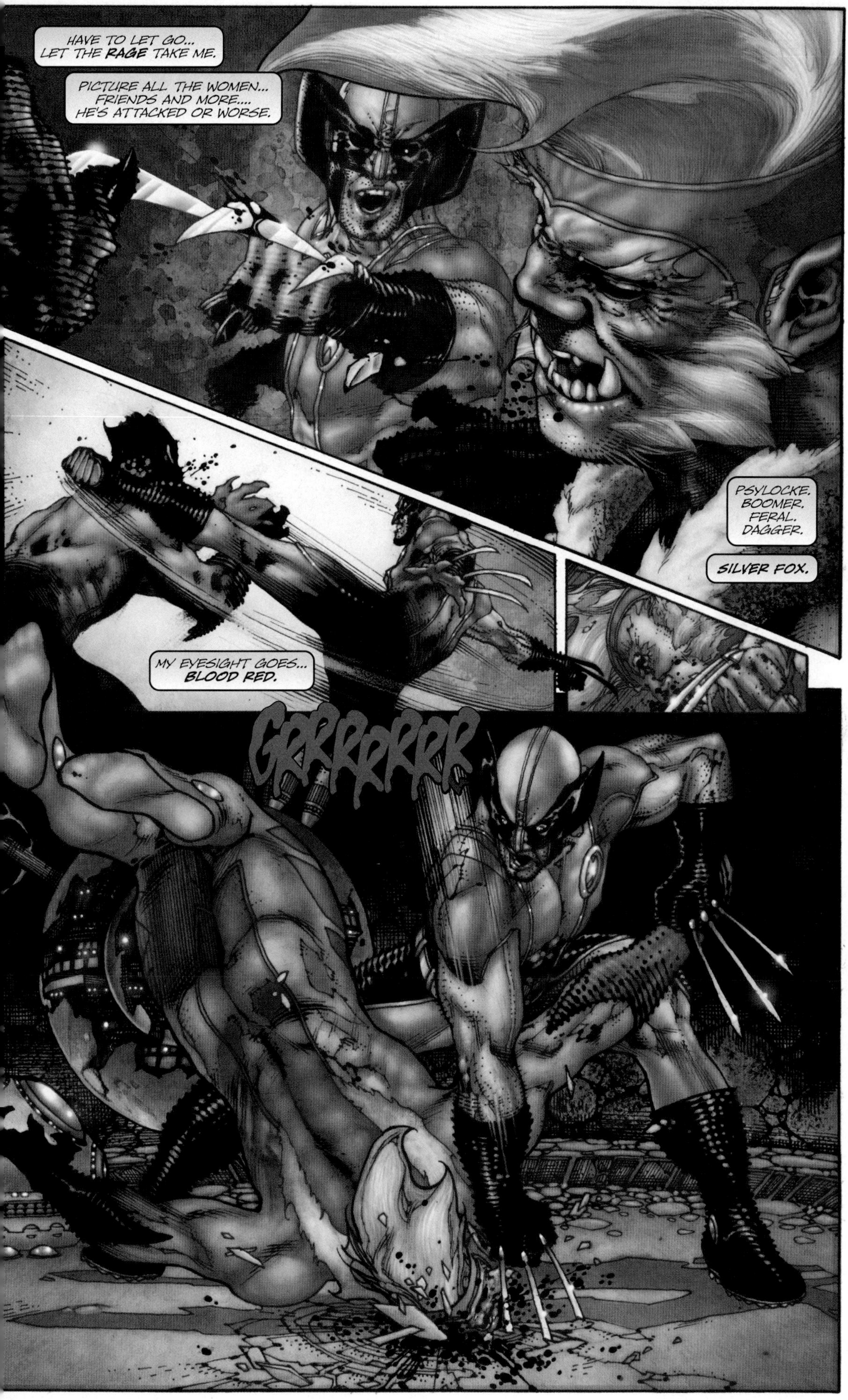
HAVE TO LET GO... LET THE RAGE TAKE ME.
PICTURE ALL THE WOMEN... FRIENDS AND MORE.... HE'S ATTACKED OR WORSE.
PSYLOCKE. BOOMER. FERAL. DAGGER.
SILVER FOX.
MY EYESIGHT GOES... BLOOD RED.
GRRRRRRR

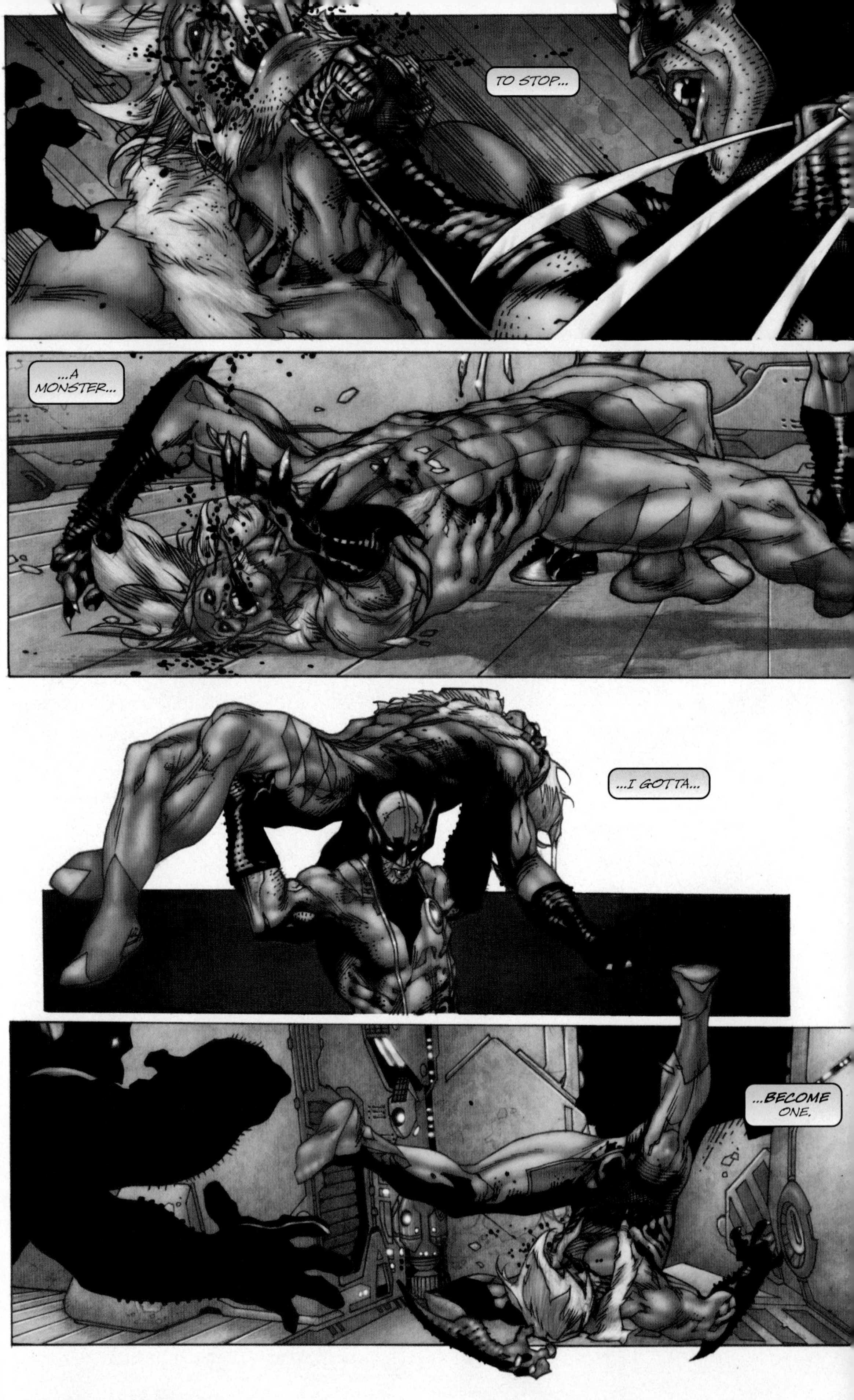
TO STOP...
...A MONSTER...
...I GOTTA...
...BECOME ONE.

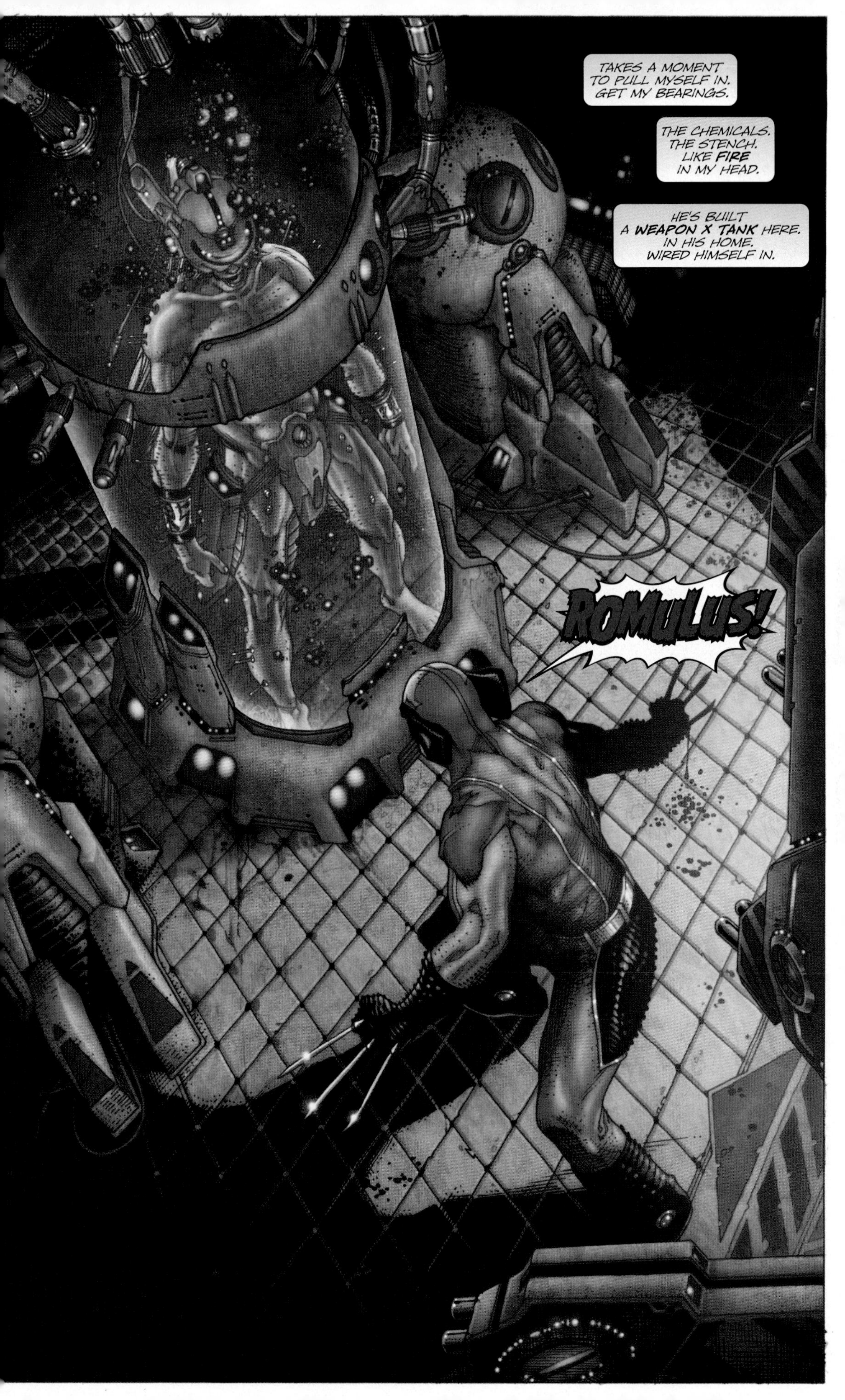
TAKES A MOMENT TO PULL MYSELF IN. GET MY BEARINGS.
THE CHEMICALS. THE STENCH. LIKE FIRE IN MY HEAD.
HE'S BUILT A WEAPON X TANK HERE. IN HIS HOME. WIRED HIMSELF IN.
ROMULUS!

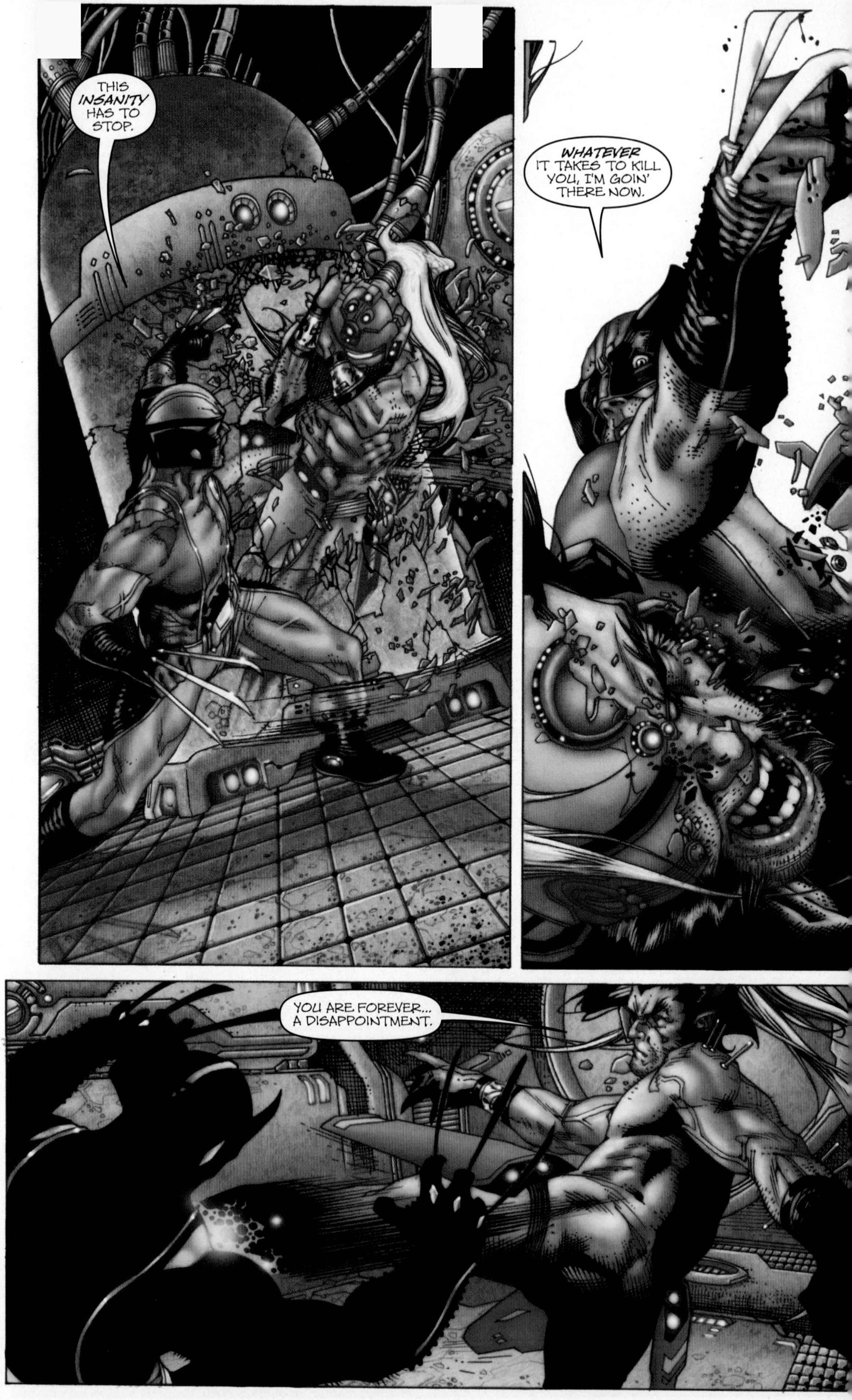
THIS *INSANITY* HAS TO STOP.
WHATEVER IT TAKES TO KILL YOU, I'M GOIN' THERE NOW.
YOU ARE FOREVER... A DISAPPOINTMENT.

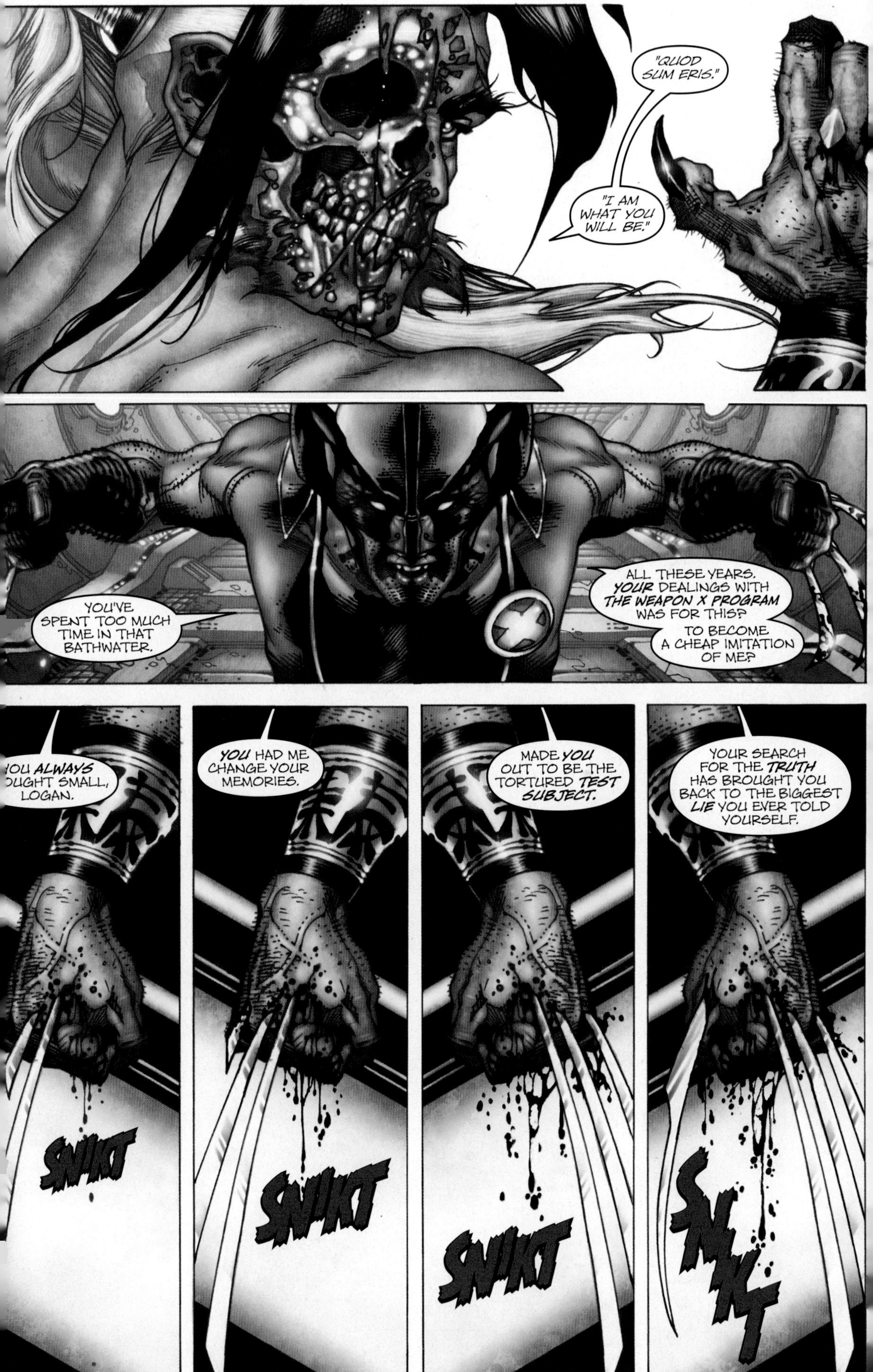
"QUOD SUM ERIS."
"I AM WHAT YOU WILL BE."
YOU'VE SPENT TOO MUCH TIME IN THAT BATHWATER.
ALL THESE YEARS, YOUR DEALINGS WITH THE WEAPON X PROGRAM WAS FOR THIS?
TO BECOME A CHEAP IMITATION OF ME?
OU ALWAYS OUGHT SMALL, LOGAN.
SNIKT
YOU HAD ME CHANGE YOUR MEMORIES.
SNIKT
MADE YOU OUT TO BE THE TORTURED TEST SUBJECT.
SNIKT
YOUR SEARCH FOR THE TRUTH HAS BROUGHT YOU BACK TO THE BIGGEST LIE YOU EVER TOLD YOURSELF.
SNIKT

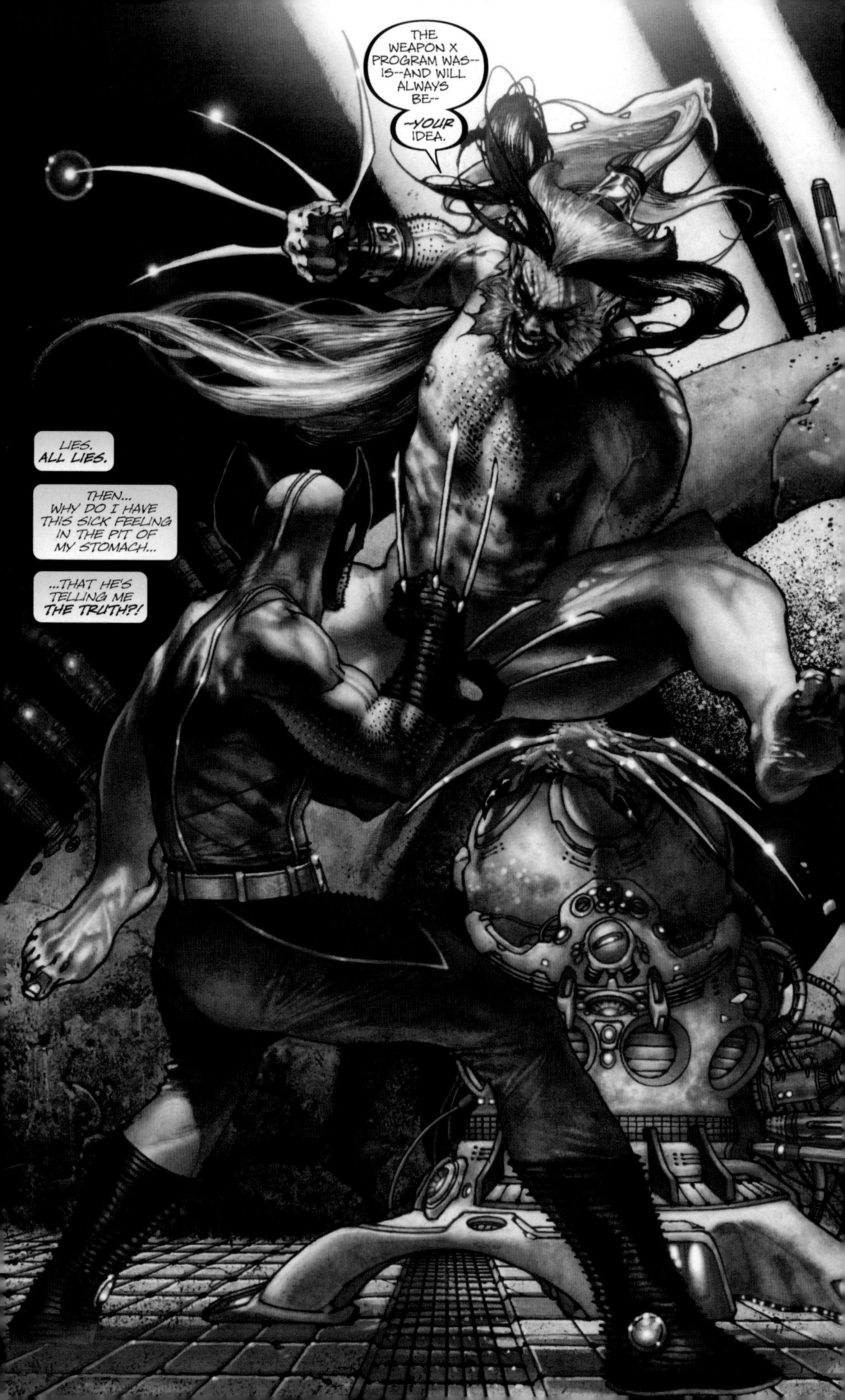
THE WEAPON X PROGRAM WAS-- IS--AND WILL ALWAYS BE--
--YOUR IDEA.
LIES. ALL LIES.
THEN... WHY DO I HAVE THIS SICK FEELING IN THE PIT OF MY STOMACH...
...THAT HE'S TELLING ME THE TRUTH?!

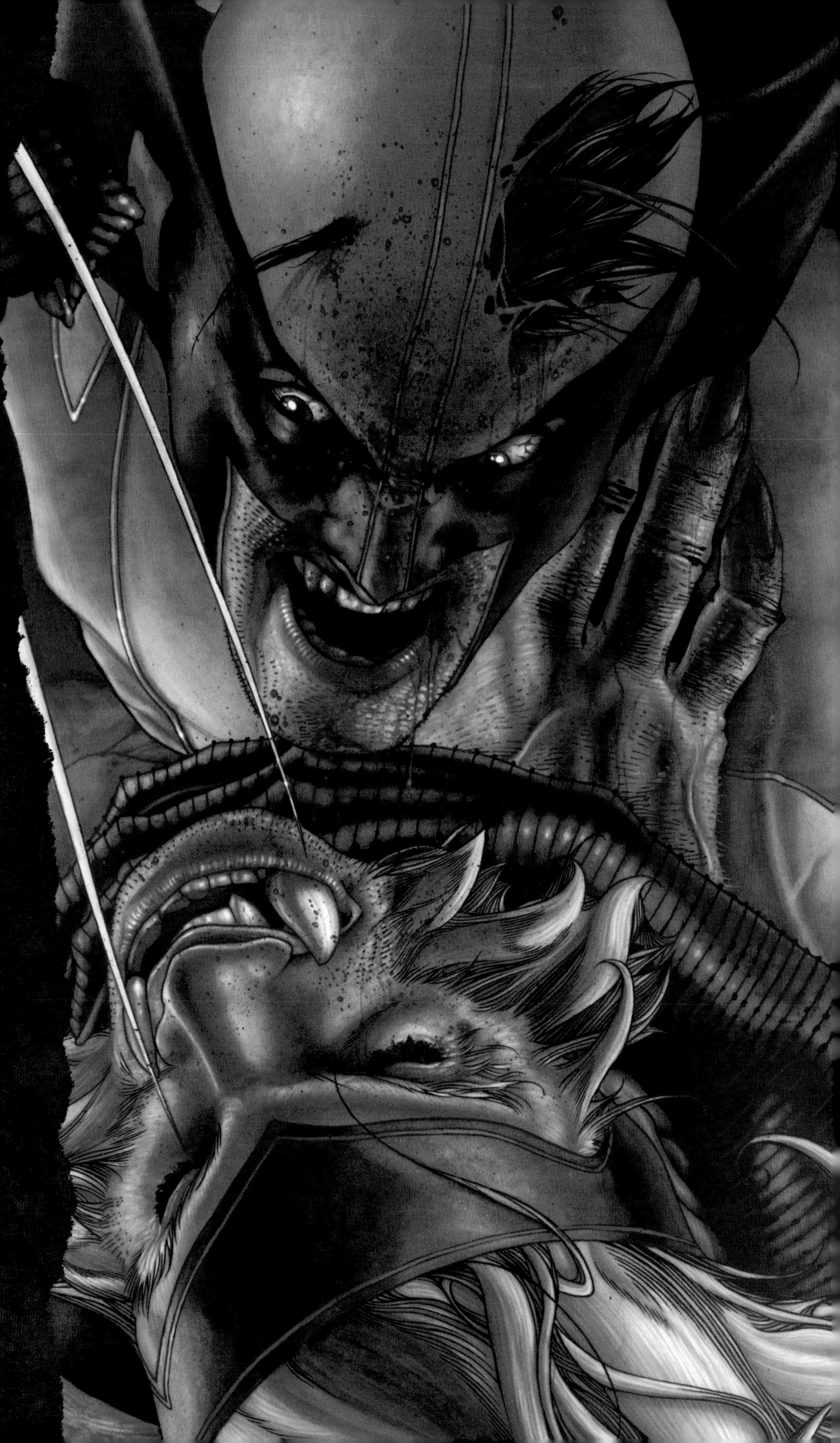

CHAPTER FOUR:
REVOLUTION

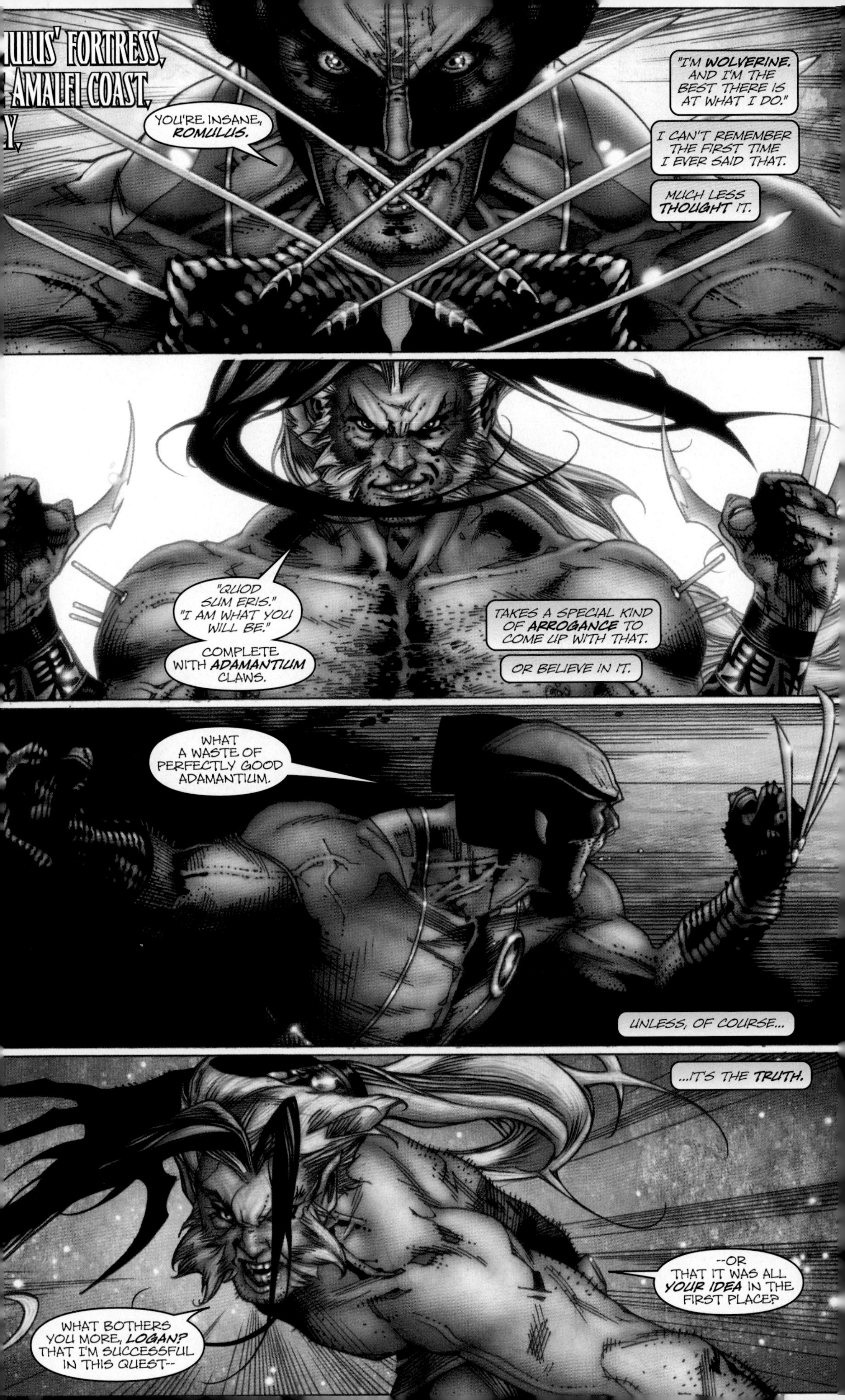
ULUS' FORTRESS,
AMALFI COAST,
Y,
"I'M WOLVERINE. AND I'M THE BEST THERE IS AT WHAT I DO."
YOU'RE INSANE, ROMULUS.
I CAN'T REMEMBER THE FIRST TIME I EVER SAID THAT.
MUCH LESS THOUGHT IT.
"QUOD SUM ERIS." "I AM WHAT YOU WILL BE."
COMPLETE WITH ADAMANTIUM CLAWS.
TAKES A SPECIAL KIND OF ARROGANCE TO COME UP WITH THAT.
OR BELIEVE IN IT.
WHAT A WASTE OF PERFECTLY GOOD ADAMANTIUM.
UNLESS, OF COURSE...
...IT'S THE TRUTH.
WHAT BOTHERS YOU MORE, LOGAN? THAT I'M SUCCESSFUL IN THIS QUEST--
--OR THAT IT WAS ALL YOUR IDEA IN THE FIRST PLACE?

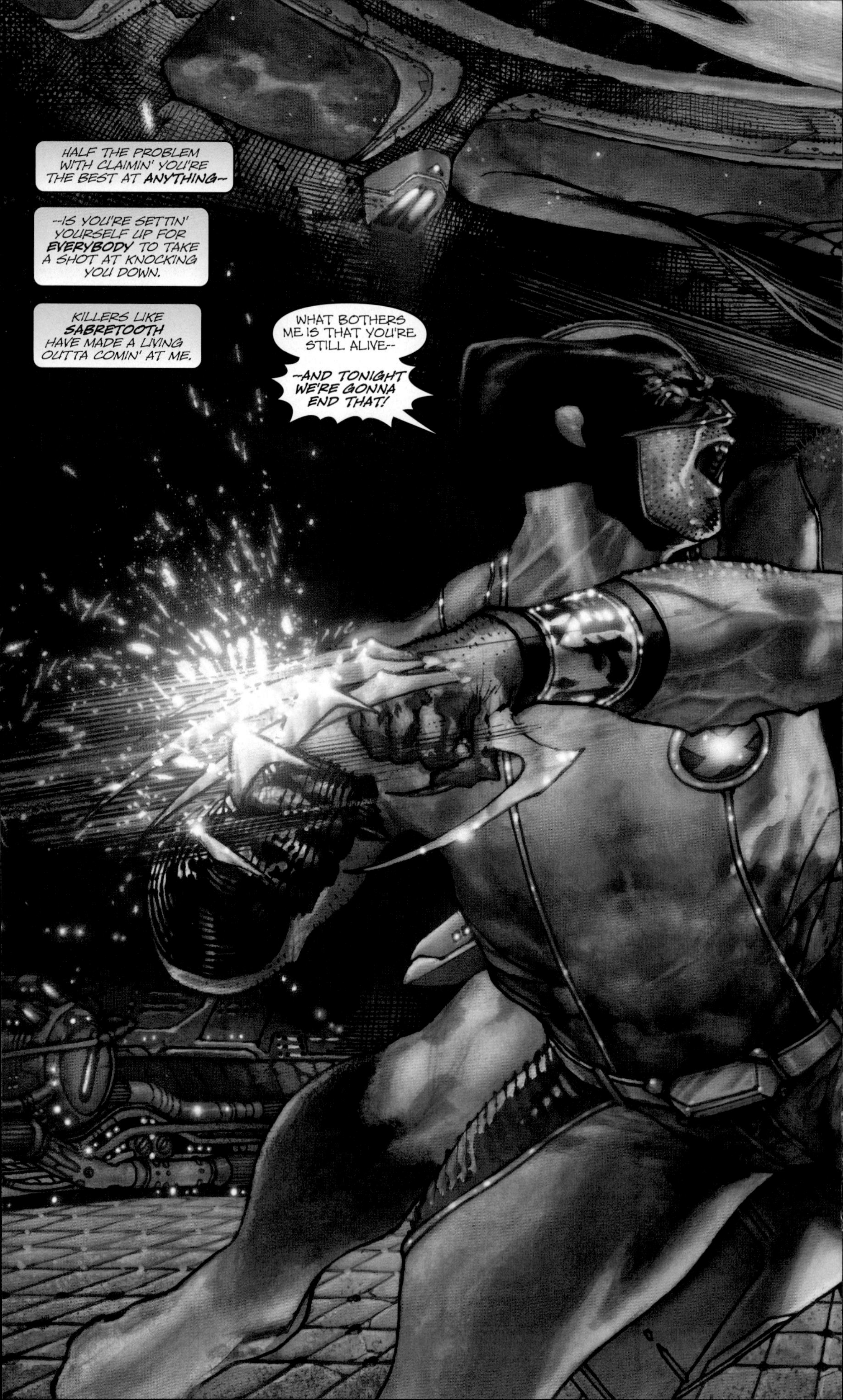

HALF THE PROBLEM WITH CLAIMIN' YOU'RE THE BEST AT ANYTHING--
--IS YOU'RE SETTIN' YOURSELF UP FOR EVERYBODY TO TAKE A SHOT AT KNOCKING YOU DOWN.
KILLERS LIKE SABRETOOTH HAVE MADE A LIVING OUTTA COMIN' AT ME.
WHAT BOTHERS ME IS THAT YOU'RE STILL ALIVE--
--AND TONIGHT WE'RE GONNA END THAT!

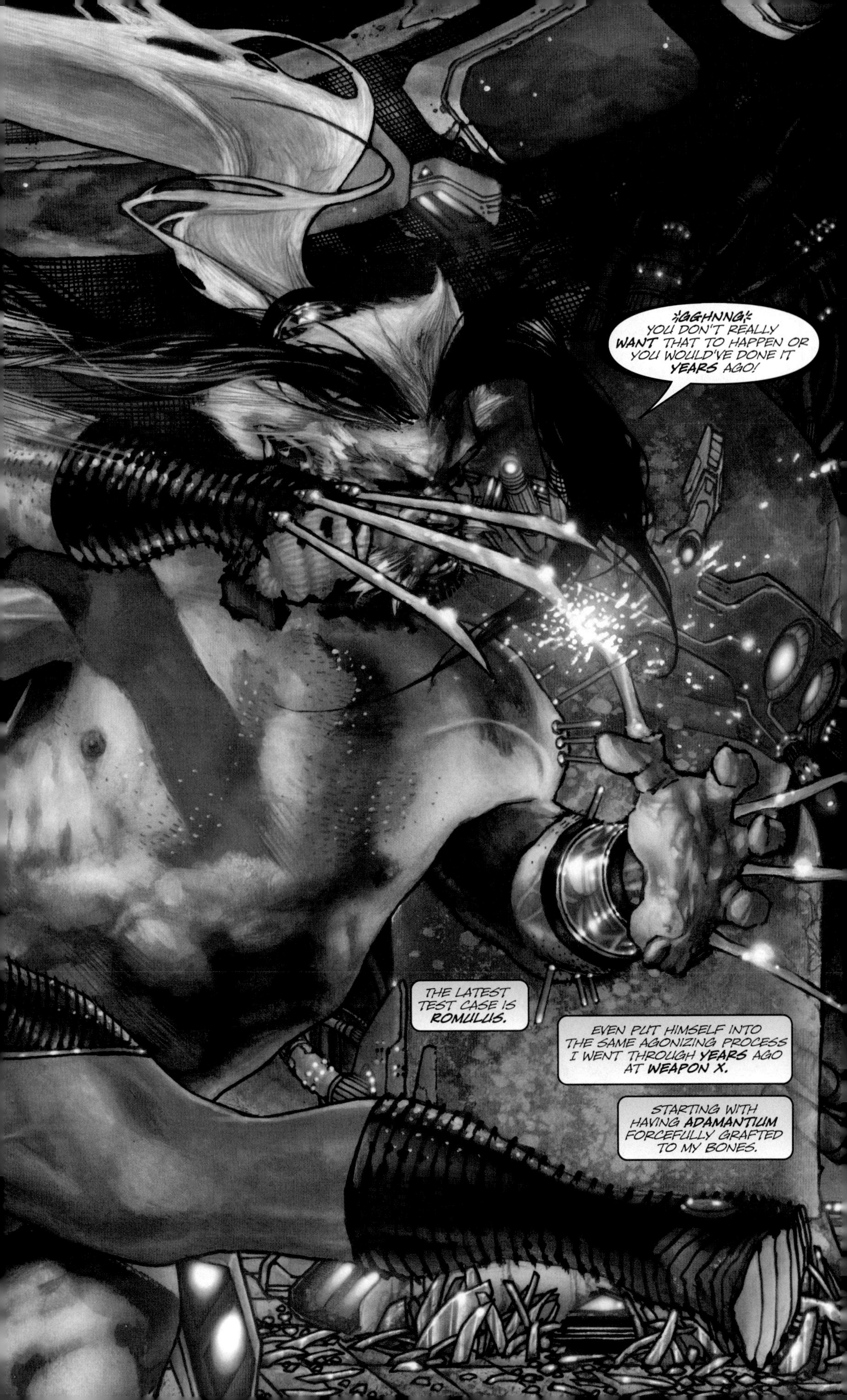

¡GGHNNG¡ YOU DON'T REALLY WANT THAT TO HAPPEN OR YOU WOULD'VE DONE IT YEARS AGO!
THE LATEST TEST CASE IS ROMULUS.
EVEN PUT HIMSELF INTO THE SAME AGONIZING PROCESS I WENT THROUGH YEARS AGO AT WEAPON X.
STARTING WITH HAVING ADAMANTIUM FORCEFULLY GRAFTED TO MY BONES.

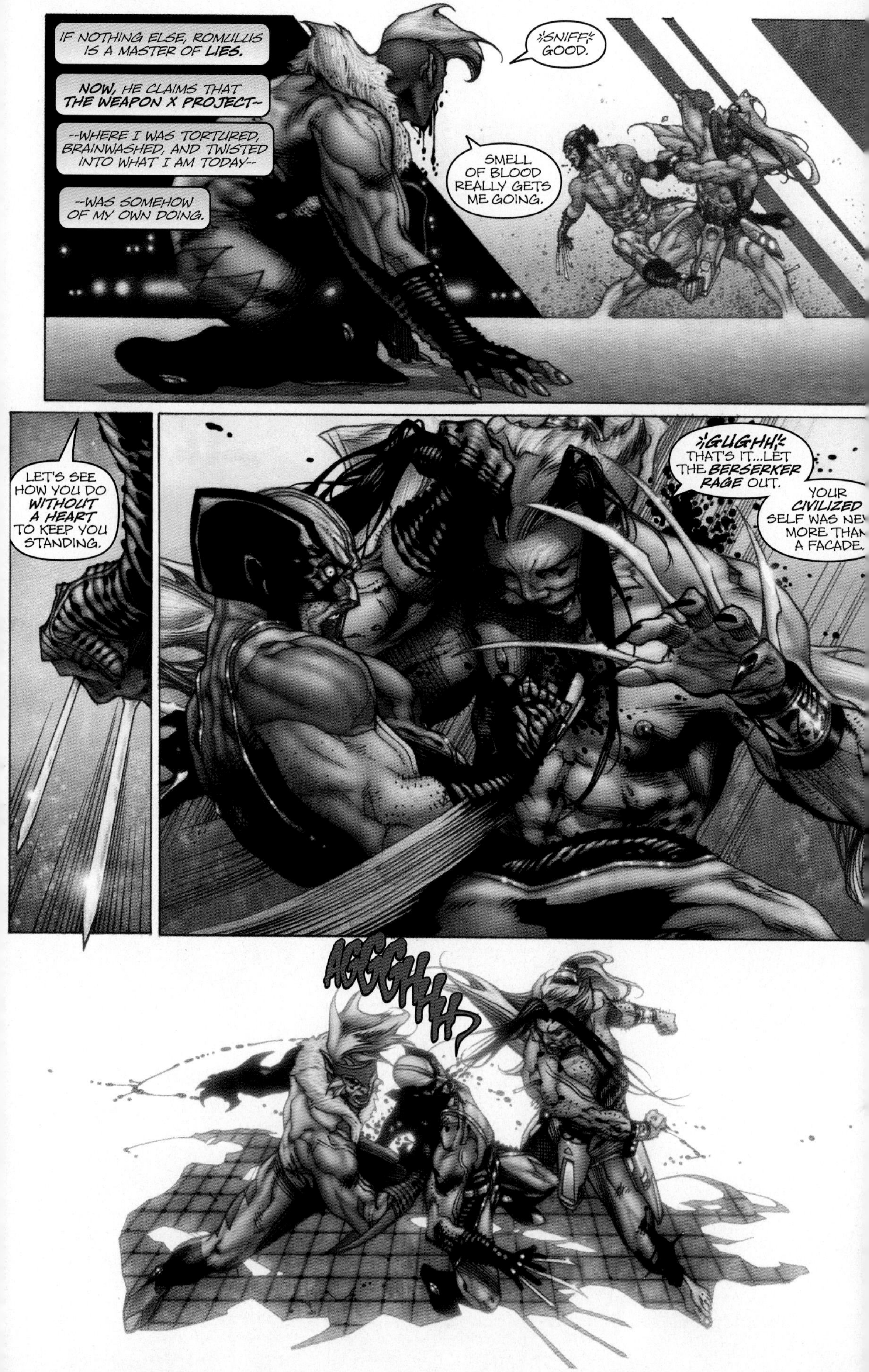
IF NOTHING ELSE, ROMULUS IS A MASTER OF LIES.
NOW, HE CLAIMS THAT THE WEAPON X PROJECT--
--WHERE I WAS TORTURED, BRAINWASHED, AND TWISTED INTO WHAT I AM TODAY--
--WAS SOMEHOW OF MY OWN DOING.
SNIFF GOOD.
SMELL OF BLOOD REALLY GETS ME GOING.
LET'S SEE HOW YOU DO WITHOUT A HEART TO KEEP YOU STANDING.
GUGHH THAT'S IT...LET THE BERSERKER RAGE OUT.
YOUR CIVILIZED SELF WAS NE MORE THA A FACADE.
AGGGHHH

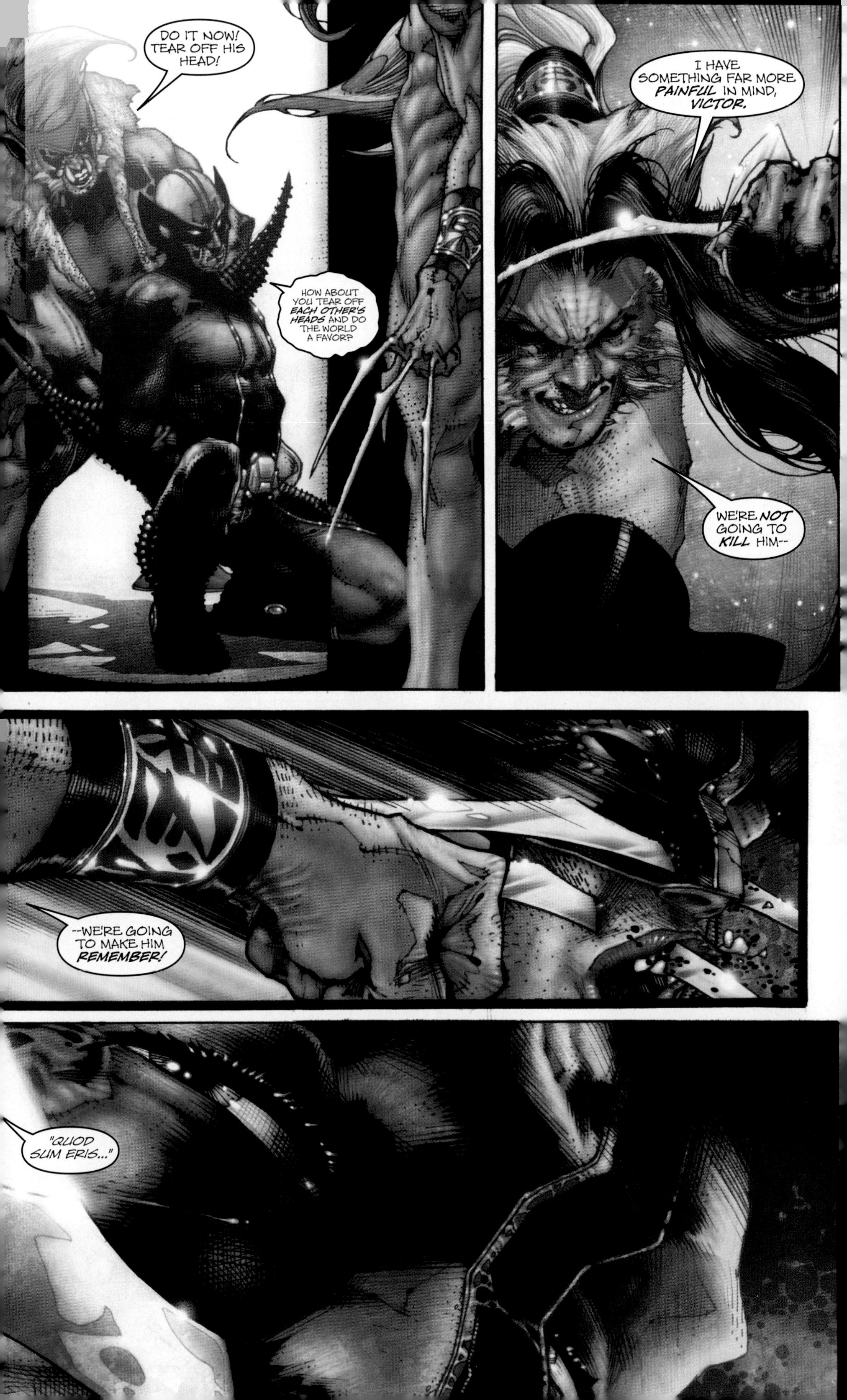
DO IT NOW! TEAR OFF HIS HEAD!
HOW ABOUT YOU TEAR OFF *EACH OTHER'S HEADS* AND DO THE WORLD A FAVOR?
I HAVE SOMETHING FAR MORE *PAINFUL* IN MIND, *VICTOR.*
WE'RE *NOT* GOING TO *KILL* HIM--
--WE'RE GOING TO MAKE HIM *REMEMBER!*
"QUOD SUM ERIS..."

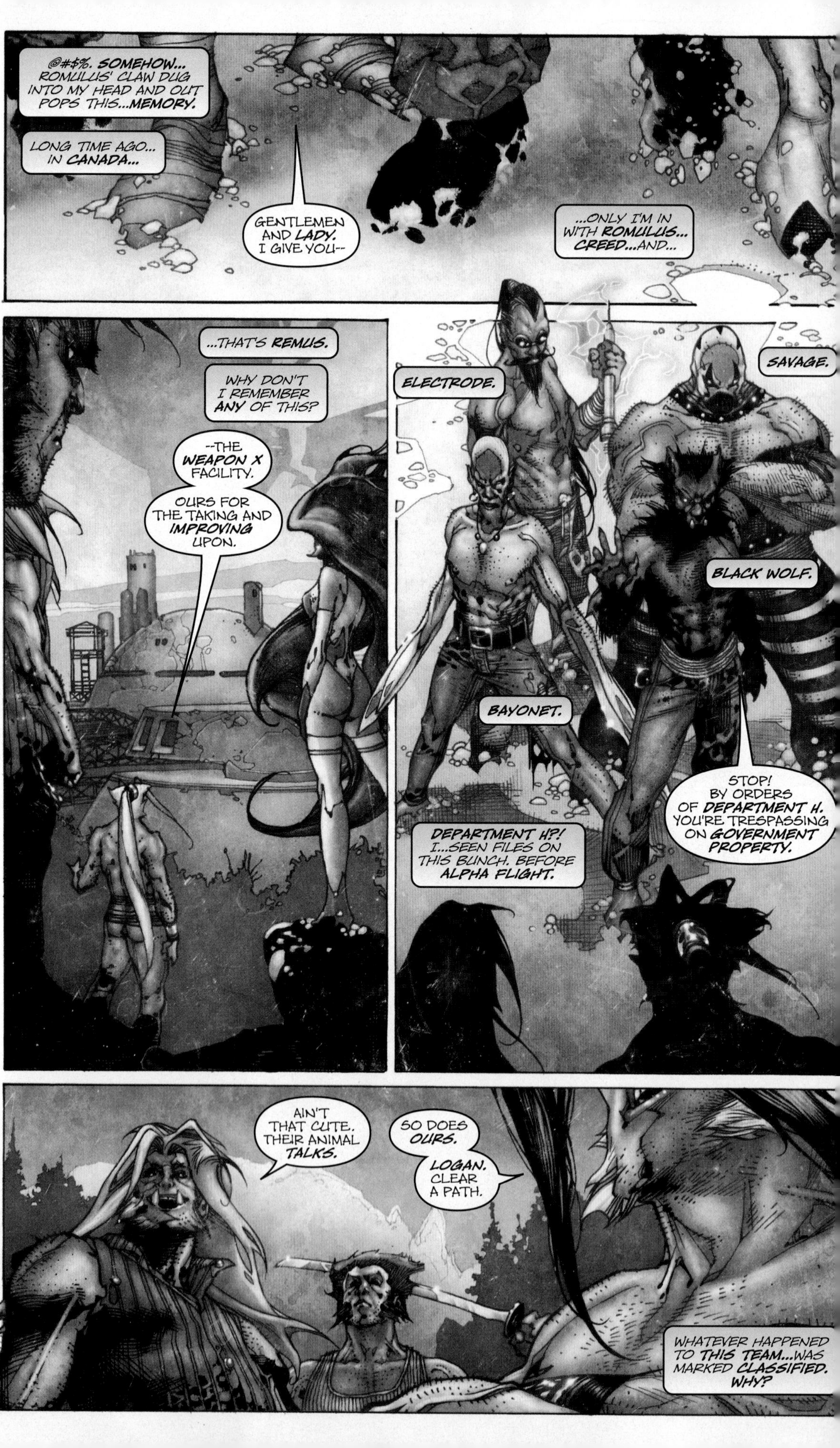
@#$%. SOMEHOW... ROMULUS' CLAW DUG INTO MY HEAD AND OUT POPS THIS...MEMORY.
LONG TIME AGO... IN CANADA...
GENTLEMEN AND LADY. I GIVE YOU--
...ONLY I'M IN WITH ROMULUS... CREED...AND...
...THAT'S REMUS.
WHY DON'T I REMEMBER ANY OF THIS?
--THE WEAPON X FACILITY.
OURS FOR THE TAKING AND IMPROVING UPON.
ELECTRODE.
SAVAGE.
BLACK WOLF.
BAYONET.
STOP! BY ORDERS OF DEPARTMENT H. YOU'RE TRESPASSING ON GOVERNMENT PROPERTY.
DEPARTMENT H?! I...SEEN FILES ON THIS BUNCH. BEFORE ALPHA FLIGHT.
AIN'T THAT CUTE. THEIR ANIMAL TALKS.
SO DOES OURS.
LOGAN. CLEAR A PATH.
WHATEVER HAPPENED TO THIS TEAM...WAS MARKED CLASSIFIED. WHY?

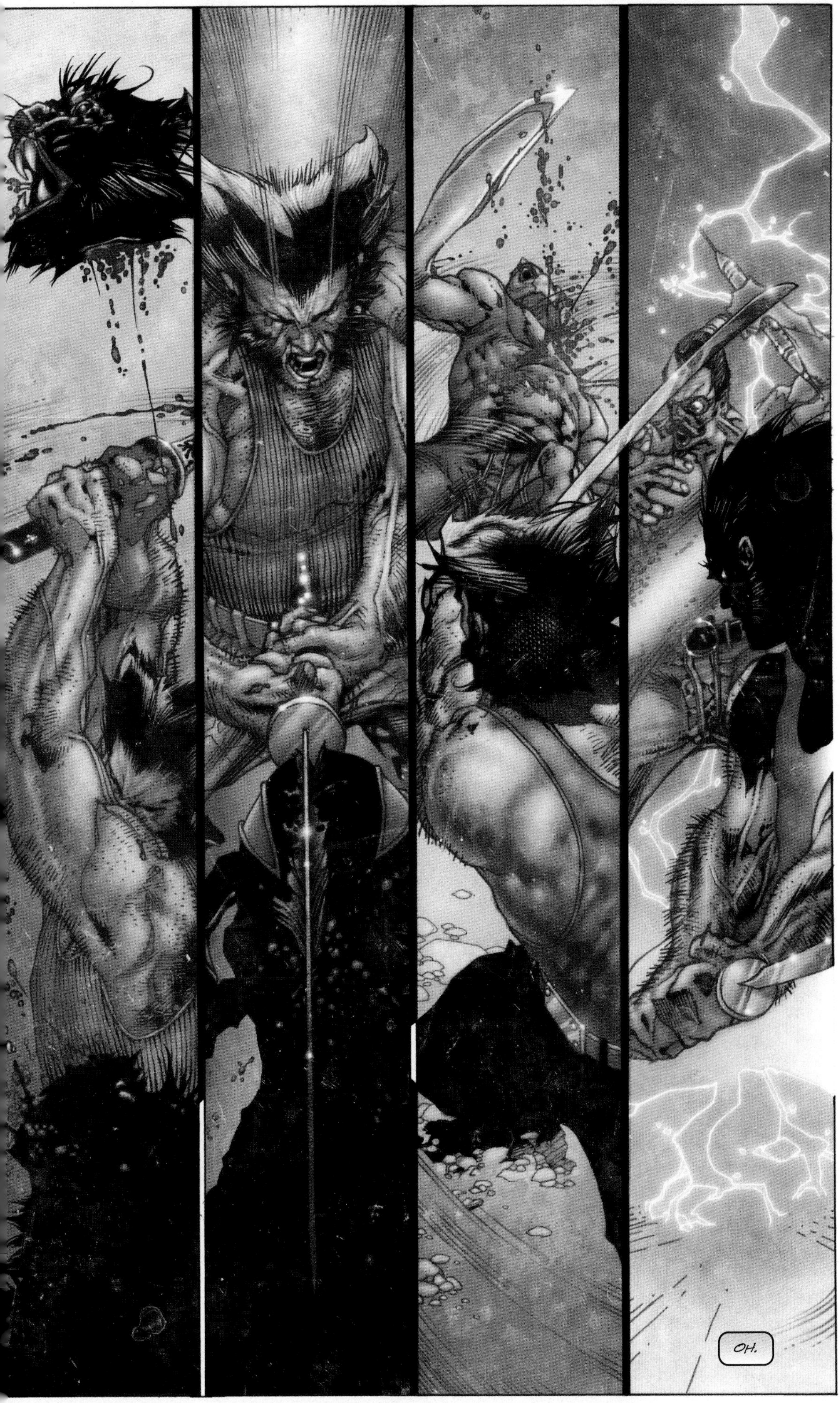
OH.

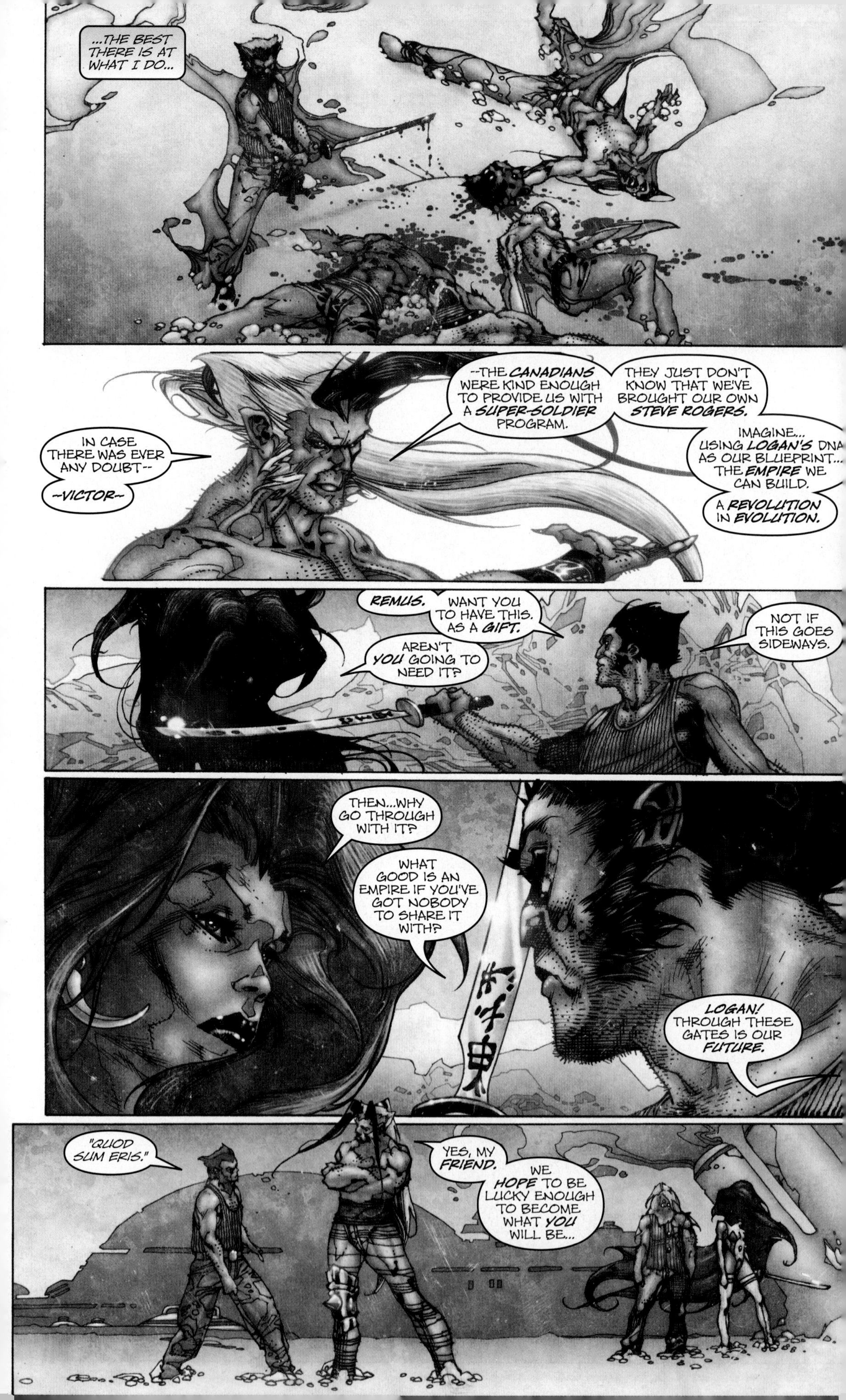
...THE BEST THERE IS AT WHAT I DO...
IN CASE THERE WAS EVER ANY DOUBT--
--VICTOR--
--THE CANADIANS WERE KIND ENOUGH TO PROVIDE US WITH A SUPER-SOLDIER PROGRAM.
THEY JUST DON'T KNOW THAT WE'VE BROUGHT OUR OWN STEVE ROGERS.
IMAGINE... USING LOGAN'S DNA AS OUR BLUEPRINT... THE EMPIRE WE CAN BUILD.
A REVOLUTION IN EVOLUTION.
REMUS.
WANT YOU TO HAVE THIS. AS A GIFT.
AREN'T YOU GOING TO NEED IT?
NOT IF THIS GOES SIDEWAYS.
THEN...WHY GO THROUGH WITH IT?
WHAT GOOD IS AN EMPIRE IF YOU'VE GOT NOBODY TO SHARE IT WITH?
LOGAN! THROUGH THESE GATES IS OUR FUTURE.
"QUOD SUM ERIS."
YES, MY FRIEND.
WE HOPE TO BE LUCKY ENOUGH TO BECOME WHAT YOU WILL BE...

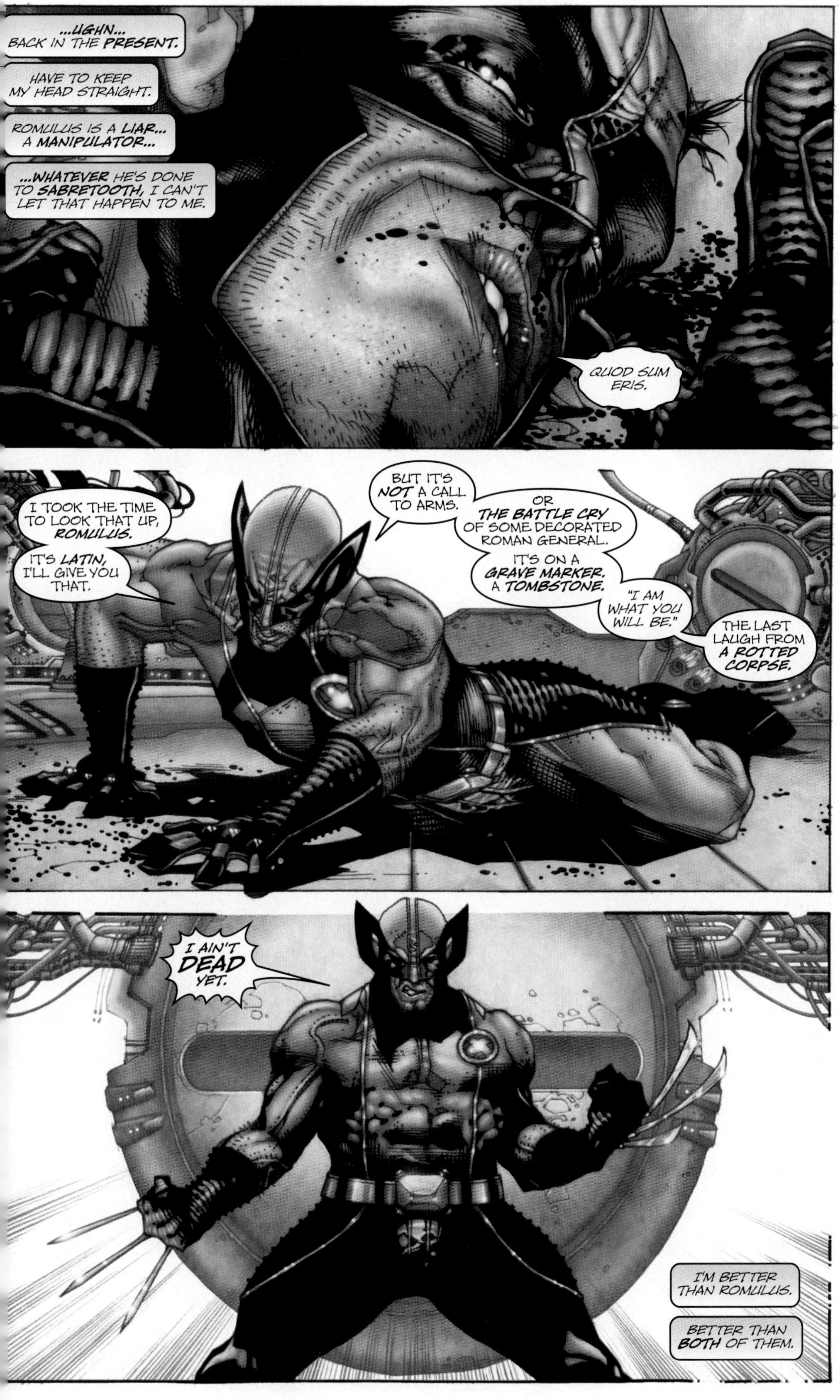
...UGHN... BACK IN THE PRESENT.
HAVE TO KEEP MY HEAD STRAIGHT.
ROMULUS IS A LIAR... A MANIPULATOR...
...WHATEVER HE'S DONE TO SABRETOOTH, I CAN'T LET THAT HAPPEN TO ME.
QUOD SUM ERIS.
I TOOK THE TIME TO LOOK THAT UP, ROMULUS.
IT'S LATIN, I'LL GIVE YOU THAT.
BUT IT'S NOT A CALL TO ARMS.
OR THE BATTLE CRY OF SOME DECORATED ROMAN GENERAL.
IT'S ON A GRAVE MARKER. A TOMBSTONE.
"I AM WHAT YOU WILL BE."
THE LAST LAUGH FROM A ROTTED CORPSE.
I AIN'T DEAD YET.
I'M BETTER THAN ROMULUS.
BETTER THAN BOTH OF THEM.

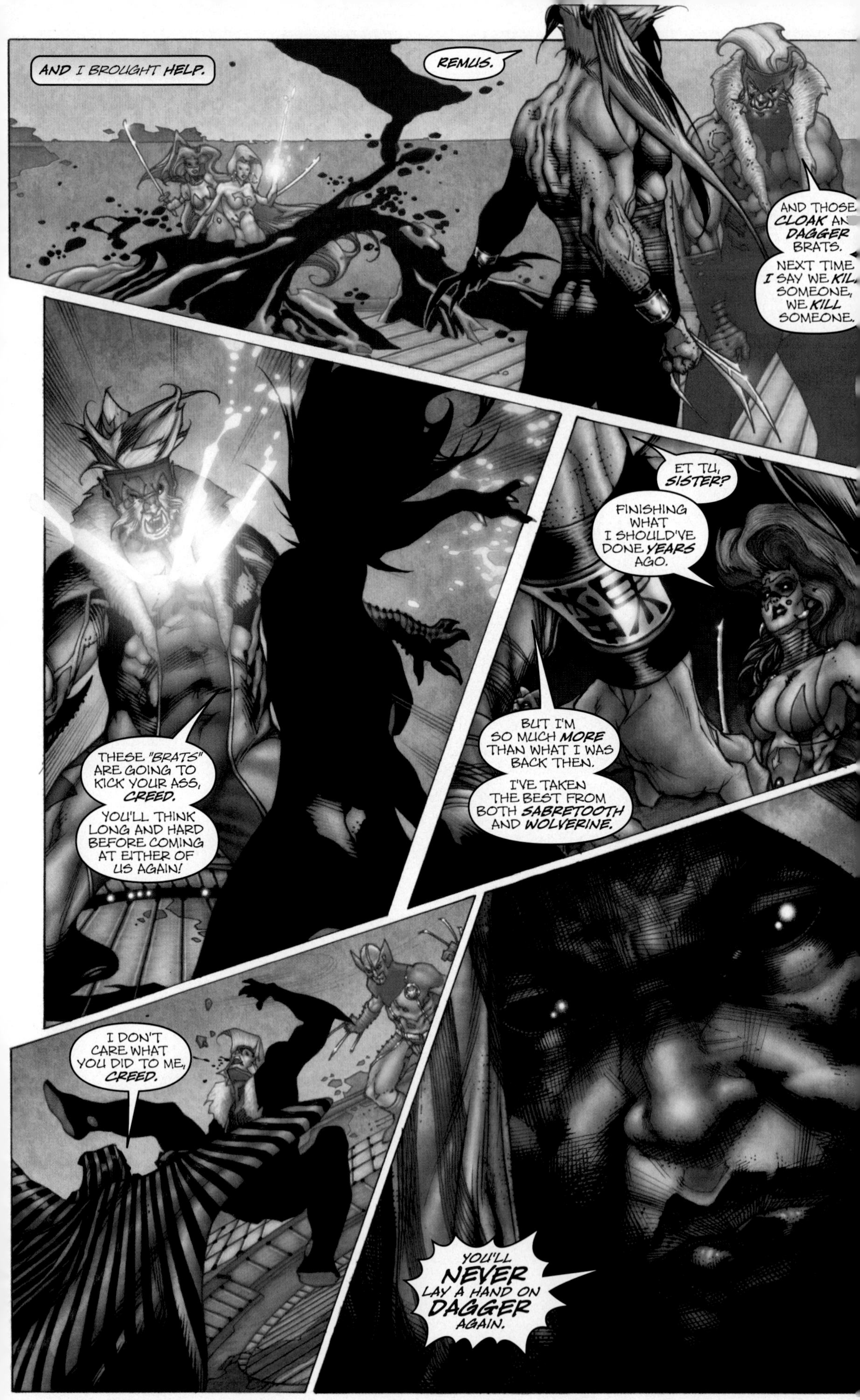
AND I BROUGHT HELP.
REMUS.
AND THOSE CLOAK AN DAGGER BRATS. NEXT TIME I SAY WE KIL SOMEONE, WE KILL SOMEONE.
THESE "BRATS" ARE GOING TO KICK YOUR ASS, CREED. YOU'LL THINK LONG AND HARD BEFORE COMING AT EITHER OF US AGAIN!
ET TU, SISTER?
FINISHING WHAT I SHOULD'VE DONE YEARS AGO.
BUT I'M SO MUCH MORE THAN WHAT I WAS BACK THEN. I'VE TAKEN THE BEST FROM BOTH SABRETOOTH AND WOLVERINE.
I DON'T CARE WHAT YOU DID TO ME, CREED.
YOU'LL NEVER LAY A HAND ON DAGGER AGAIN.

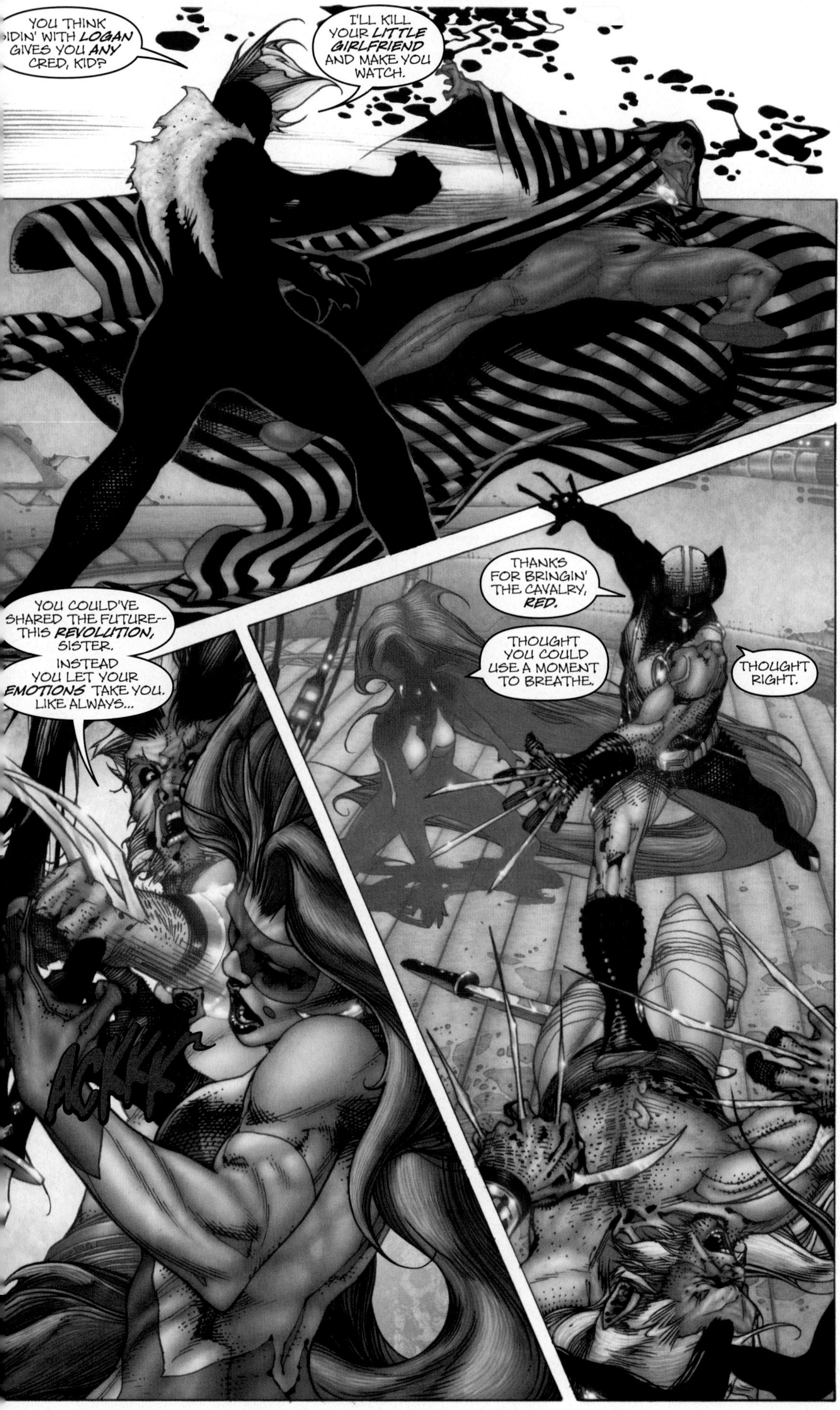
YOU THINK RIDIN' WITH LOGAN GIVES YOU ANY CRED, KID?
I'LL KILL YOUR LITTLE GIRLFRIEND AND MAKE YOU WATCH.
THANKS FOR BRINGIN' THE CAVALRY, RED.
THOUGHT YOU COULD USE A MOMENT TO BREATHE.
THOUGHT RIGHT.
YOU COULD'VE SHARED THE FUTURE-- THIS REVOLUTION, SISTER.
INSTEAD YOU LET YOUR EMOTIONS TAKE YOU. LIKE ALWAYS...
ACKK!

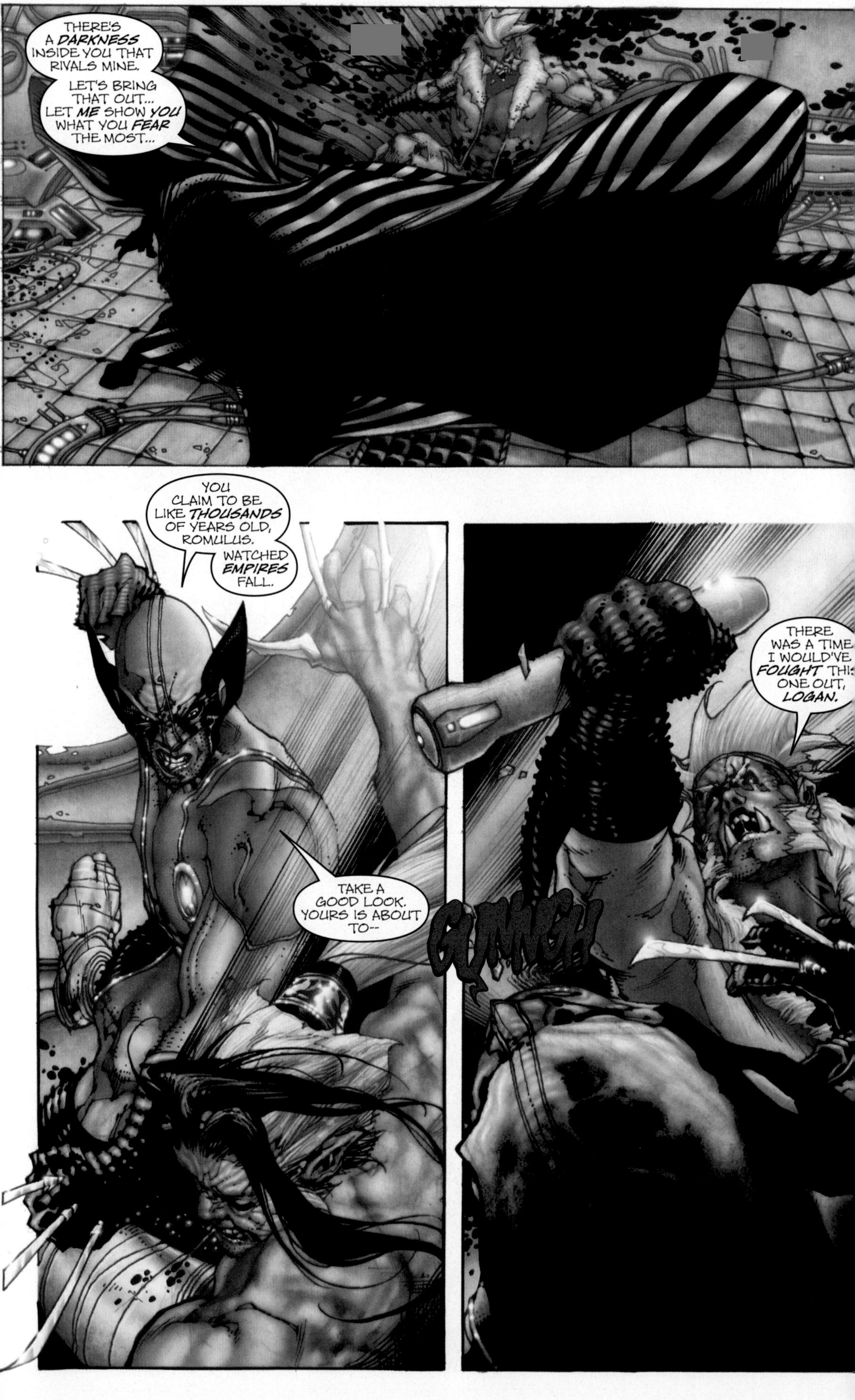
THERE'S A DARKNESS INSIDE YOU THAT RIVALS MINE.
LET'S BRING THAT OUT... LET ME SHOW YOU WHAT YOU FEAR THE MOST...
YOU CLAIM TO BE LIKE THOUSANDS OF YEARS OLD, ROMULUS.
WATCHED EMPIRES FALL.
TAKE A GOOD LOOK. YOURS IS ABOUT TO--
GUNNGH
THERE WAS A TIME I WOULD'VE FOUGHT THI ONE OUT, LOGAN.

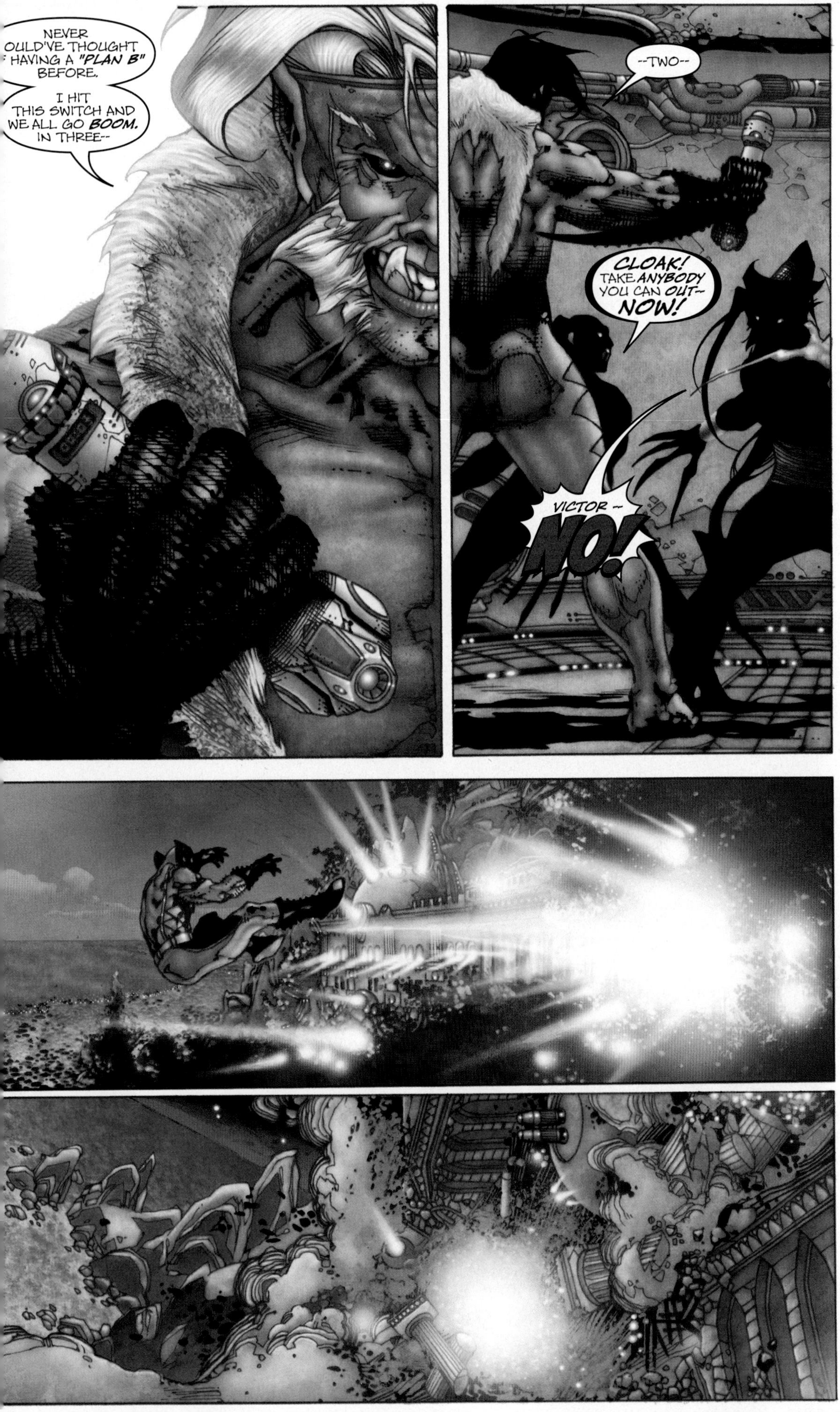
NEVER OULD'VE THOUGHT F HAVING A "PLAN B" BEFORE.
I HIT THIS SWITCH AND WE ALL GO BOOM. IN THREE--
--TWO--
CLOAK! TAKE ANYBODY YOU CAN OUT-- NOW!
VICTOR -- NO!

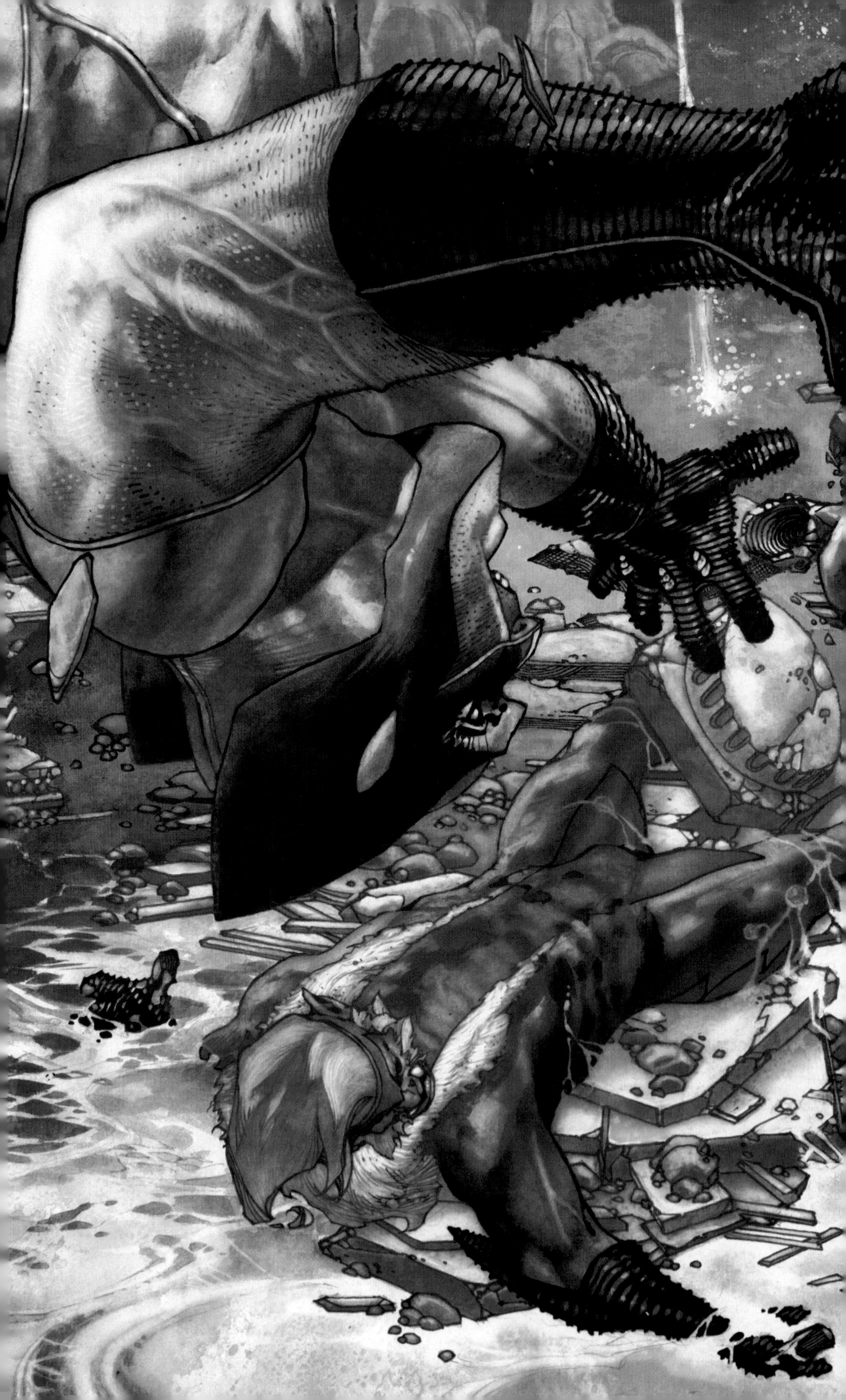

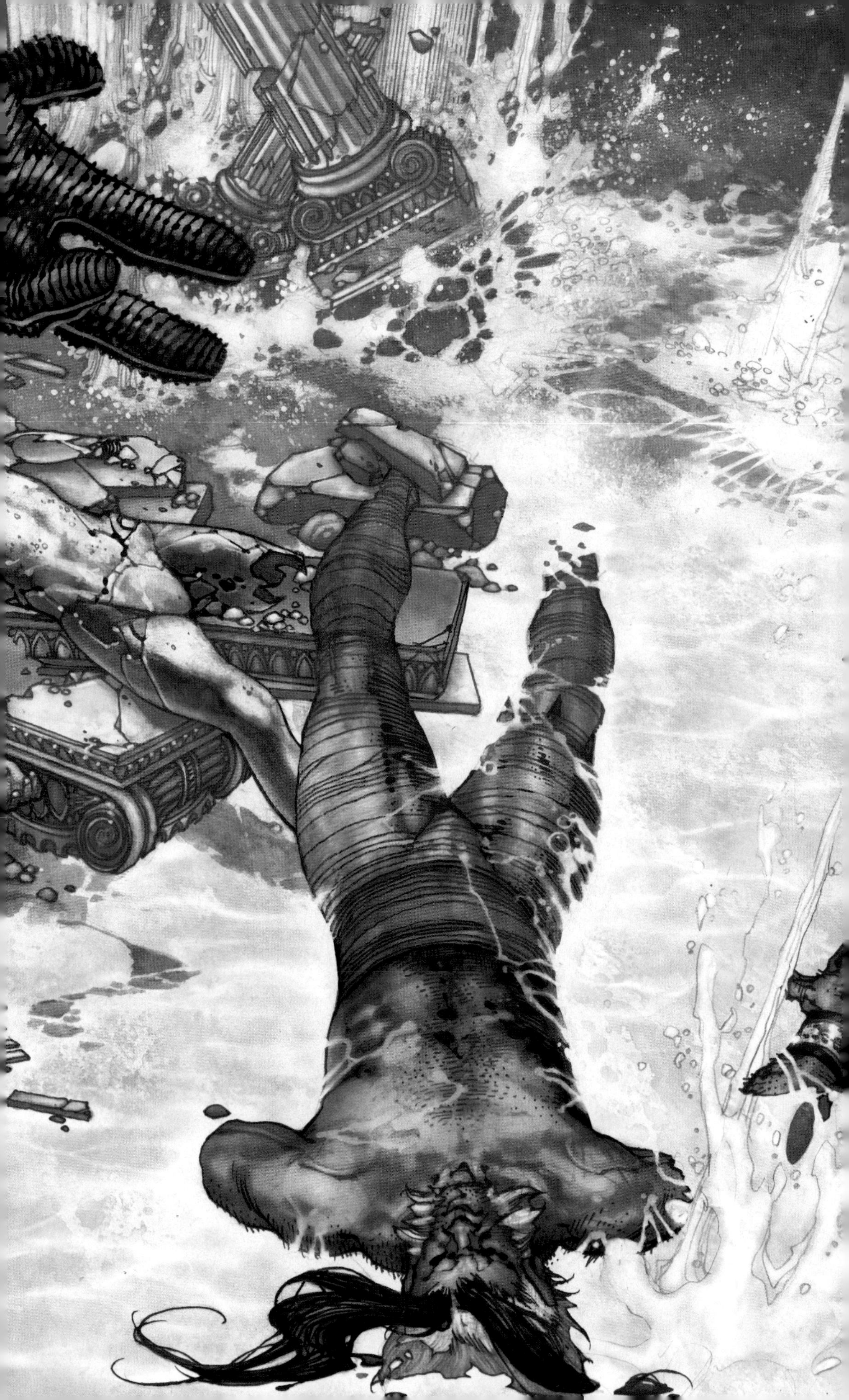

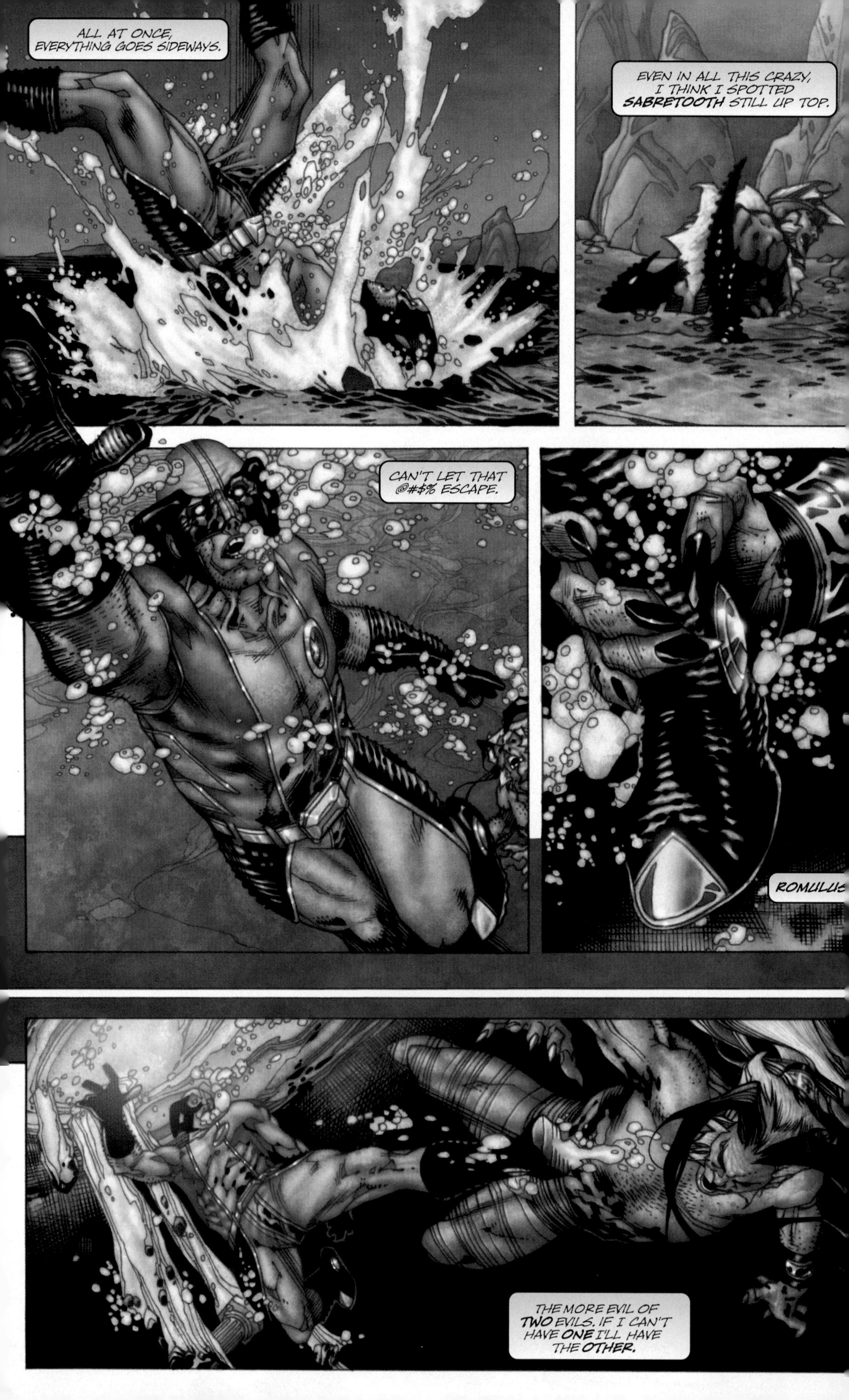
ALL AT ONCE, EVERYTHING GOES SIDEWAYS.
EVEN IN ALL THIS CRAZY, I THINK I SPOTTED **SABRETOOTH** STILL UP TOP.
CAN'T LET THAT @#$% ESCAPE.
ROMULUS
THE MORE EVIL OF **TWO** EVILS. IF I CAN'T HAVE **ONE** I'LL HAVE THE **OTHER**.

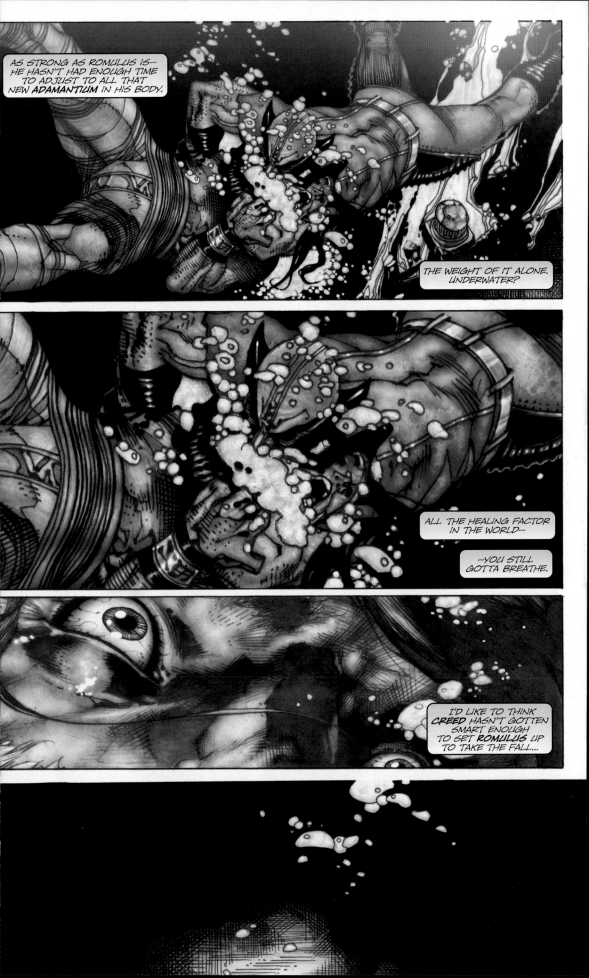

AS STRONG AS ROMULUS IS-- HE HASN'T HAD ENOUGH TIME TO ADJUST TO ALL THAT NEW **ADAMANTIUM** IN HIS BODY.

THE WEIGHT OF IT ALONE. UNDERWATER?

ALL THE HEALING FACTOR IN THE WORLD--

--YOU STILL GOTTA BREATHE.

I'D LIKE TO THINK **CREED** HASN'T GOTTEN SMART ENOUGH TO SET **ROMULUS** UP TO TAKE THE FALL...

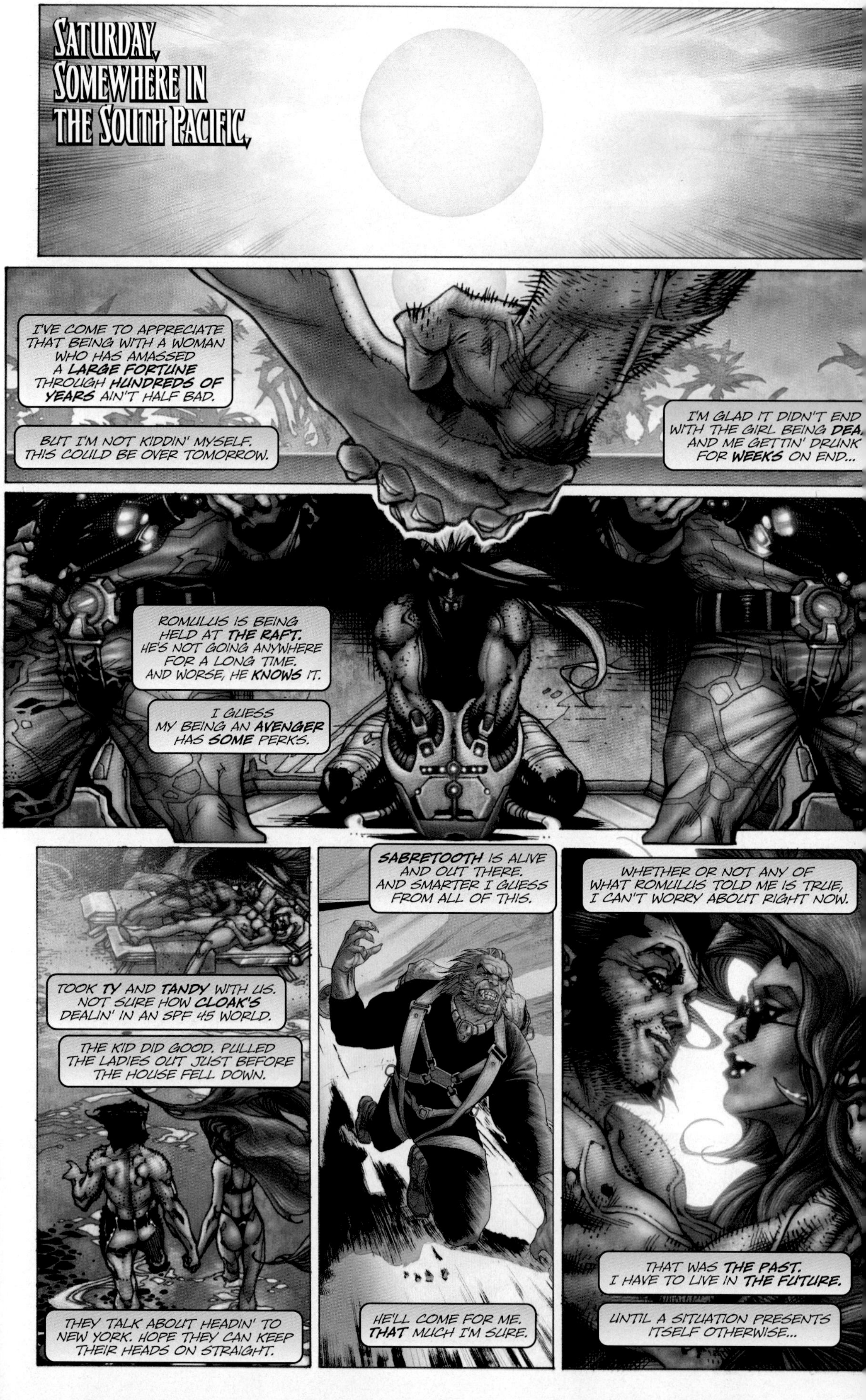
SATURDAY, SOMEWHERE IN THE SOUTH PACIFIC.
I'VE COME TO APPRECIATE THAT BEING WITH A WOMAN WHO HAS AMASSED A LARGE FORTUNE THROUGH HUNDREDS OF YEARS AIN'T HALF BAD.
BUT I'M NOT KIDDIN' MYSELF. THIS COULD BE OVER TOMORROW.
I'M GLAD IT DIDN'T END WITH THE GIRL BEING DEA AND ME GETTIN' DRUNK FOR WEEKS ON END...
ROMULUS IS BEING HELD AT THE RAFT. HE'S NOT GOING ANYWHERE FOR A LONG TIME. AND WORSE, HE KNOWS IT.
I GUESS MY BEING AN AVENGER HAS SOME PERKS.
TOOK TY AND TANDY WITH US. NOT SURE HOW CLOAK'S DEALIN' IN AN SPF 45 WORLD.
THE KID DID GOOD. PULLED THE LADIES OUT JUST BEFORE THE HOUSE FELL DOWN.
THEY TALK ABOUT HEADIN' TO NEW YORK. HOPE THEY CAN KEEP THEIR HEADS ON STRAIGHT.
SABRETOOTH IS ALIVE AND OUT THERE. AND SMARTER I GUESS FROM ALL OF THIS.
HE'LL COME FOR ME. THAT MUCH I'M SURE.
WHETHER OR NOT ANY OF WHAT ROMULUS TOLD ME IS TRUE, I CAN'T WORRY ABOUT RIGHT NOW.
THAT WAS THE PAST. I HAVE TO LIVE IN THE FUTURE.
UNTIL A SITUATION PRESENTS ITSELF OTHERWISE...

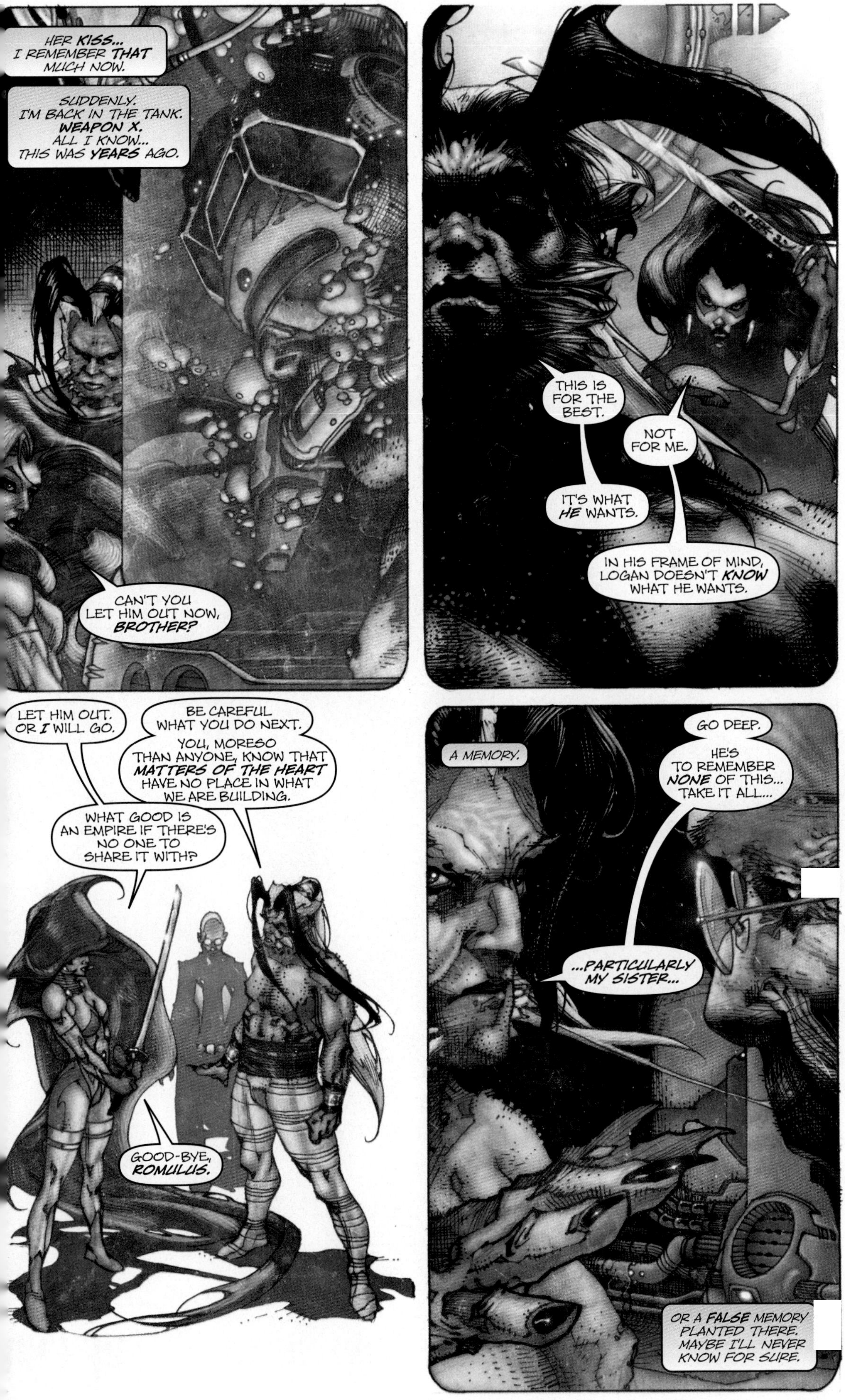
HER KISS... I REMEMBER THAT MUCH NOW.
SUDDENLY. I'M BACK IN THE TANK. WEAPON X. ALL I KNOW... THIS WAS YEARS AGO.
CAN'T YOU LET HIM OUT NOW, BROTHER?
THIS IS FOR THE BEST.
NOT FOR ME.
IT'S WHAT HE WANTS.
IN HIS FRAME OF MIND, LOGAN DOESN'T KNOW WHAT HE WANTS.
LET HIM OUT. OR I WILL GO.
BE CAREFUL WHAT YOU DO NEXT.
YOU, MORESO THAN ANYONE, KNOW THAT MATTERS OF THE HEART HAVE NO PLACE IN WHAT WE ARE BUILDING.
WHAT GOOD IS AN EMPIRE IF THERE'S NO ONE TO SHARE IT WITH?
GOOD-BYE, ROMULUS.
A MEMORY.
GO DEEP.
HE'S TO REMEMBER NONE OF THIS... TAKE IT ALL....
...PARTICULARLY MY SISTER...
OR A FALSE MEMORY PLANTED THERE. MAYBE I'LL NEVER KNOW FOR SURE.

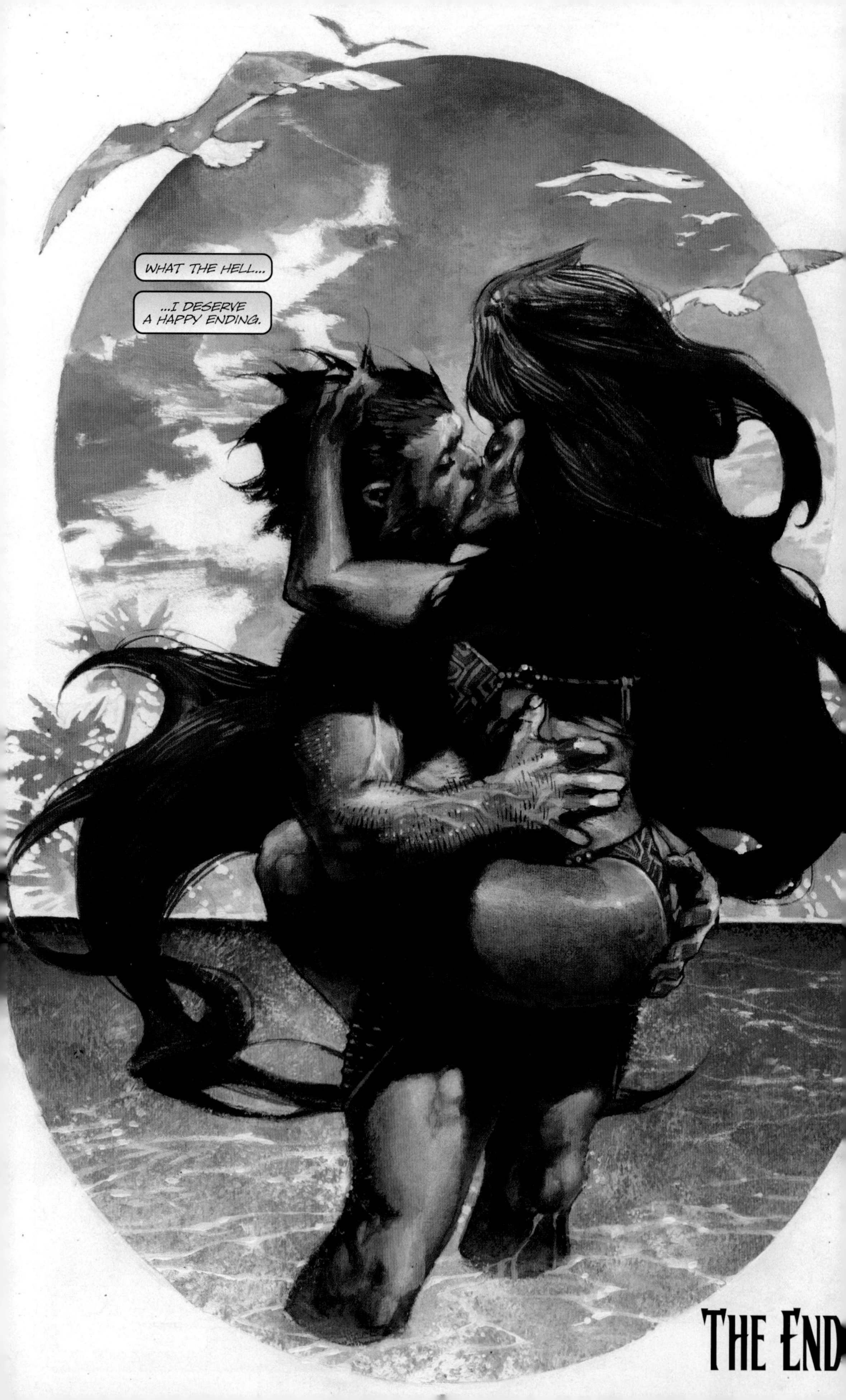
WHAT THE HELL...
...I DESERVE A HAPPY ENDING.
THE END

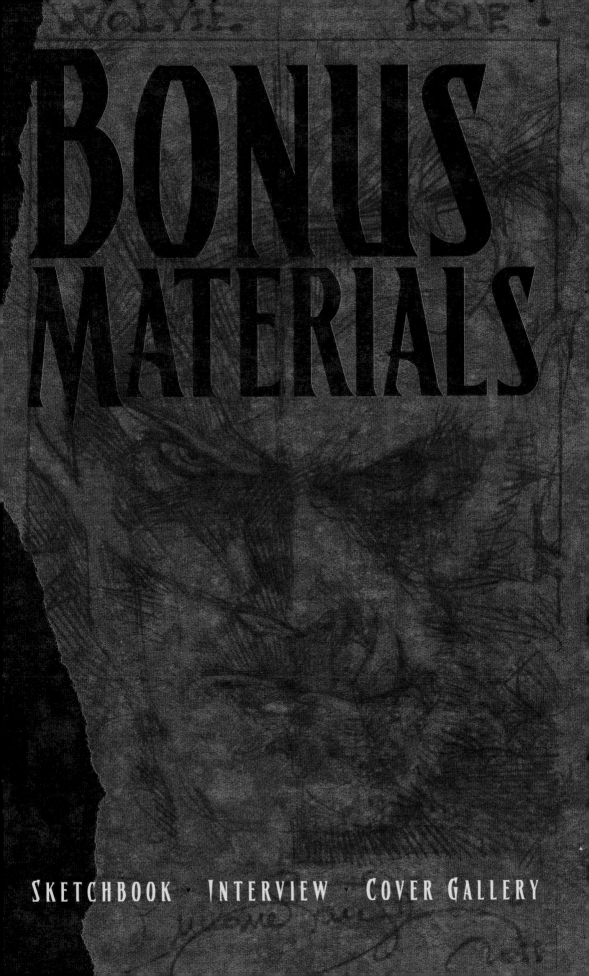

BONUS MATERIALS

SKETCHBOOK · INTERVIEW · COVER GALLERY

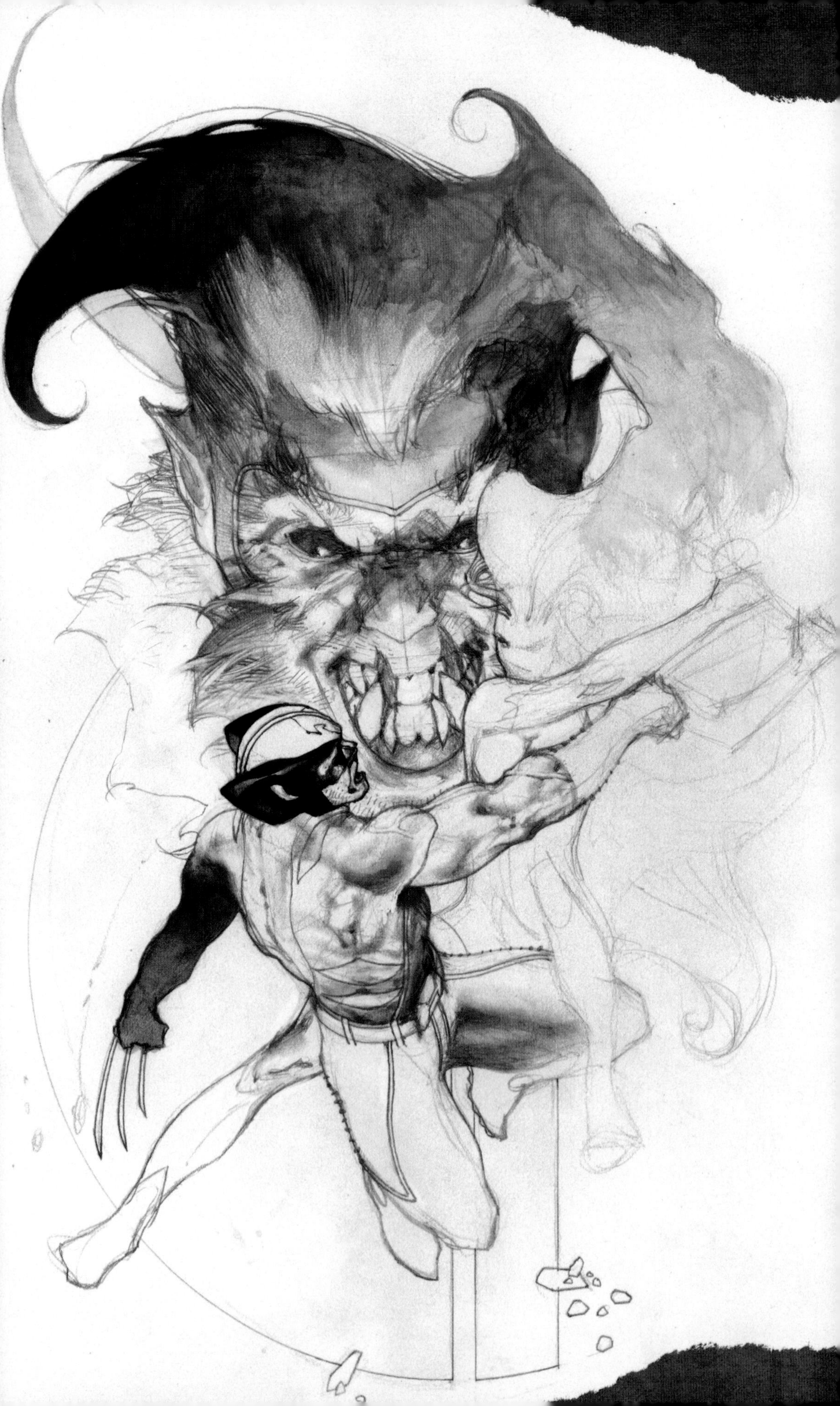

JEPH LOEB AND SIMONE BIANCHI TALK WOLVERINE

When you were coming to the end of WOLVERINE: EVOLUTION, what was it like laying down the seeds for SABRETOOTH REBORN?

JL: It was more like knowing where the rest of the story had to go. We never saw EVOLUTION as the full story — it was the first part of an epic struggle between Wolverine and Sabretooth and we knew someday we'd be back for the rest. The only question in our minds was — when? Answer: Now!

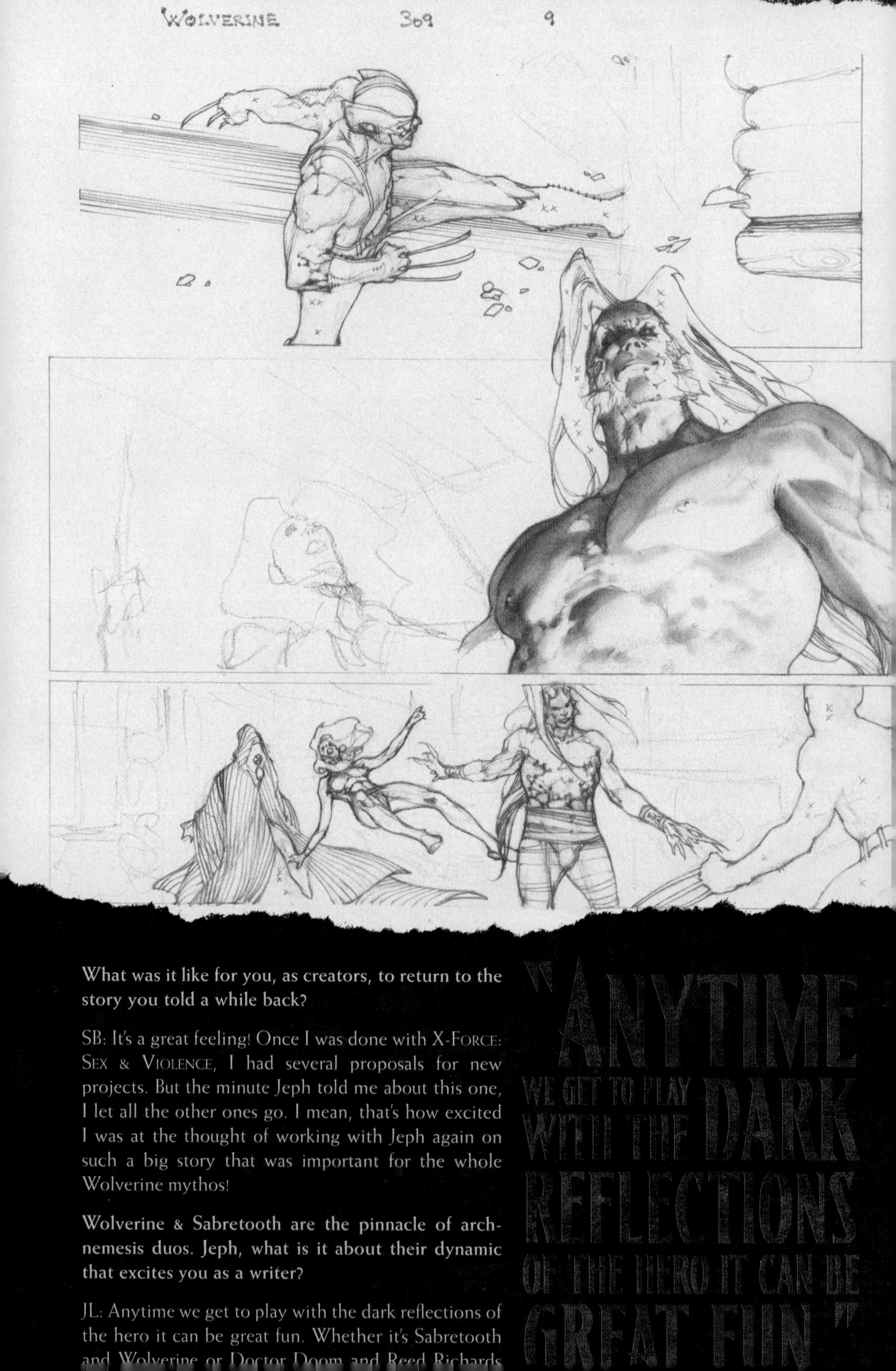
WOLVERINE
309
9

What was it like for you, as creators, to return to the story you told a while back?

SB: It's a great feeling! Once I was done with X-FORCE: SEX & VIOLENCE, I had several proposals for new projects. But the minute Jeph told me about this one, I let all the other ones go. I mean, that's how excited I was at the thought of working with Jeph again on such a big story that was important for the whole Wolverine mythos!

Wolverine & Sabretooth are the pinnacle of arch-nemesis duos. Jeph, what is it about their dynamic that excites you as a writer?

JL: Anytime we get to play with the dark reflections of the hero it can be great fun. Whether it's Sabretooth and Wolverine or Doctor Doom and Reed Richards

"ANYTIME WE GET TO PLAY WITH THE DARK REFLECTIONS OF THE HERO IT CAN BE GREAT FUN."

WOLVERINE 309 9

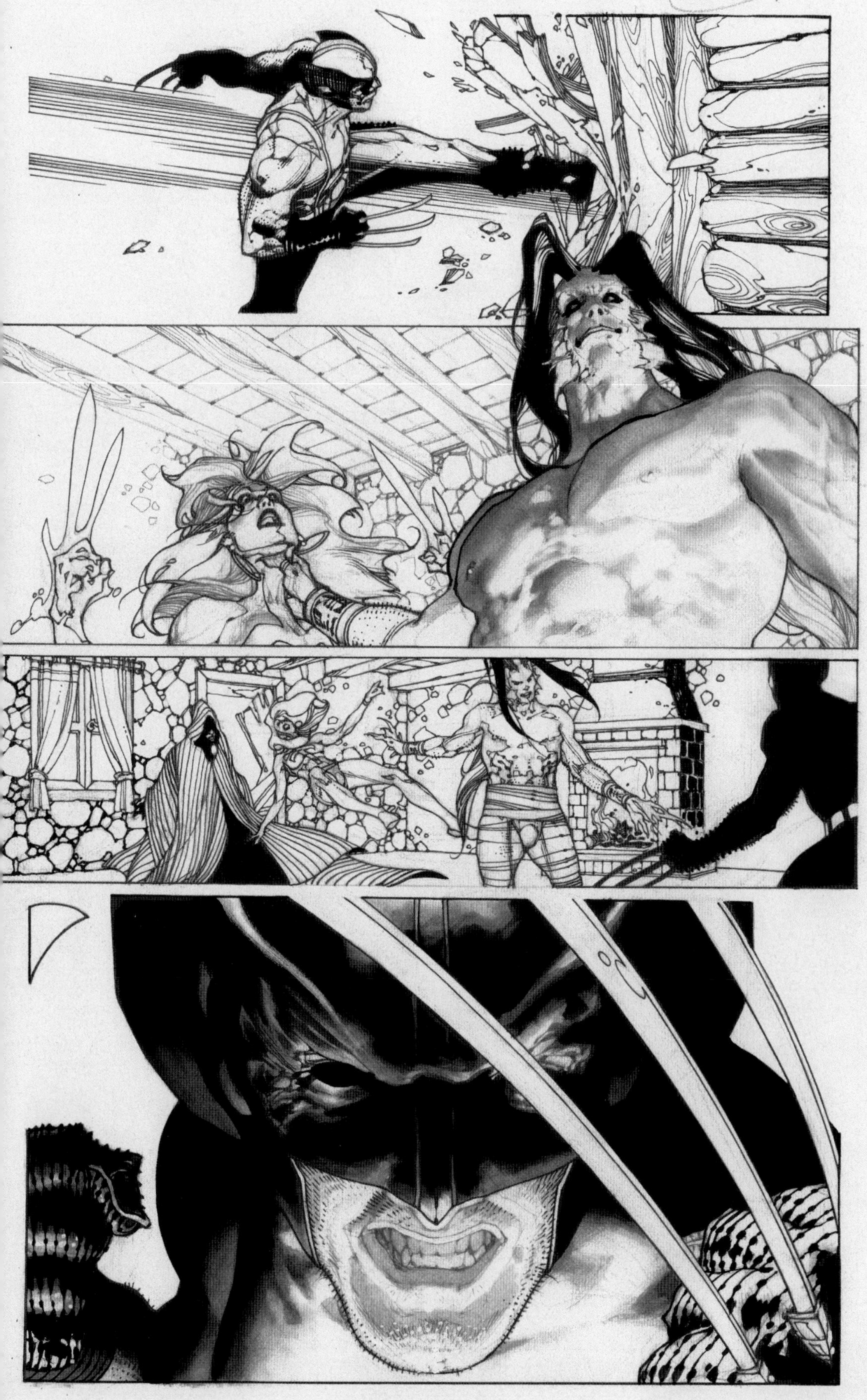

2012

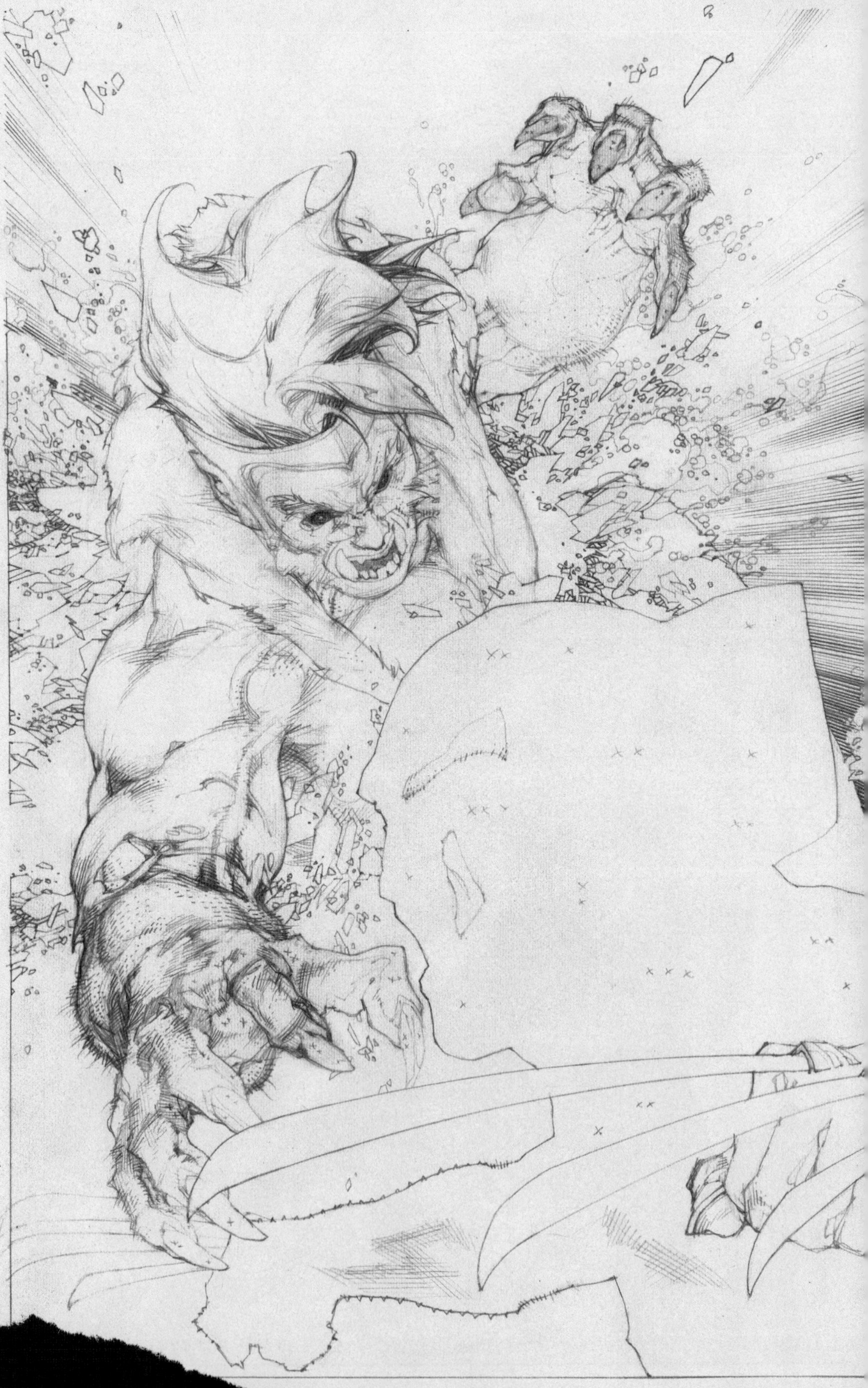

> "SABRETOOTH IS THAT ROAD NOT TAKEN BY WOLVERINE — HE KILLS WITHOUT MERCY AND ACTUALLY ENJOYS IT."

or Captain America and the Red Skull — the villain actually serves to better showcase the heroic aspects of the main character.

Sabretooth is that road not taken by Wolverine — he kills without mercy and actually enjoys it. Logan is by far the better, and in some ways, more evolved character. But make no mistake they are metaphorical brothers who are dealing with their own personal demons.

How does SABRETOOTH REBORN have a different tone than WOLVERINE: EVOLUTION?

JL: Where Sabretooth has been and what he's learned in the time since his death will have a profound — and hopefully long lasting — effect on the character. That was always important to us — and to our Editor in Chief Axel "Basketball" Alonso, X-Men Editor Supremo Nick "Mr. Television" Lowe and our own Editorial Goddess Jeanine "Sniktress" Schaefer — that he couldn't come back and just pick up where he left off.

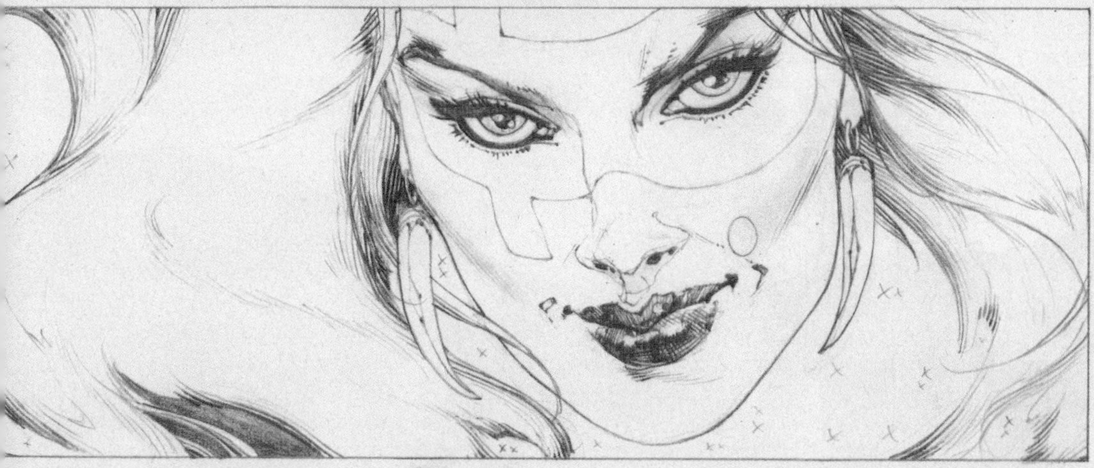

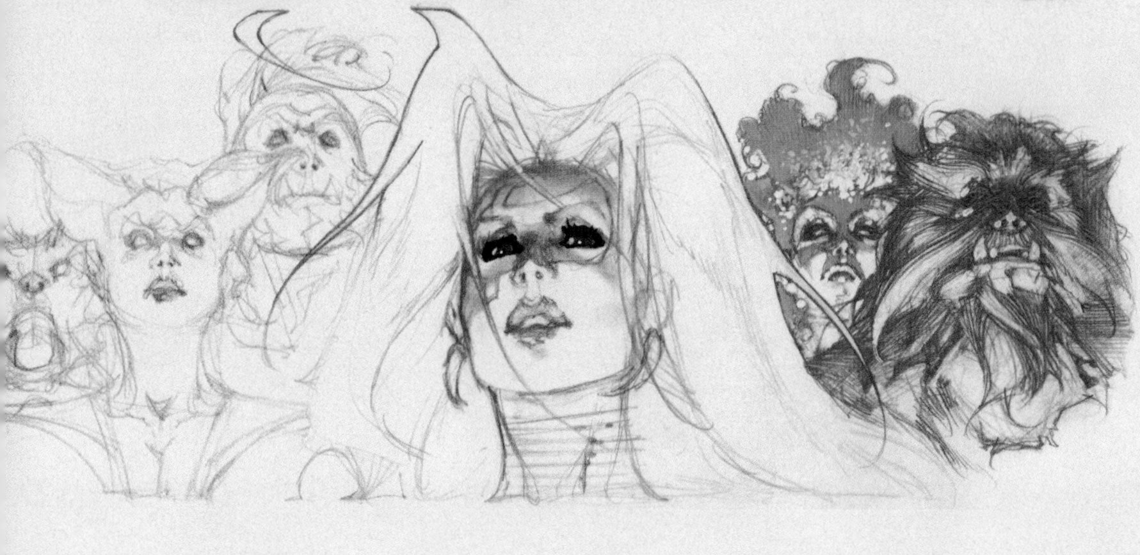

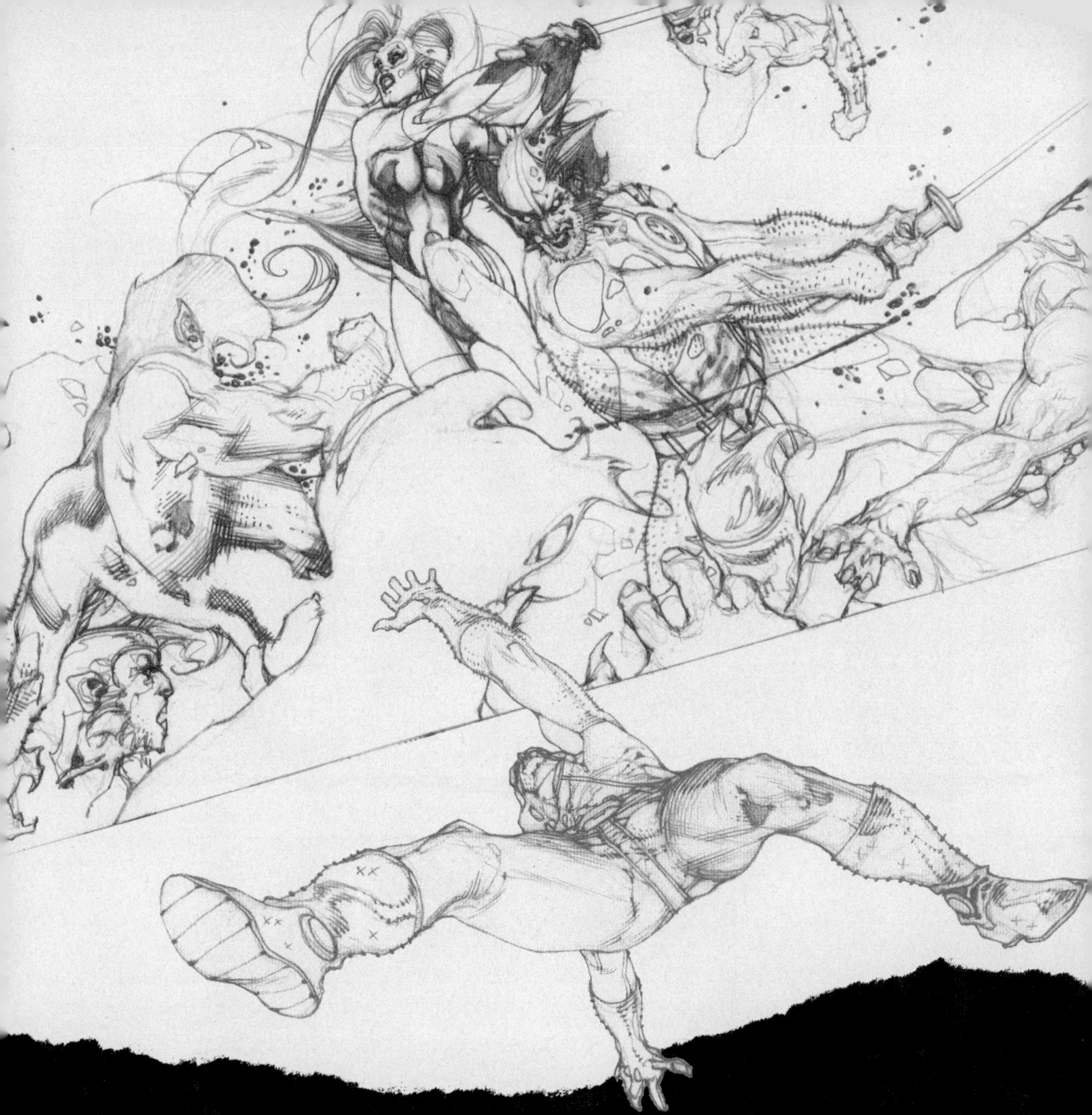

Simone, how has your artistic style and approach evolved since your last epic team-up with Jeph?

SB: I basically gave up ink wash and half-tones and went straight for a purer black and white look. I think it makes the pages lighter and clearer, making it better for storytelling. Also, it gives my colorist Simone Peruzzi the chance to show off his amazing skills in an even stronger way. Plus, the layouts have gotten much simpler and direct. I've adapted the use of straight panels and less crazy layouts in order to give the story and the storytelling more fluidity.

Jeph, what aspect do you like best when working with Simone?

JL: He draws so elegantly — and with such passion. There's nothing he won't try to do (and I've certainly pushed him!) and it always is so breathtaking. What can I say — he's a mad Italian genius! I'm very lucky to have worked with him as much as we have.

"SIMONE DRAWS SO ELEGANTLY AND WITH SUCH PASSION. THERE'S NOTHING HE WON'T TRY TO DO."

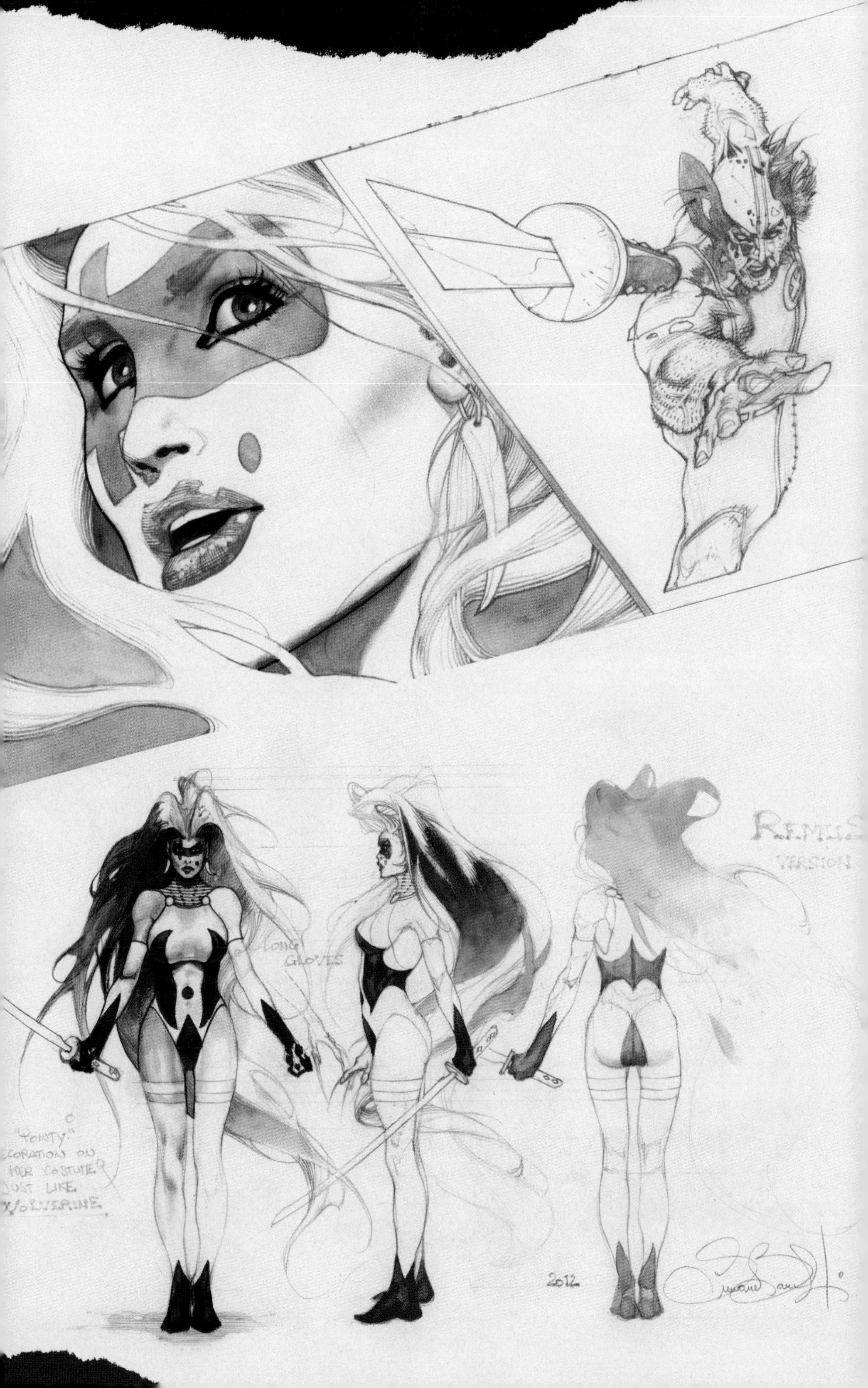

VERSION
LONG GLOVES
"POINTY"
ECORATION ON
HER COSTUME?
JUST LIKE
WOLVERINE
2012

WOLVERINE 310 13

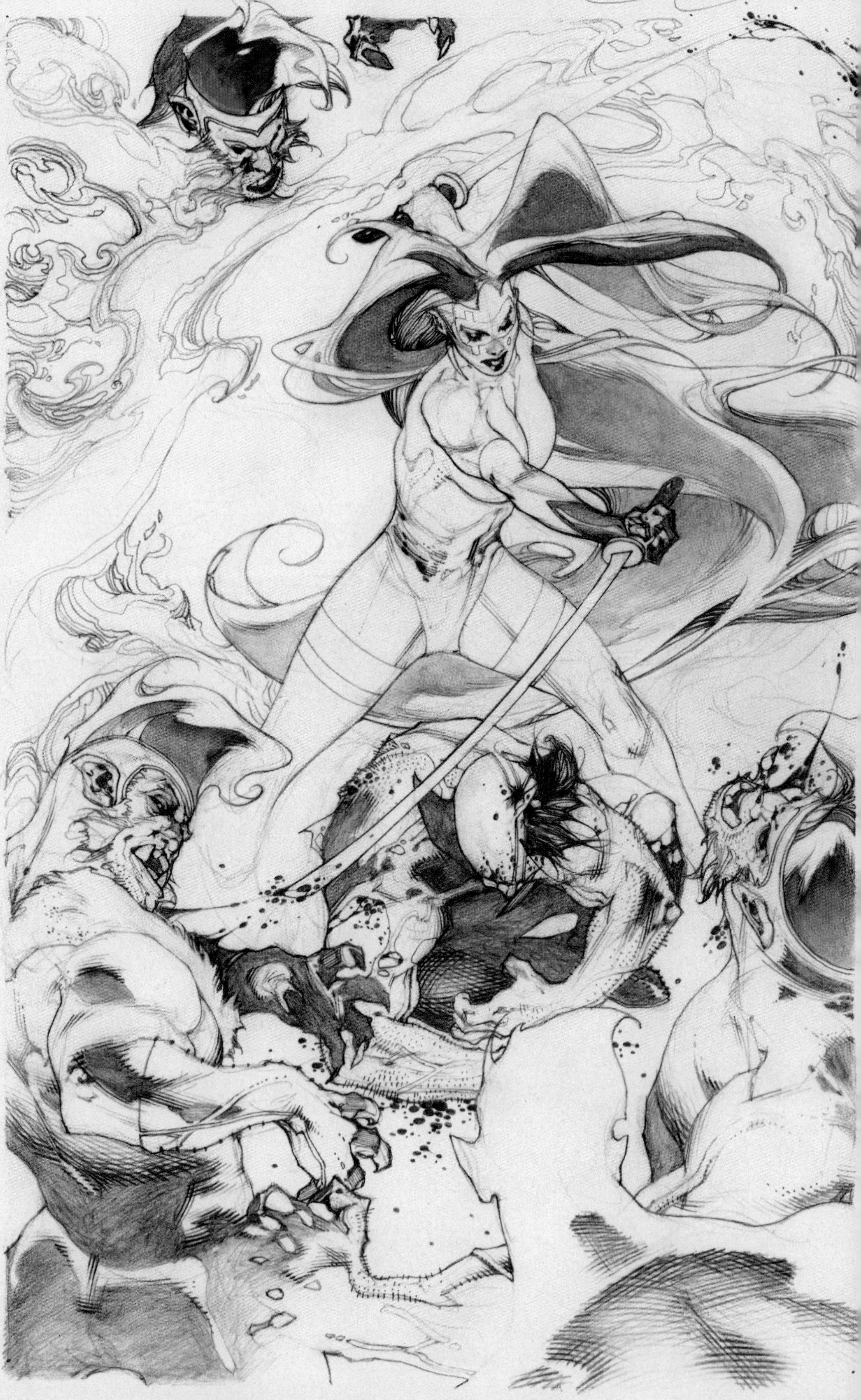

"I DON'T THINK THEY WILL EVER EXCHANGE FLOWERS AND BLOW KISSES TO EACH OTHER."

Sabretooth's return is a major event for the Marvel Universe — one of the biggest this year; in what ways has Sabretooth evolved as a character?

SB: It's too early for me to say. He still shows the same hate and anger towards Logan the way he has always done over the years. It goes without saying, I don't think they will ever exchange flowers and blow kisses to each other.

What ramifications will arise with Sabretooth's return to the Marvel Universe?

JL: We've always believed that Sabretooth is the baddest of bad when it comes to mutant villains. And now with Simone and I showing how he came back, you can be sure he's going to cause all sorts of headaches in the Marvel Universe. He's fair game now!

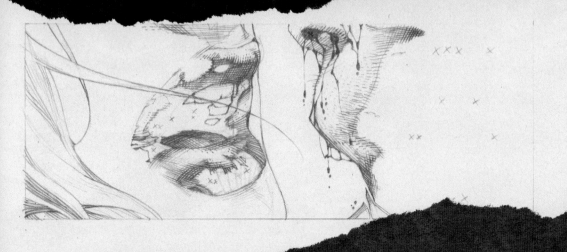

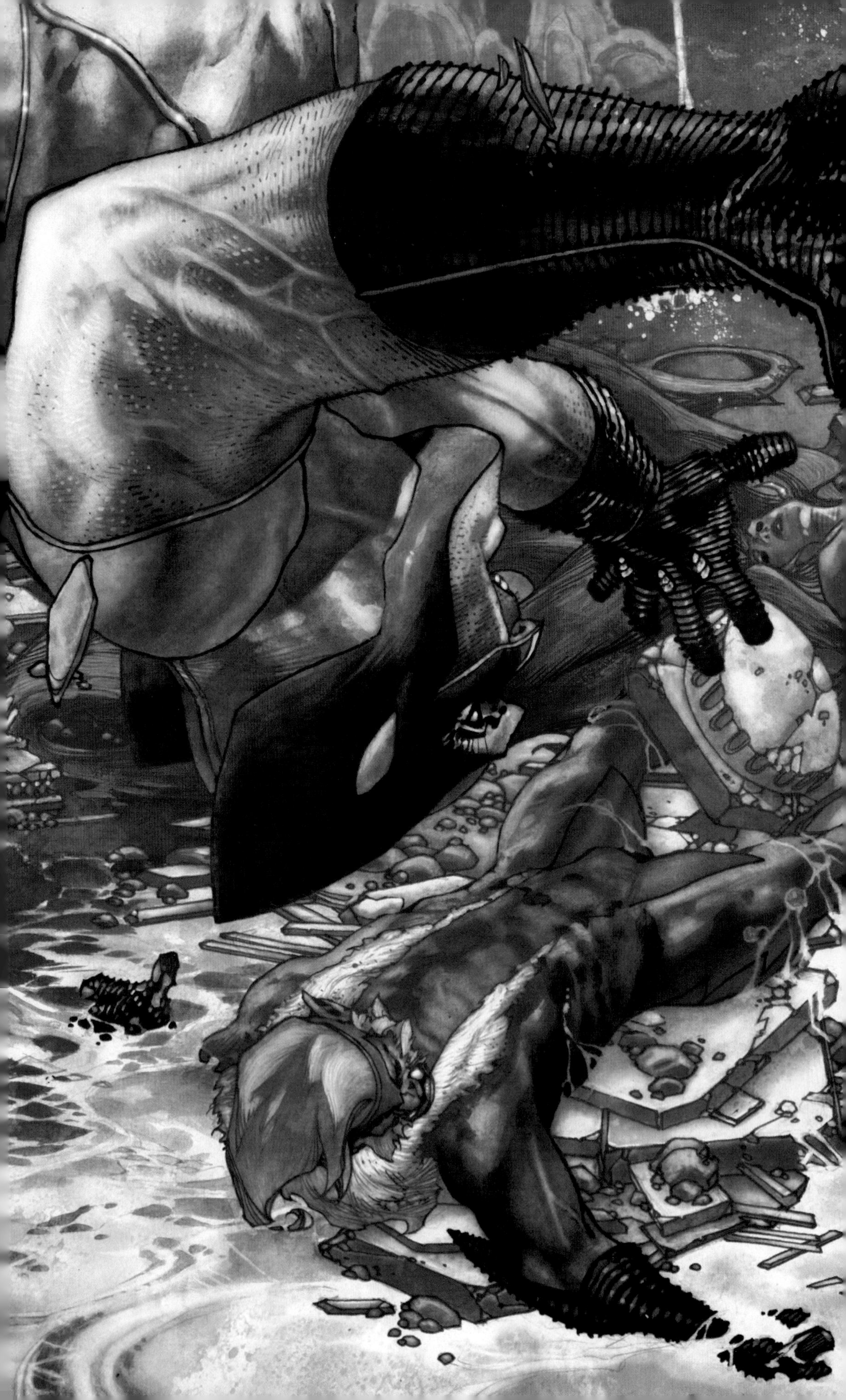

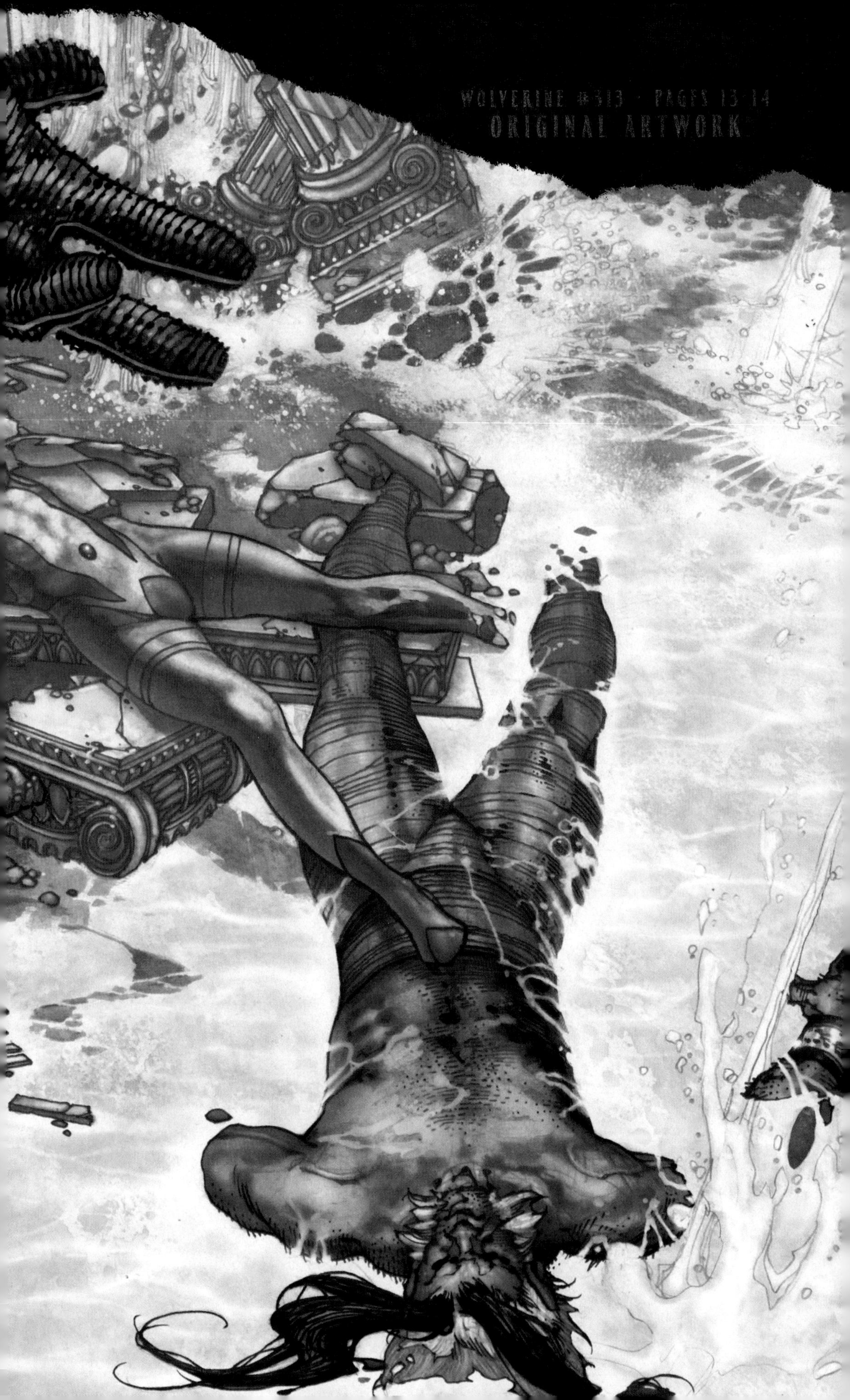
WOLVERINE #313 · PAGES 13-14
ORIGINAL ARTWORK

WOLVERINE #310 VARIANT COVER

ED MCGUINNESS & JASON KEITH

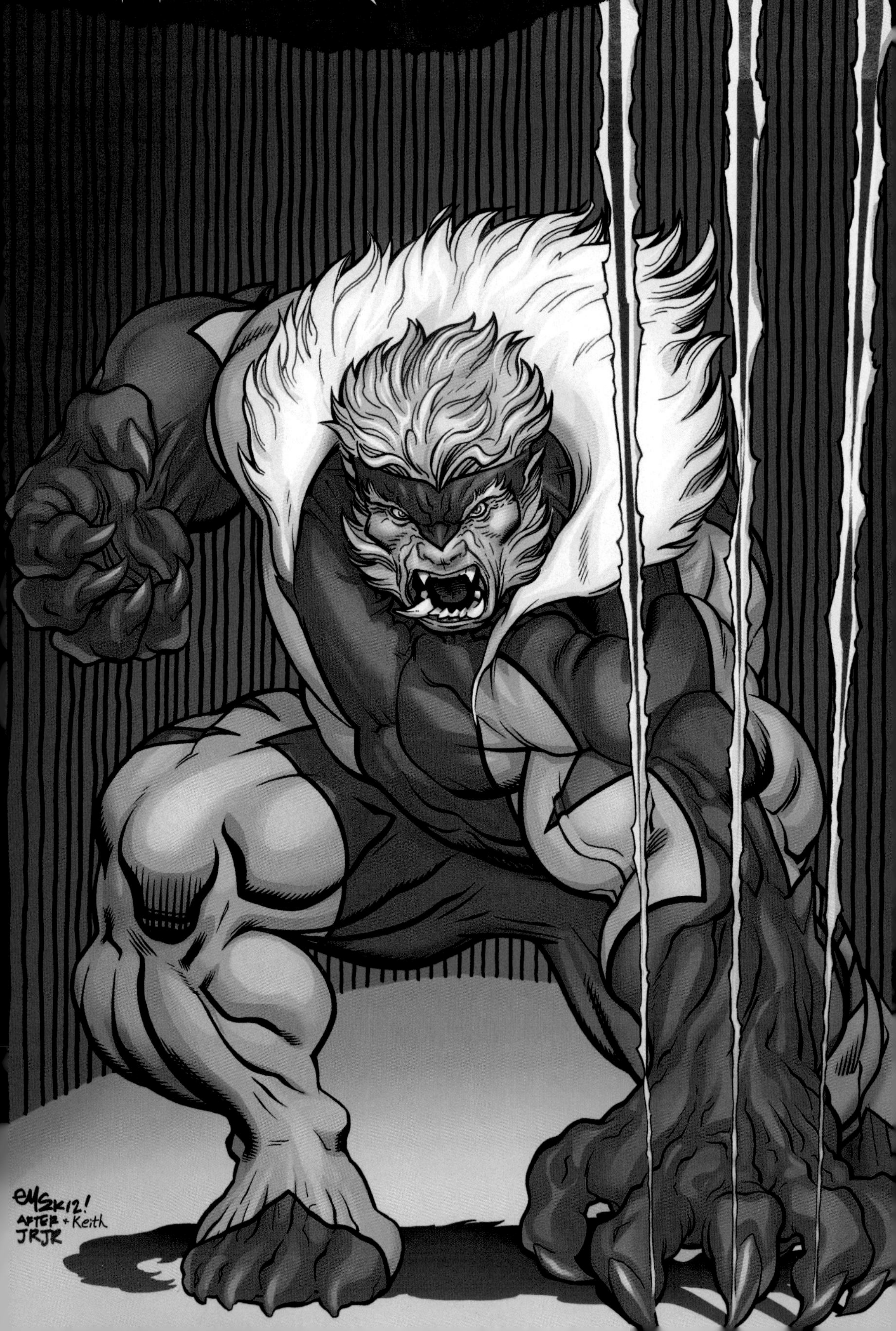

EMSK12!
AFTER + Keith
JRJR

WOLVERINE #310 VARIANT COVER

STEPHEN PLATT

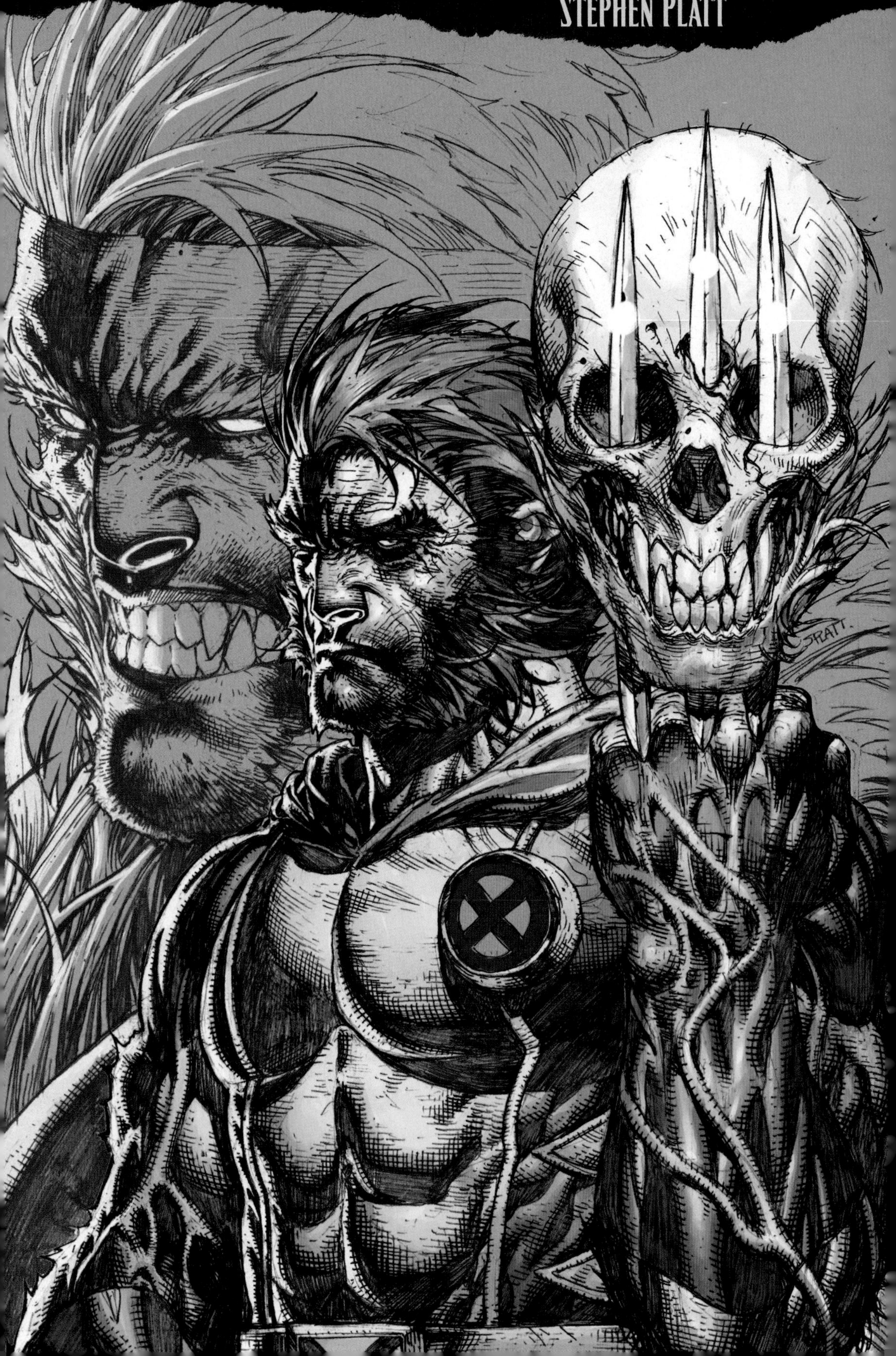

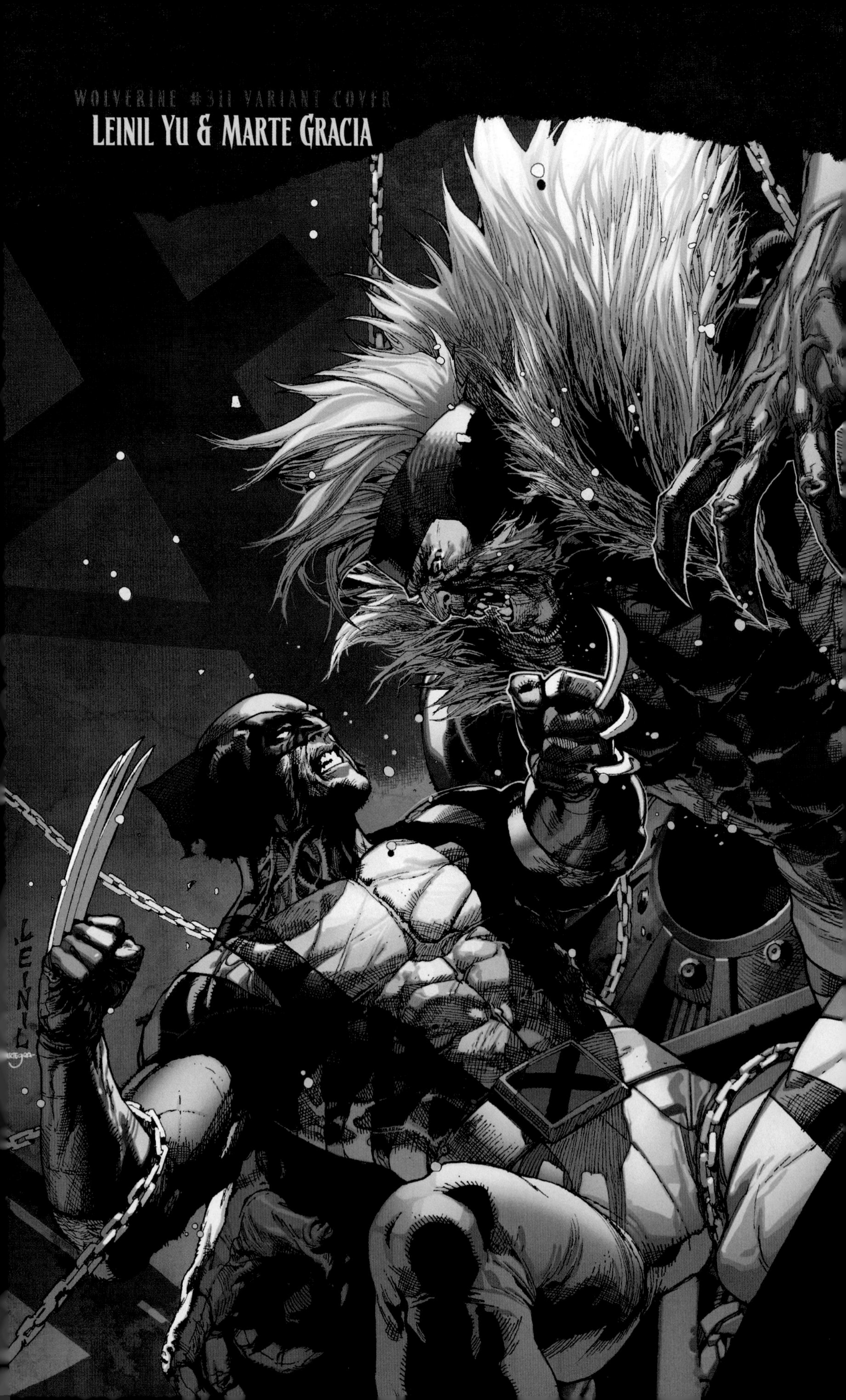

WOLVERINE #311 VARIANT COVER

LEINIL YU & MARTE GRACIA

WOLVERINE #312 VARIANT COVER

J. SCOTT CAMPBELL & EDGAR DELGADO

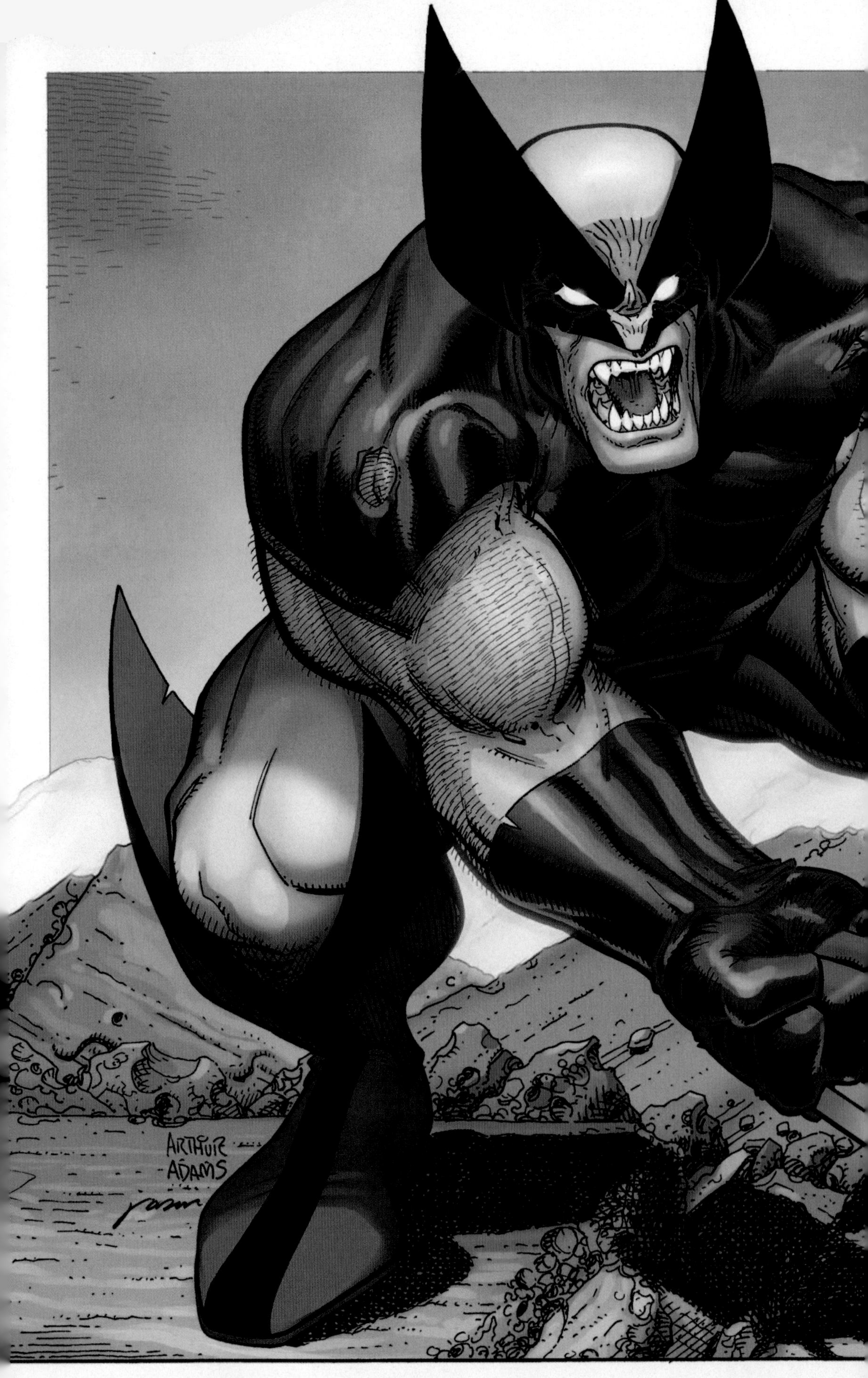
ARTHUR ADAMS

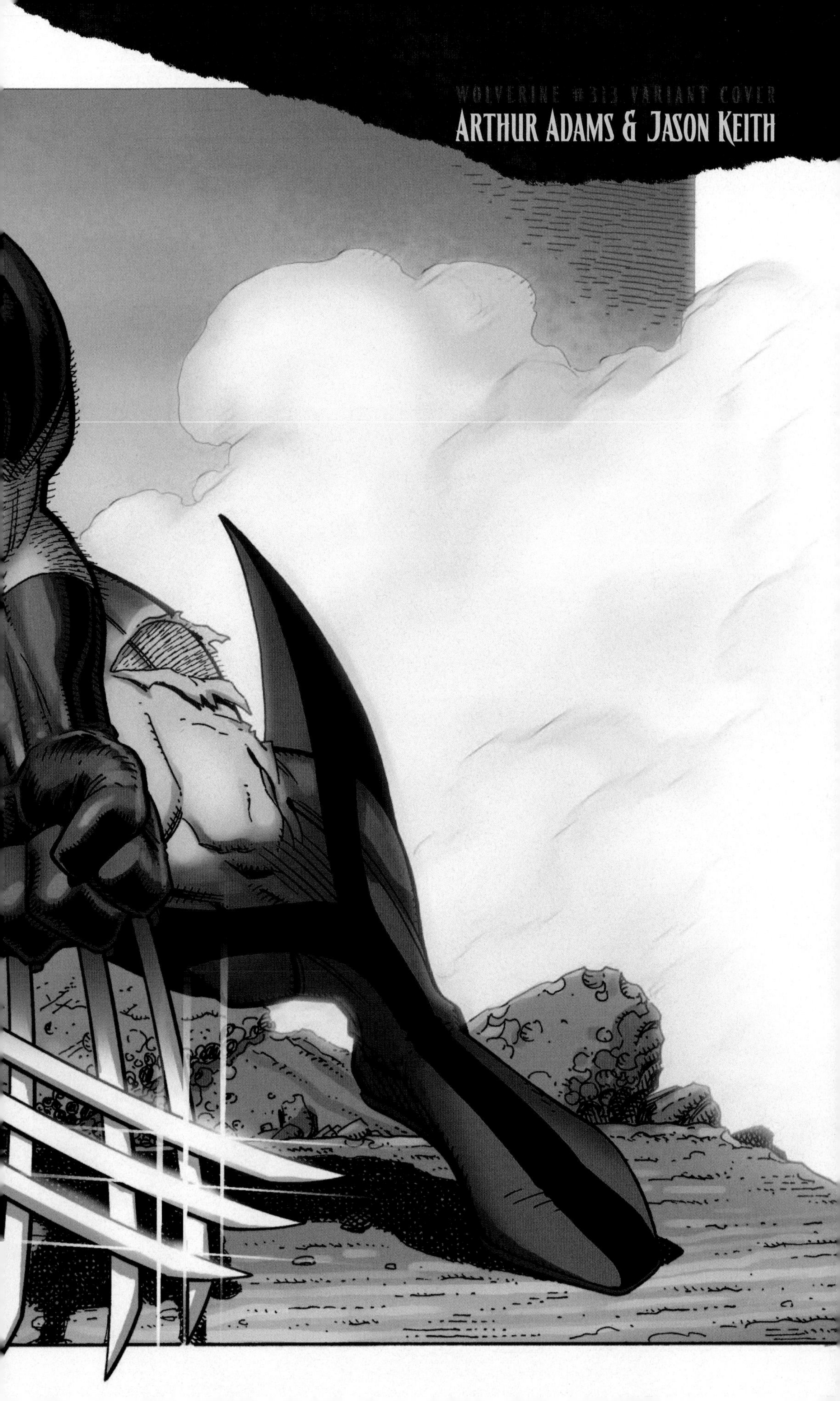

WOLVERINE #313 VARIANT COVER
ARTHUR ADAMS & JASON KEITH

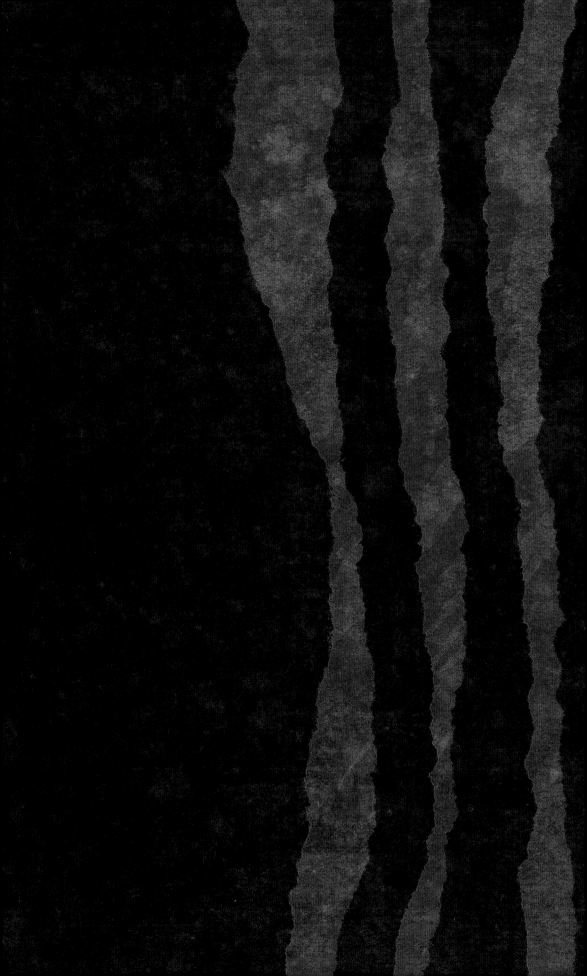

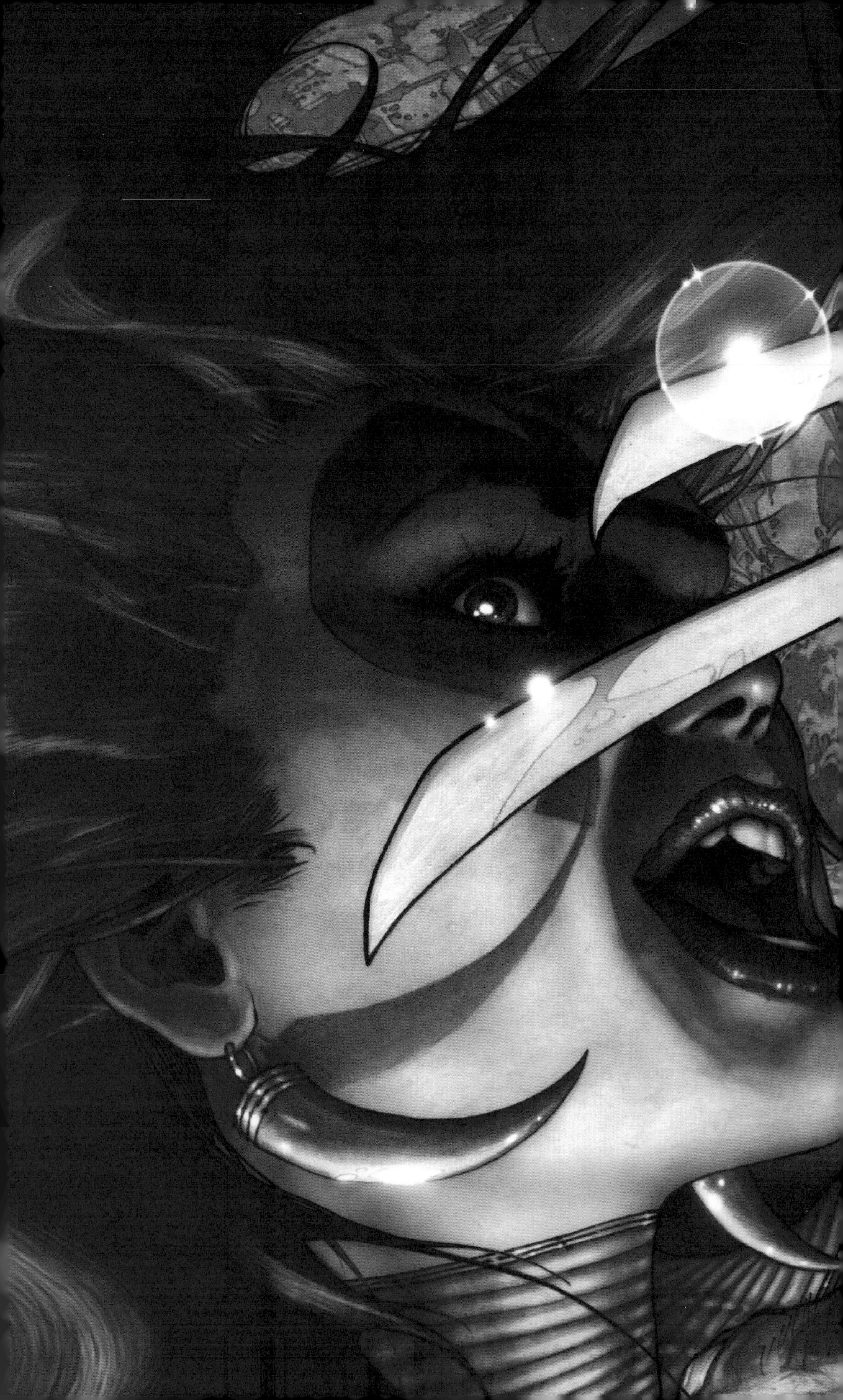